Somewhat More Independent

Somewhat More Independent

THE END OF SLAVERY
IN NEW YORK CITY,
1770–1810

Shane White

THE UNIVERSITY
OF GEORGIA PRESS
Athens and London

© 1991 by the University of Georgia Press
Athens, Georgia 30602
All rights reserved

Designed by Betty Palmer McDaniel
Set in eleven on thirteen Janson Text
The paper in this book meets the guidelines for
permanence and durability of the Committee on
Production Guidelines for Book Longevity of the
Council on Library Resources.

Printed in the United States of America

91 92 93 94 95   C   5 4 3 2 1
95 96 97 98 99   P   5 4 3 2 1

Library of Congress Cataloging in Publication Data
White, Shane.
Somewhat more independent : the end of slavery in
New York City, 1770–1810 / Shane White.
p. cm.
Includes bibliographical references.
ISBN 0-8203-2374-8
1. Slavery—New York (N.Y.)—History.   2. New York
(N.Y.)—History—1775–1865.   3. Afro-Americans—
New York (N.Y.)—History.   4. New York (N.Y.)—Race
relations.   I. Title.
F128.44.W54   1991
974.7´1—dc20   90-10843

British Library Cataloging in Publication Data available

Portions of this book have previously appeared as "Impious Prayers: Elite and Popular Attitudes Towards Blacks and Slavery in the Middle-Atlantic States, 1783–1810," *New York History* 67 (1986), 261–83; "A Question of Style: Blacks in and Around New York City in the late Eighteenth Century," *Journal of American Folklore* 102 (1989), 24–45; "Pinkster: Afro-Dutch Syncretization in New York City and the Hudson Valley,: *Journal of American Folklore* 102 (1989), 69–76; and " 'We Dwell in Safety and Pursue Our Honest Callings': Free Blacks in New York City, 1783–1810," *Journal of American History* 75 (1988), 445–70.

For Mavis and Chalky White,
and for Lexie Macdonald

Contents

Maps and Figures

Tables

Preface

IN THE BEGINNING this was to be a study of the end of slavery in the North. After a couple of years I realized that I had bitten off more than I could satisfactorily chew and the topic was cut back to the end of slavery in the Middle Atlantic states. A while later Pennsylvania got the chop. Then large areas of New York and New Jersey began to go the way of an ever-increasing proportion of American territory. This book is presented now in its current form—an analysis of the end of slavery in a loosely defined New York City—before it degenerates to the point where it is little more than an account of slavery on Wall Street on a dark night in November 1789.

Perhaps it was inevitable that I should end up concentrating on New York City. I am a city lad. The countryside unsettles me. I know from experience that cows, given the chance, will walk over me. In fact animals of any sort, even very little animals, sensing my tenseness, will bail me up. After two days in the country I have to stick my head near the exhaust pipe of a car to get a breath of real air. In short, few would describe me as being at one with nature. On the other hand I feel comfortable in a city. Probably I had fallen for New York City before I saw it; the reality, once I arrived, was even better. After being reluctantly ejected from libraries and archives each afternoon and having no desire to return to the dump financial exigency forced me to sleep in, I walked all over Manhattan, often until the early hours of the morning. On my first night in New York, without sleep for forty hours and a trifle disoriented, I made my way to the southern tip of the island. There, while drinking a cup of coffee and idly consulting a 1789 street map, I was approached by a gentleman who had definitely seen better days. He informed me that, in an earlier incarnation, he had lived in eighteenth-century New York, and for the price of a few cigarettes he was prepared to divulge all. What putative historian could resist such an opportunity? Where else but in New York could it have occurred?

Yet no matter how congenial I may have found New York City, this history clearly has been written by an outsider. I am not black and I am not American. I traveled to America twice while research-ing this book — once for about nine weeks and a second time for five days (predictably, the latter was the more productive trip). Since then I have been back twice, but only for brief, jet-lagged visits to attend conferences. Distance from America has probably affected my interpretation of slavery and of blacks in New York, but that, in the end, is for others to judge. Here, I would like to mention briefly the impact that distance has had on the sources employed in this book. Although my quick but extraordinarily expensive raids on manuscript collections have yielded much useful material, par-ticularly from the District Attorney's Indictment Papers in the Mu-nicipal Archives, for the most part this work is based on sources such as the census, newspapers, the *Early American Imprint Series* that have been microfilmed (or unfortunately microcarded) and are readily available in Australia. For more years than I care to remem-ber I have read enormous quantities of such sources, carding every reference to blacks or slavery: a small-meshed seine was, in effect, dragged through a considerable body of water, and although the yield was seldom large, index cards gradually accumulated. Geog-raphy may have imposed constraints on the material used, but it also forced me to try and tease out the meaning from what often appeared to be very unpromising sources. A year's solid work in the archives in America might well have allowed me to finish a book on the end of slavery in New York City within a more reasonable time span, but the resulting work would, I believe, have differed considerably.

My primary interest was always in the lives of the blacks them-selves. Strongly influenced by the flowering of black history in the 1970s, I tried to sketch in an answer to the question: what did it mean to be black and living in New York City at the end of the eighteenth century? I quickly discovered, however, that such an en-deavor depended on knowing rather more about slavery and slaveowners in New York City than I, at least, was able to glean from the work of previous scholars. (This frustration has resulted in a certain tartness in some of the historiographical discussions in this book, an acidity that although sweetened somewhat by the advice of more experienced hands is, I believe, justified.) Consequently part 1 of this book is devoted to the whites. Here I try to work out answers to such basic questions as who owned slaves, what they used them for, and how white New Yorkers conceived of blacks, slaves, and slavery. In part 2 the focus shifts first to the slaves and then finally in the last chapters to the free blacks.

As the unseemly length of the following acknowledgments in-dicates I have received a lot of support and help from a variety of people. First I must thank the staffs of archives and libraries at which I carried out my research. These include the New York Public Library, the New-York Historical Society, the Library of Congress, and the Historical Documents Collection at Queens College. Par-ticularly helpful were the staff at the State Library of New York in Albany (who on a cold and miserable winter's day found it difficult to believe that the only two people perusing New York documents not only were from Australia but also had never met before), and at the Municipal Archives of the City of New York where, I was in-formed, I did not just break but shattered all previous photocopying records. In Australia the staff in the microfilm section and in the interlibrary loans department at the University of Sydney's Fisher Library have also been very helpful.

I have been promising students for years that the next sentence would take pride of place in this section. Much of the work for this book was mind-numbingly boring, tedious, and frustratingly slow, and it could never have been completed without the aid of vari-ous drugs, among which nicotine, caffeine, and Springsteen must be named. Funnily enough, one student purloined this phrase and used it as a campaign slogan in a student election (it was nice to know that someone had listened to at least part of the lecture).

I would also like to acknowledge with gratitude the help of a number of American academics who have taken the time to read and to criticize bits and pieces of this study. These include Roger Ekirch, Paul Gilje, Michael Kammen, Jonathan Prude, and Daniel

Walkowitz. Thomas J. Davis and Graham Hodges, fellow toilers in the rich field of black New York history and, I suppose, technically rivals or competitors, have been unusually generous, reading and commenting on this work and aiding me in many other ways. In this country the small scholarly community interested in things American have, with remarkable patience, at the biennial conferences of the Australian and New Zealand American Studies Association, sat through a number of papers on New York blacks and offered many useful comments. Two prominent members of that community, Paul Bourke and Don DeBats, were external examiners for the thesis from which this book is derived and supplied me with helpful critiques. Members of the history department at the University of Sydney also have assisted in a number of ways: here I would like to single out Tony Cahill, Brian Fletcher, David Goodman, Neville Meaney, Ros Pesman, and Craig Reynolds.

Stanley L. Engerman, Philip D. Morgan, and Gary B. Nash have read most of this book chapter by chapter, a burden made more difficult by the fact that the order in which those chapters sporadically emerged while I was writing my thesis was neither chronological nor logical. I am very grateful to all three for taking a lot of time from their own work to send me the sort of detailed comments and suggestions that have saved me from a number of graduate-student excesses and improved this work immeasurably.

Many who read this will be well aware of the sense of futility that, for varying lengths of time, afflicts those writing a thesis or a book. Encouragement and the odd word of praise from other historians deadened the pain by suggesting that something worthwhile could eventually emerge. Donna Merwick's infectious enthusiasm is always intellectually stimulating. Similarly, Charles Joyner's effusive reaction to a paper I delivered at a conference in Auckland and his subsequent help both in reading chapters and in finding a publisher for this work gave me a huge boost. Not only did Jim Gilbert set a standard that future Fulbright visitors to this country will find difficult to match, but his intellectual vivacity and presence in the history department were also of considerable help as I tried to kill off the first draft of this manuscript. Ira Berlin read an early version of chapter 6 and then incisively commented on the thesis that forms the basis of this work.

As a young graduate student I was enthralled, in particular, by the work of two outstanding historians: I am pleased to acknowledge my extensive debts to both of them. Larry Levine not only read and commented on this manuscript, but his splendid support of my work also has been extraordinarily helpful. My admiration for Rhys Isaac and for his scholarship knows few bounds. I am flattered that he has managed to discern something worth encouraging in my work and grateful for the exuberant manner with which he has offered that encouragement.

It is also a pleasure to thank publicly a number of good friends who have cheered me on from the beginning. Ian Mylchreest has ferreted out obscure material on New York in Cornell University's libraries and acted as the intermediary for my valiant attempt, through the buying of books, to keep the American economy afloat, as well as encouraging the completion of this work. Richard Bosworth, a distinguished historian of Italy, managed to overcome his profound distaste of things American for long enough to serve as my "average historical person on the street." His acerbic marginal comments about both America and my writing — after one particularly labyrinthine and statistical portion he was moved to say that, if ever released, the section in question could end the market for Valium — were always useful, and his belief that I was constructing something of value gave me, from time to time, a much-needed injection of confidence.

My largest intellectual debts, however, are to two men who have been my teachers, critics, colleagues, and, most important, very good friends. Graham White (no relation) has prodded and encouraged me from the inception of this study. One of the largest problems I faced in this work is my almost total inability to write more than about two sentences without committing some heinous crime against the Queen's English. Graham White, on the other hand, has an extraordinary talent with words. He has been over numerous drafts of this work, patiently correcting my many egregious sins and coaxing a text out of me that (I hope) is at least readable. Richard Waterhouse has also exhibited a considerable amount of patience with me: he was a young man when he began supervising my dissertation. Over the years I have been at work on this manuscript he has given me much astute advice and guidance. But even more important in my development as a historian than the formal relationship between student and teacher (which thankfully hasn't been formal at all) have been the almost daily conversations I have had with him about his own work and about the scholarship of other historians. It was there that I picked up at least some of his passion for history and fascination with the subtleties of the past. I can only hope that some of this comes through in the text of this work. My historical training has been largely at the hands of these two men: whatever merits this book may have (and this could be a backhander) are largely attributable to their efforts.

Graham White has hardly been the only person to sweat over the style of my prose. I would like to thank *New York History*, the *Journal of American Folklore*, and the *Journal of American History* for permission to reprint articles first published in their pages; and Wendell Tripp, Bruce Jackson, David Thelen, and Susan Armeny for their assistance with those pieces. Thanks are also due to Cynthia Carter Ayers, Madelaine Cooke, and Malcolm Call for helping a novice author through the process of turning a manuscript into a book.

The last acknowledgments I would like to make are to three people who have not read this work (and probably only a gun pointed at their heads will induce them to do so). My parents have offered much support, both financial and otherwise, over the years, and I am very grateful. And finally I would like to thank Lexie Macdonald for her companionship, her sense of humor, and for much else besides that has made the last few years so enjoyable.

Introduction

OVER RECENT YEARS historians of black Americans have demonstrated a high level of historical consciousness about their own field. August Meier and Elliot Rudwick, relying on scores of interviews with practitioners, have documented its rise from a Jim Crow specialty ignored by nearly all to its present status as one of the liveliest and most important areas in the profession. *Black History and the Historical Profession, 1915–1980* is a veritable who's who of specialists in the field, providing brief biographical snippets about every major historian of black Americans and many minor ones as well.[1] Other historians have attended learned symposia and contributed historiographical articles assessing the significance of the flood of scholarly work published on the subject. At a conference sponsored by the American Historical Association in 1983 prominent scholars ruminated over the "current state" of black history and suggested several areas deserving of future attention. The quantity and length of the footnotes in these pieces attest to the current vigor of the genre.[2]

If in all of this there is a hint of the celebratory it is not without good reason. It is only about twenty-five years ago that Leon Litwack, currently one of the more prominent specialists, was urged by a senior professor at Berkeley to turn to another area lest he damage his career.[3] Now, however, practitioners of black history hold influential positions in the profession, and books and articles on their area of expertise have probably won more than their fair share of the numerous prizes that are nowadays on offer.

It was the realization that blacks were not passive ciphers but had a history and a highly developed culture of their own, a revelation largely spurred by the concerns of the 1960s and given substance by

the publication of the federal Works Project Administration interviews, that prompted the vigorous reassessment of the black experience.[4] Yet this reassessment has proceeded unevenly. Of course the
task of writing blacks back into American history is a large one, but
surprisingly there are still significant lacunae, areas where there has
been little interest and where the intellectual vigor that has characterized the reinterpretation of the slave South has not been in
evidence. One such area is the study of slavery and its demise in
New York and New Jersey.

The neglect of this area is surprising. Throughout the eighteenth
century New York and New Jersey were more reliant on slave labor
than were any other regions in the North, and slaves constituted
more than 20 percent of the total population in parts of these colonies. In 1790, when the first national census was taken, every third
inhabitant of Kings County on the western end of Long Island was
black and almost six in every ten white households owned slaves. In
the town of New Utrecht, 38 percent of the population was black
and three out of every four households owned slaves. As late as 1810,
more than 60 percent of white households in Flatbush, another
town in Kings, contained slaves. Yet in spite of these quite striking
figures and the obvious importance of the topic, there have been
few attempts to analyze slavery in New York and New Jersey.

Moreover, the issues considered by those who have ventured
into the field have generally remained within parameters set by
the studies written at the turn of the century. Those early mono-
graphs reflected the dominance of political and institutional history
and, in each case, concentrated on the operation of slavery within
one colony or state.[5] Relying heavily on colonial statutes and legal
cases, historians were concerned not with blacks but with the effect
of slavery on white institutions. Their studies followed a set pattern: a discussion of when the first black entered the colony and
how slavery was established, followed by a consideration of slavery
couched in the negative terms of what colonial laws forbade, followed by a history of the opposition to slavery, from early attempts
to limit the importation of slaves to the emergence of antislavery
groups in the second half of the eighteenth century. At their best, as
with Edmund Raymond Turner's *The Negro in Pennsylvania*, these
accounts provided well-researched institutional histories of their
respective states. A. Judd Northrup's history of New York, on the

other hand, contained little more than undigested slabs of primary material strung together with a few words of facile commentary. Henry S. Cooley's *A Study of Slavery in New Jersey* was more useful, but hardly distinguished.

Though a few articles were published in the next seventy years, there was no full-length study of slavery until Edgar McManus published two rather similar volumes, *A History of Negro Slavery in New York* in 1966 and *Black Bondage in the North* in 1973.[6] Both these works are institutional histories, and although McManus assumed a harsher view of slavery and emphasized slave resistance, his framework differed little from that of earlier studies. Chapters on early settlement and the establishment of a system of bondage led to an analysis, based on colonial laws, of the nature of the institution and finally to accounts of slavery's demise. McManus's purpose, as he explained in the preface to *Black Bondage in the North*, was to tell his story "with a minimum of generalization or interpretation" and, in particular, to avoid "imposing a conceptual framework on the study."[7]

Although no satisfactory general account of slavery in either New York or New Jersey yet exists, historians have extensively covered two aspects of the institution.[8] Slave rebellions, in particular the well-known slave conspiracy of 1741, have attracted a considerable amount of interest.[9] Paradoxically, however, the abundance of material on the latter appears to have stymied a broad consideration of the nature of black resistance. On the face of it the conspiracy would appear to have almost endless possibilities as a point of entry into the world of the slaves. Instead, detailed narrative accounts of the complex events that led up to the trial of those involved have been preferred to sustained attempts to analyze the meaning and significance of the conspiracy itself. Further, concentration on this dramatic episode has inhibited investigation of the more typical (and more successful) forms of everyday black resistance.[10] We are left with little more than the inadequately substantiated conclusion of Edgar McManus, who, writing of the entire North, declared that black resistance to slavery "turned the racial hegemony of the whites into a regime of mutual terror and repression."[11]

The second aspect of New York and New Jersey slavery that has received a good deal of attention is its eventual end. In their seminal works David Brion Davis and Winthrop Jordan have placed the emergence of antislavery thought in the wider perspective of European and American intellectual history from the sixteenth to the nineteenth century.[12] At a less ambitious level, the history of the passage of the gradual manumission laws has also been treated at length.[13] But again, accounts of antislavery societies and legislative proceedings have taken the place of a considered analysis of the impact of the end of slavery either on slaveholders or, even more noticeably, on blacks.

The 1741 conspiracy and the legislative end of slavery are important topics, but concentration on them has skewed our understanding of slavery in New York and New Jersey. Generally, the existing historiography gives the impression that slavery was solely a political, social, and moral problem of the white elite. Blacks are either relegated to the role of grateful and usually invisible beneficiaries of white philanthropy or depicted simplistically as incipient Nat Turners, threatening the white order. Detailed analysis of the writings and activities of antislavery advocates, or even close examination of slave codes, may reveal much about the fears and expectations of white society; it can tell us virtually nothing about the region's blacks.[14]

The historiography of slavery in New York and New Jersey prompts a series of questions that have not satisfactorily been answered. How extensive was slavery? Who were the slaveholders and to what uses did they put their slaves? What was the effect of the end of slavery on the slaveholders? Neither has there been any sustained attempt to consider the slaves themselves. Though methods used over the past two decades by historians of southern slavery, and questions raised by them, have had some impact on newer studies of New York and New Jersey, it is still the case that little is known of slave culture, of the influence on these slaves of the African past, or of the impact on them of the end of slavery.[15]

One indication of the lackluster and limited nature of the historiography is the way in which other scholars working on New York and New Jersey have virtually ignored it. Often, in studies of these colonies or states, slavery has been completely omitted or dismissed in a few lines. The extent and importance of the institution in some parts of New York and New Jersey are simply not recognized. In an examination of Newtown on Long Island, modeled on the New England town studies, slavery is mentioned on fewer than 20 of its

270 pages.[16] Even this paltry figure overstates the relative weight the author gives to the institution, for many of these pages contain only the most fleeting references. Nowhere is there an account of the establishment and rise of slavery or a detailed assessment of the role the institution played in the town's scheme of things, let alone any consideration of the blacks. Yet at the time of the 1790 census about 25 percent of Newtown's inhabitants were black and slightly in excess of one in every two white households contained slaves. Admittedly the author ends her account in 1775, but from the scanty population figures that appear in her book, it would appear that blacks had constituted a similar proportion of the population for much of the eighteenth century. To all intents and purposes Newtown, with every other household owning blacks, was a slave society, yet only the most perceptive reader could have drawn such a conclusion from the text of this book.

It is not easy to account for the scholarly neglect of slavery in New York and New Jersey. No doubt the refractory and unyielding nature of the sources is partly to blame. Interestingly, the historiography is most comprehensive in the areas where there are easily exploitable sources. Antislavery leaders were nothing if not highly articulate and literate, and they have left much material for historians in tracts, magazine and newspaper pieces, and correspondence. Similarly, Daniel Horsmanden, the presiding judge at the 1741 conspiracy trial, left a lengthy and readily available account of the proceedings, including the testimony of many of the accused slaves.[17] But for the most part sources on black life in and around New York City are hard to come by. Blacks were a minority of the population, were for the most part illiterate, and left few obvious traces on the historical record. These comments are also applicable to Pennsylvania, and yet historians writing about that state, most notably Gary Nash, have imaginatively exploited material with similar limitations to produce some excellent studies of slavery and blacks.[18] This book, which examines the last years of slavery in New York City and its surrounds,[19] is a further contribution toward a reassessment of black life and slavery in the North.[20]

This, then, is in the first place a book about slavery. The "peculiar institution" is most commonly associated with the South, but thousands of blacks were also enslaved in New York and elsewhere in the North. The record of their plight—and in spite of complacent assertions about the mildness of northern slavery this is the correct word—and of the way in which they adapted to the exigencies of their situation should be written back into American history. Yet more is involved than some liberal attempt to redress the imbalance of history, although this too is a factor. As we shall see, New York City provides a strikingly different ground on which to investigate the creation of black culture, offering a new perspective that can contribute to an overall understanding of the complex process of acculturation.

This is also a book about freedom. I have sought, among other things, to outline the impact of the end of slavery on both the white and black populations of the city and to make a contribution to the field of "emancipation studies," which Armstead Robinson has asserted are already at the cutting edge of scholarly inquiry into the black experience.[21] Although there has been a commendable comparative dimension to the many studies of the impact of freedom on southern blacks, historians have used the Caribbean, or even Russia, as a basis for their analyses.[22] They have not so far looked to the North. Yet emancipation (and indeed slavery) in New York City may provide an equally useful perspective on the experience in the South.

Finally, this is a book about New York City. I do not claim that New York is America writ small: the city is idiosyncratic, probably representative only of itself. But by the early years of the nineteenth century it was rapidly emerging as the most important and vital urban center in the new nation, and the lives and activities of its inhabitants have continued to be a focus of interest for historians, particularly in recent years.[23] Sean Wilentz has written about class formation, Christine Stansell about gender relations, and Paul Gilje about popular disorder and violence. The following account of the end of slavery is a contribution to the historiography of slavery and freedom; it should also reveal something new about New York City itself.

A Note to the Reader

Population Statistics

THE POPULATION STATISTICS for New York in this book are taken from the 1790, 1800, and 1810 federal censuses. My figures differ from the totals used by other historians for a number of reasons. Anyone who has worked with these early censuses soon discovers that they are riddled with errors. I have assumed that the individual entries are correct and that the errors lie in the additions. (On occasion it is possible to see where the census taker has made mistakes, such as omitting the totals from one page in his computations.) I have reworked the statistics for the whole of New York State in these three censuses on this basis. I have then adjusted the figures for the total population by the error in the black population, both slave and free. For example, in 1800 the census taker for Kings County calculated that the total population was 5,740 and that there were 1,479 slaves. However, if one adds up the slaves recorded in the manuscript census against the individual heads of households in Kings County the total is 1,506. According to my reckoning, the census taker made the following errors—in Flatbush he counted ten too many slaves, in Flatlands, one too many; but in Bushwick, he omitted eight, and in New Utrecht thirty slaves. Consequently, I have entered Kings County in my calculations as having 1,506 slaves and a total population of 5,767. Undoubtedly errors exist in the figures for the white population, but these, I am afraid, are someone else's problem. Generally the errors in the figures for New York City are small; those for the rest of the state are sometimes more serious.

Another factor contributing to the discrepancy between these and other statistics is that I have eliminated from the original city census returns data relating to the area of Manhattan Island north of the city itself. This area was made up largely of small farms and the country estates of the rich, which are not particularly relevant to a study of patterns in the city. Matching the 1789 tax list and the 1790 census (see below) enabled me to establish which households, listed in the outward of the 1790 census, were located "north of the line." For 1800 I used the city directories to work out approximately where in the Seventh Ward the limits of the city were. For 1810 I excluded the Ninth Ward completely. There is one other major source of discrepancy. Free blacks were listed in a column in the census entitled "all other free persons." Generally this description signified free blacks, and many census takers actually used this term rather than the official title. However, sometimes the census takers included other groups in this total. For example, in 1810 in the Sixth Ward the census taker included 204 inmates of the prison. Some of these were undoubtedly black; the majority were not. I have excluded all such entries from the total, a procedure that does the least injury to the accuracy of the total.

Comparison of the 1790 Census with the 1789 Tax List

TABLE 1 WAS CONSTRUCTED by comparing and matching the 1789 tax list with the 1790 census. The tax list, over two hundred pages long, is a difficult document to deal with and presents a number of problems. Leaving aside the issues of the legibility of eighteenth-century handwriting and the at times bewildering lack of consistency in spelling, there are problems arising from multiple property ownership by the Smiths and Browns of this world. Although I took every possible care—for example, using the abstracts of several hundred New York wills to check property ownership wherever possible—probably no two people undertaking this exercise would end up with the same result. Even so, such differences would I hope not be large enough to alter my conclusions. There was, however, another important problem: the time lag of a year between the two lists. Leases in New York usually expired on May 1, and it was perhaps inevitable that May 1, 1790, would fall between the time the tax list was drawn up in 1789 and the date on which the census was completed in 1790. At times it seemed to me as though the whole of New York was on the back of a cart, moving, on that critical day in 1790. Under the circumstances it was fortunate that the city directories for 1789, 1790, and 1791 made it possible to trace many of these movements.

All individuals living north of the line (marked on the tax list) were excluded, as were institutions and deceased estates not redistributed at the time the tax list was taken. Table 1 thus contains an approximation of the wealth on Manhattan Island of the inhabitants of New York City. It should be emphasized that the figures are only approximations—values for both personal and real estate were usually rounded off to such sums as £20 or £100.[1] It should also be remembered that wealth and income are not the same.[2] Nevertheless, providing the figures are used sensibly, they give a rough guide to the distribution of wealth in New York City.

The 4,237 individuals on the 1789 tax list were matched with the 1790 census and 1789, 1790, and 1791 city directories to work out, wherever possible, their occupations and whether they owned slaves or not. The individuals were then ranked according to wealth and divided into deciles. Where a number of individuals were on the border between two deciles they were randomly separated (by a rather unscientific card-shuffling process). Bruce Wilkenfield also has worked out the wealth distribution from the tax list, although he did not match his results to the census. He used the whole list (including institutions, deceased estates, and residents living north of the line), and consequently his figures are marginally different from mine. His totals are 4,406 assessment ratings adding up to £2,234,605, as opposed to the 4,237 individuals owning £2,129,577 here; his top 10 percent owned 54.5 percent of the wealth and bottom 50 percent owned 6.9 percent (here the figures are 55.6 and 6.6 percent).[3]

Comparison of the Censuses with the Directories

CENSUS ENTRIES INCLUDED the name of the head of the household and, in columns across the page, the numbers of members of the household in different age and sex categories. Free blacks and slaves were listed in the last two columns, undifferentiated until 1820 by either age or sex. Thus the censuses make it possible to identify the black heads of households in New York City. The city directories, on the other hand, contained in alphabetical order the name, address, and occupation of a large proportion of the adult work force. The New York directories made no mention of race. Many historians have used these directories, and for a variety of purposes, but no one seems to have noticed that among the names listed were those of many free blacks, although names like Pompey Valentine and Congo Clark are rather conspicuous. By linking the name of the head of the black household in the census entry with the names in the directories it is possible to find out the occupations and addresses of many free blacks. Most of the heads of free black households in the 1790 census were identified only by their given or first names, so only a couple can be matched with the directories. But by 1800 most were listed with a surname. Table 24 was constructed by matching the 1800 census with the 1799, 1800, and 1801 directories and the 1810 census with the 1810 and 1811 directories.

The tables listing the occupations of the white heads of households containing free blacks or slaves (for example, tables 2 and 3) were constructed in much the same manner by matching the various censuses with the city directories.

Maps

THE CENSUS AND DIRECTORY MATERIAL was also the basis for maps 1, 3, 4, 5, 6, and 7. Again, the process is best illustrated by using the maps containing free black households as an example. The comparison between the census and the directories provided the addresses of a small proportion of the free black heads of households. These black households can be plotted on a map. If the census was no more than a random list of the heads of black households in a particular ward this would be the limit of the usefulness of the material. The census, however, is not random. There was a system behind the 1790, 1800, and 1810 New York City censuses. The census taker made his entries while walking up and down the streets of New York, and it is possible with the use of the city directories to follow his path. By checking the addresses of thousands of other households, particularly those around black households, I have been able to locate the street for every black household included in the three censuses. Further, by using the cross streets (the census takers tended to walk up one side of a street and then turn at the first cross street, often working their way around the block) I have been able to estimate the positions of the black households on those streets. Though I cannot claim 100 percent precision, I think that the maps provide a reasonably accurate picture of the residential pattern of *all* free black households listed in the 1790, 1800, and 1810 New York City censuses. The same process was used to map the households of slaveowners.

PART ONE

Whites

1

Slavery in New York City

IN THE EARLY HOURS of a September morning in 1794, the *Fair American* drifted gently on the tide into New York harbor. Awakened by unaccustomed sounds and eager for his first glimpse of America, William Strickland, an English gentleman farmer, hurried on deck. His first reaction was one of disappointment. He had expected to be intrigued by the unfamiliar sights of a New World city. Instead, he beheld "a forest of masts, some hundreds of vessels surrounding," just as one might expect to see "on the Thames below London bridge." As Strickland poked inquisitively around the city during the next few days his sense of disappointment deepened. Had he traveled so far, he wondered, merely "to be sett down again in the country I quitted?" One contrast, however, was too vivid to miss: the "greater number of the Blacks particularly of women and children in the streets who may be seen of all shades till the stain is entirely worne out."[1]

What Strickland considered remarkable New Yorkers must easily have accepted, for slavery and blacks had long been important and familiar elements in their lives. Through most of the eighteenth century their city had ranked second only to Charlestown in the number of slaves owned by its inhabitants. According to the 1771 census, the last taken during the colonial period, blacks were 14.3 percent of the total population. Patrick M'Robert, a traveler visiting New York City in 1774, had commented in a similar fashion to Strickland that "it rather hurts an Europian eye to see so many negro slaves upon the streets." Slavery was well established in the immediate hinterland too, since farmers on the western end of Long Island and in the parts of New Jersey that supplied New York with food customarily relied on black slaves for their labor requirements. In 1771, 20 percent of the population in Richmond and Queens counties were slaves. Even more strikingly, one in every three residents of Kings County was a slave, a ratio that would not have been out of place in the South.[2] Yet the extent and significance of such slaveholding in and around New York in the eighteenth century have remained hidden, in large part because those who have studied the subject have rarely gone beyond the sporadic comments of travelers and the odd total from an eighteenth-century census. For a more accurate and comprehensive picture of the institution we must turn to the precise statistical data collected in the post-Revolutionary period in census schedules, tax lists, and city directories.

NEW YORK RECOVERED rapidly from the devastation of the British occupation. Its population was probably not much more than 12,000 when the war ended, but by the time of the first federal census in 1790 there were 31,229 people living within the city limits.[3] Slavery, too, had been reestablished, and the number of slaves would continue to increase until after the turn of the century. But the institution never regained fully its former standing in the city. The growth of the slave population in the two decades after the Revolution, although substantial, could not match the dramatic expansion in the number of New York residents. Furthermore, in the colonial period virtually all blacks had been slaves, but in the aftermath of the Revolutionary war this was no longer the case. Of 3,092 blacks residing in New York in 1790 about two-thirds were slaves.[4] Consequently, although blacks composed about 10 percent of the city's inhabitants at the time of Strickland's arrival in 1794, the dependence of New Yorkers on slavery, as measured by the slave proportion of the total population, was at a lower level than earlier in the century.

Nevertheless, slavery was far from being of negligible importance in the city. Even though the enslaved percentage of the population was slipping, this was attributable in large part to the vigorous demographic growth of New York. It was still the case that in absolute terms the number of slaves was increasing significantly. Of course gross or percentage figures can give only the bare outlines of the institution of slavery, particularly when, as in New York, slave-

TABLE 1

Wealth and Slaveholding in New York City in 1789–1790

Decile	N	Matched to Census	Wealth	%	Slaveholders		Slaves	
					N	%	N	%
£1,210–16,430	424	318	£1,184,175	55.6	224	29.6	645	39.9
650–1,200	424	269	378,870	17.8	162	21.4	339	21.0
400–650	424	268	206,745	9.7	113	14.9	217	13.4
250–400	424	257	131,800	6.1	63	8.3	110	6.8
180–250	424	234	88,637	4.2	62	8.2	109	6.8
100–180	424	242	57,463	2.7	28	3.7	34	2.1
80–100	424	225	40,890	1.9	33	4.4	41	2.6
50–80	423	225	23,365	1.1	34	4.5	58	3.6
20–50	423	216	14,156	0.7	28	3.7	44	2.7
0–20	423	173	3,476	0.2	10	1.3	18	1.1
	4,237	2,427	£2,129,577	100.0	757	100.0	1,615	100.0

Sources: New York City Tax List for 1789, microfilm copy, Library of Congress; U.S. Bureau of the Census, *Heads of Families at the First Census of the United States Taken in the Year 1790: New York* (Washington, D.C., 1909). For a more detailed account of the construction of this table, see A Note to the Reader.

holdings were small and slaves were a minority of the total population. But a much clearer image of the involvement of New Yorkers with slavery comes into focus if we use the census schedules to work out the ratio of slaveholding to nonslaveholding households. Such a study reveals the surprising fact that even in 1790 about one in every five households in the city owned at least one slave.

When combined with other sources, the census schedules can also be used to draw a collective profile of New York City slaveholders. By comparing the 1789 tax list, which valued personal property and real estate on Manhattan Island, with the 1790 census, which listed slaveowners, it is possible to correlate economic status, as measured by assessable wealth, with slaveholding (see table 1). Slightly fewer than 60 percent (2,427 out of 4,237) of the heads of households enumerated in the tax list were matched with the census. This included 75 percent of the 1790 slaveholders, who between them owned 80 percent of the slaves.

Certain characteristics of slaveownership become clear from this data. Not surprisingly, the majority of slaveholders were in the upper economic strata, with nearly 30 percent of the slaveholders matched with the census being in the top decile of wealth. Thomas

Smith, an attorney-at-law, owned a house at 9 Wall Street valued at
£1,100 and personal property worth £800, which ranked him in the
first decile. According to the census he also owned four slaves. More
than 70 percent of the matched heads of households in this decile,
and in fact, more than one in two of the whole decile, even including those not matched with the census, owned slaves. Furthermore,
slaveholders in the top decile owned on average nearly three slaves
each as compared with two or less for persons in other deciles. But
the most interesting point to emerge from the data is the extent to
which slaveholding had penetrated the lower deciles. These slaveowners were not at the very bottom of the white social structure
but, as Herbert Klein and Edmund Willis have pointed out, should
be considered as the "propertied poor," a group that probably ap-
proximated an upper lower class.[5] Hastings Stackhouse, a grocer
who lived on Cherry Street near the New Slip, owned no real estate
and had personal property valued at only £50, which ranked him
in the eighth decile, but he is recorded in the 1790 census as owning a slave. Similarly, William Stymets, a tailor, rented his house
on Crown Street from John Alsop, a wealthy merchant, and owned
personal property assessed at only £25, placing him in the ninth
decile of wealth in the city. Yet within a few months, by which time
he had moved around the corner to Queen Street, the census taker
listed him as owning one slave. Slaveholding was considerably more
evenly distributed than wealth. The bottom 50 percent of the city's
population owned 6.6 percent of the assessable wealth but 12.1 percent of the slaves. Gary B. Nash's analysis of the Philadelphia tax
list for 1767 shows that only 5 percent of the slaveholders were in
the bottom 50 percent of the wealth distribution. James Henretta
has found that the comparable figure for Boston in 1771 was 5.4
percent.[6] But in New York in 1789 the figure was 17.6 percent, more
than three times that of Boston and Philadelphia.

The profile of the slaveholders can be further sharpened by using
the city directories. Published annually in New York after 1786,
these listed the names, addresses, and occupations of a majority of
heads of households. Working from the 1789, 1790, and 1791 directories I have located an entry for 921, or 90.1 percent, of the 1,022
slaveholders. The results obtained by comparing the census with
the city directories are set out in tables 2 and 3. Though listings
in the directories were not complete — 4,280 people appeared in the

TABLE 2

Male-Headed White Households Containing Blacks in New York City in 1790

	Slaveowning Households				White Households with Free Blacks				Total White Households Containing Blacks			
	Household		Slaves		Household		Free Blacks		Household		Total Blacks	
	N	%	N	%	N	%	N	%	N	%	N	%
Merchant	178	21.9	449	27.3	55	31.8	82	33.3	205	22.2	531	28.1
Retail	179	22.0	295	18.0	22	12.7	25	10.2	193	21.0	320	16.9
Professional	59	7.2	144	8.8	19	11.0	25	10.2	68	7.4	169	8.9
Official	34	4.2	81	4.9	8	4.6	9	3.6	38	4.1	90	4.4
Artisan	225	27.6	426	25.9	41	23.7	61	24.8	259	28.2	487	25.8
Service	35	4.3	55	3.4	8	4.6	9	3.7	39	4.2	64	3.4
Maritime	28	3.4	38	2.3	4	2.3	5	2.0	30	3.3	43	2.3
Miscellaneous	25	3.1	39	2.4	5	2.9	12	4.9	30	3.3	51	2.7
No occupation	51	6.3	117	7.1	11	6.4	18	7.3	58	6.3	135	7.1
	814	100.0	1,644	100.0	173	100.0	246	100.0	920	100.0	1,890	100.0
Not matched	76		144		34		42		104		186	
	890		1,788		207		288		1,024		2,076	

Sources: U.S. Bureau of the Census, *Heads of Families at the First Census of the United States Taken in the Year 1790: New York* (Washington, D.C., 1909); *The New York Directory, and Register, for the Year 1789* (New York, 1789); *The New York Directory, and Register, for the Year 1790* (New York, 1790); *The New York Directory, and Register, for the Year 1791* (New York, 1791). For a more detailed account of the construction of this table, see A Note to the Reader.

TABLE 3

Female-Headed White Households Containing Blacks in New York City in 1790

	Slaveowning Households		White Households with Free Blacks		Total White Households Containing Blacks	
	Household	Slaves	Household	Free Blacks	Household	Total Blacks
Retail	14	26	2	2	16	28
Professional	3	4	3	5	5	9
Skill	7	7	0	0	7	7
Service	20	29	8	9	25	38
Widow	43	91	8	10	47	101
No occupation	20	53	8	11	25	64
	107	210	29	37	125	247
Not matched	25	48	12	24	35	72
	132	258	41	61	160	319

Sources: U.S. Bureau of the Census, *Heads of Families at the First Census of the United States Taken in the Year 1790: New York* (Washington, D.C., 1909); *The New York Directory, and Register, for the Year 1789* (New York, 1789); *The New York Directory, and Register, for the Year 1790* (New York, 1790); *The New York Directory, and Register, for the Year 1791* (New York, 1791). For a more detailed account of the construction of this table, see A Note to the Reader.

1790 directory, whereas according to the census there were 5,590 white households in the city—they are more comprehensive than many have realized, even including, as we shall later see, information about quite a few free blacks.

Male slaveholders were distributed over a diverse range of occupations, but there was a concentration in the categories of merchant, retailer, and artisan (see table 2). The total number of people from these and other groups listed in the directories gives a rough indication of the prevalence of slaveholding within the various occupational categories. Of New York's merchants, for instance, more than two out of every three owned slaves. In the retailing category, which ranged from a few pedlars to grocers and shopkeepers, who were the vast majority, somewhere between one in three and one in four owned slaves. Similarly, about one in three of the professionals in the city were slaveowners. Though a smaller proportion of New York artisans, about one in eight, possessed slaves, artisans were still in 1790 the largest group of slaveholders.[7]

One other important group of eighteenth-century slaveholders, a group not so far studied extensively, was made up of women.

Although the vast majority of women married at some time in their lives, a much smaller percentage of the total female population was married at any given time. Consequently quite a few women in New York, usually widows, were heads of households.[8] Even according to the 1790 directory, a source that plainly underestimates the number of such women, about one in twelve households was headed by a woman. By 1800 this figure had risen to about one in nine. The census schedules for 1790 reveal that about 13 percent of New York slaveholders were women. Table 3 contains the results of the comparison of female slaveholders listed in the census with the directories. Most of these slaveholders were widows, but when an occupation was also listed for a woman she has been included under that heading. A few women who headed households were quite well off. Ann M'Adam, listed in the directory as having no occupation, owned three slaves. According to the tax list she also owned her house on Broadway and some property north of the city line, which when combined with her personal estate totaled some £2,790. That placed her comfortably in the first decile of wealth in the city. But many other women must have had difficulties making ends meet. The directory listed the widow M'Cullen as running a boardinghouse. She rented her dwelling and her personal property was valued at only £20, which situated her in the lowest wealth decile, yet she owned two slaves. Slaveholding women were most prominent in the service category, within which in 1790 probably about one in three women were slaveowners. This service category was largely made up of women who, like M'Cullen, ran a boardinghouse, a traditional means of support for widows.

One of the main characteristics of slavery in New York as in other urban settings was the small size of the slaveholding unit. In 1790, 75 percent of slaveholders owned only one or two slaves. Though the divorce between living space and work space associated with the transition to a more capitalistic economy had begun, many New Yorkers, whether merchants, grocers, or artisans, still conducted their business in the building in which they lived.[9] Almost invariably their slaves slept in the garrets or cellars of these houses, which severely limited the number of slaves city dwellers could own. In spite of the difficulties of space, however, in 1790 there were seventy-six households containing five or more slaves. Numbered in this group were such prominent New York families as the Beekmans and the Livingstons. Governor George Clinton owned eight slaves, Chief Justice Richard Morris six, and Aaron Burr five. John Jay, the president of the Manumission Society, also owned five slaves.

The issue of how New York slaves were employed is problematical. Travelers' accounts, such as those of Henry Wansey or Strickland, generally suggest that most slaves were domestic servants.[10] But such comments are impressionistic and are based on a rather narrow experience of New York society. Those who made them came armed with letters of introduction to important officials, lawyers, merchants, and gentlemen and circulated mainly among them, so that their judgments are really applicable only to slaveholding among such elite groups. Though some slaves belonging to the socially prominent were probably hired out or worked around the docks, the travelers were undoubtedly correct in assuming that the vast majority were house servants. Runaway advertisements for New York in the 1790s and early 1800s contain many descriptions of blacks trained as coachmen, cooks, and servants. Morris, an eighteen-year-old runaway, was "well acquainted with the duties of a servant in a gentleman's family" and Joshua, who absconded from his master's house on Greenwich Street, had "long been accustomed to the driving of a carriage and taking care of horses."[11] However, the range both of occupations and of assessable wealth of slaveholders strongly suggests that many slaves performed more economically productive functions. It is possible, for example, that slaves owned by ships' masters merely helped the masters' wives while the ships were away at sea. But given the large role played by blacks in the maritime work force it seems more likely that such slaves actually worked on ships earning money for their owners.[12]

A similar question arises with regard to artisan slaveholders: were the slaves held by this group domestics or were they employed in craft production? (In this case the distinction may be largely artificial, as artisan production was still mainly based on the household unit and apprentices, women, and slaves were probably all involved in production usually carried on in the front room or the cellar.) It is, of course, difficult enough to find information on artisan production, let alone the part played in it by blacks, but runaway advertisements again strongly suggest that many of the slaves owned by artisans were themselves skilled in the various trades. Adam Mount, a baker, described his seventeen-year-old runaway slave Andrew as a "tolerable good hand at the baking business." Charles, a forty-year-old fugitive owned by the coachmaker James Hallet, was "a harness maker by trade." Slave labor was also used in some of the heavier crafts, particularly tanning and ropemaking. Gideon Carstang's slave Tom "was bred to the rope making business," and West, who ran away in 1796, was "bought of the widow Ivers and has been accustomed to working in the ropewalk." [13] Some of these artisans were large slaveowners, at least by New York standards. According to the census, James Hallet owned eight slaves. James Rivington employed eight slaves in his printing shop, most of Anthony Lispenard's seven slaves were probably used in his brewery, and it is likely that Abraham Polhemus's six slaves worked in his tannery.

Although there are a number of excellent studies of New York artisans in the years after the Revolution those studies barely mention the artisan slaveholders. [14] Sean Wilentz, for example, implies that slavery was of little importance for most of the latter part of the eighteenth century and specifically comments that, although most of the wealthiest craft entrepreneurs probably had a servant, only "a very few owned slaves" in the period before the completion of emancipation in 1827. [15] These conclusions underestimate both the extent and the longevity of slaveholding among New York artisans and suggest that most slaves of artisans were servants. Yet throughout the eighteenth century the artisans' demand for labor was met not, as in Philadelphia, by indentured servants but by slaves. [16] While it is not possible to determine the incidence of slaveholding among New York's colonial artisans, the much better documented and researched example of Philadelphia suggests that the figures for artisan slaveholding in New York in 1790 probably represent a decline from those at midcentury. [17] A large number of New York artisans, ranging from the struggling tailor Hercules Mulligan, who ranked in the second-lowest wealth decile, to the relatively well-to-do house carpenter Thomas Ogilvie, whose property placed him in the second-highest decile, owned slaves. In fact, the comparisons between the 1789 tax list, the city directories, and the 1790 census clearly demonstrate that the artisans were the most prominent group of slaveholders in every decile of the wealth distribution apart from the top one, which was dominated by merchants, and the bottom one, which was made up largely of widows.

Some indication of the extent to which New York's artisans used slave labor can be gained by examining slaveholding among members of the most prominent artisan organization – the General Society of Mechanics and Tradesmen of the City of New York. The society was founded in 1785, although its origins can be traced back to the Mechanics' Committee of the 1770s. A semipolitical organization for independent mechanics, it aimed also to capture, in Wilentz's words, "the ideal of mutuality and craft pride essential to artisan fraternities since the Middle Ages." Members of the organization came from over thirty trades and generally included the more prominent and well-to-do master craftsmen in each occupation – those whom Wilentz labels "craft entrepreneurs."[18] Significantly, of the 164 artisans who were members of the society at its incorporation in 1792, a minimum of 62, or 37.8 percent, owned slaves at some stage in the 1790s.[19] A sailmaker owned two slaves as did Malcom M'Ewen, a plumber and pewterer. Daniel Tooker, a tanner and currier, owned five. A further five members of the General Society had free blacks residing in their households. In effect, therefore, at least four out of every ten members of the organization used some form of black labor.

Although the evidence is rather fragmentary it is likely that many of the skilled slaves owned by artisans were mulattoes. Cornelius Stevenson's slave William, who had "learnt the Taylor's trade," was a mulatto. Edward Bellesin, described by his master, one C. Rousseau, as a "taylor by trade," was an eleven-year-old French mulatto. Two skilled slaves described in a runaway advertisement in the *Daily Advertiser* in 1800 – a thirty-year-old who "used formerly to serve masons" and a left-handed barber named Nicholas – were mulattoes. Two other runaways, who were specifically described as apprentices by their masters, Abel Buntier and Abraham Cannon, were also mulattoes.[20] Additional indirect evidence of the link between the skilled trades and mulattoes comes in the record of occupations of free blacks. As we shall later see, a large proportion of skilled free blacks were categorized in the 1800 census as mulattoes.

Although it was not until 1820 that the census differentiated slaves by either gender or age, there were two other enumerations of the population in this period that did separate black women from black men. Unfortunately only the totals survive, but they show that females significantly outnumbered males.[21] Evidence of female slave occupations is, however, extremely fragmentary.[22] Not only are there far fewer runaway advertisements for female slaves, but their owners were even more reticent than the owners of male slaves about listing their occupations. Those skills included in runaway advertisements—cooking, washing, ironing—were all in the domestic sphere. Occasionally a stray piece of evidence will suggest that female slaves worked in other areas. For instance, when a fire broke out in the workshop of Slidell's soap and tallow manufactory in 1790, the boiling turpentine erupted into flames "instantly to burn a negro girl and to scorch her mother considerably."[23] Nevertheless it seems probable that most female slaves toiled as domestics. And while it must remain as little more than speculation, I suspect that artisan slaveholders were less likely than either merchants or shopkeepers to own female slaves.[24]

For a large proportion of the slaveholders of New York, slaves were not simply servants but an economic investment. One in three of the slaveowners matched with the tax list owned no real estate on Manhattan Island and lived in rented dwellings. More than one in two of the retailers who owned slaves fell within this category. Evidently these people chose to invest their money in slaves rather than in real estate.[25] Slaves were regarded in a similar fashion in wills. Males clearly envisaged that slave labor would help to provide for widows. There were, of course, the usual tortuous procedures to ensure that women did not assume control of the property, particularly if they remarried. The merchant Barnadus Swarthout, who left the use of his "negro wench" Flora to his wife, stipulated that Flora was to be sold on his wife's death. Similar provisions were made for children. James Baker directed that Dinah should be put out to service and her wages applied toward the support of his two sons. If his estate proved to be insufficient for this purpose she was to be sold.[26]

An examination of the landscape of the city and the spatial distribution of the slaveholders casts further light on the nature of slavery in New York. To one observer who arrived in 1787 the city appeared little more than a conglomeration of "miserable wooden hovels and strange looking brick houses, constructed in the Dutch fashion."[27] But as the economy prospered and the city expanded, an enormous amount of building occurred, changing the visual impact of the city. By the 1790s visitors were much more likely to comment favorably on what they saw. On his arrival in 1797 the French

traveler François La Rochefoucauld-Liancourt was particularly impressed with the rebuilding of the lower West Side, a portion of the
city that had been burned to the ground during the Revolution. He
even went so far as to claim that there was not "in any city in the
world a finer street than Broadway," with its generous breadth of
one hundred feet and pleasing views of the water. The lower East
Side, which had survived pretty well intact, was less deserving of
approbation: here, the houses were generally mean, small, low, and
wooden; the streets small and crooked; and the footpaths, if there
were any, narrow and interrupted by stairs from the houses, making
walking on them extremely inconvenient.[28]

The locations of the 1,022 slaveholding households in the city in
1790 can be pinpointed by combining the information in the directories with the census (see map 1, and see A Note to the Reader
for an account of how the maps were constructed). Although the
resulting pattern reveals a slight concentration of such households
in Dock and East wards, where nearly two out of every five owned a
slave, it is clear that slaveholders were well distributed throughout
the city. Every street in New York had slaveholders residing in it,
and very few New Yorkers lived more than a few doors from a slaveholder. It is true that by the end of the eighteenth century the mixed
neighborhoods of the colonial city were beginning to give way to
the more specialized residential areas of the nineteenth-century
city.[29] Many merchants lived on Broad, Wall, and Pearl streets in
what was becoming New York's financial heart. Tanners were concentrated in what was commonly known as the "Swamp" near Ferry
and Franckfort streets, and artisans involved in boatbuilding often
lived around Cherry Street in close proximity to the shipyards. But
although there was some specialization and economic differentia-
tion among the city wards, the process had not yet advanced very
far. It was still not at all unusual to find merchants, artisans, and
laborers living on the same street.

NEW YORK'S INFLUENCE spread well beyond the city limits. The
farmers dwelling in the surrounding countryside made a living, and
often a very comfortable one, supplying the growing metropolis
with grain, vegetables, fish, meat, and firewood. On his trip through
Long Island, Timothy Dwight, later president of Yale, commented

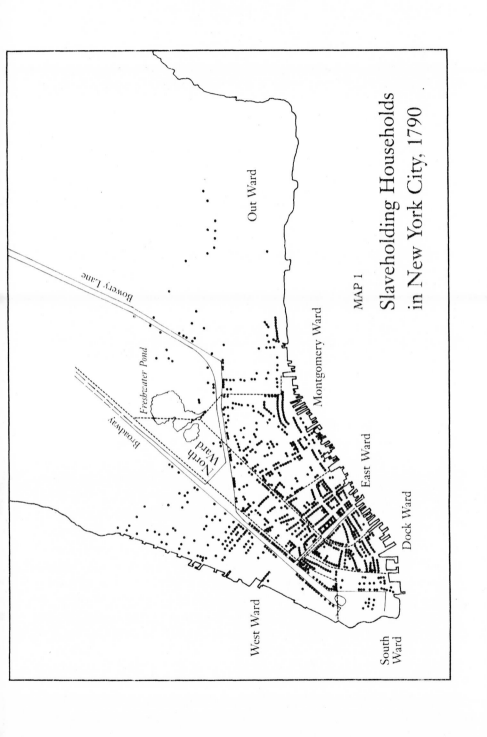

MAP 1

Slaveholding Households
in New York City, 1790

on the contrasting landscapes of Suffolk County, a sparse and wild scrubby country, and the western end of Long Island, where "the effects of the vicinity to New York are abundantly conspicuous, in the wealth of the farmers, and in the beauty of the villas with which they are handsomely ornamented." [30] Only when this urban system of New York is considered as a whole does the extent of the city's reliance on slavery become fully apparent. Alexander Coventry, an Englishman who migrated to New York in the 1780s, recorded in his memoirs that "in the vicinity of New York, every respectable family had slaves—negroes and negresses who did the drudgery," and the figures from the 1790 census support his observation (see map 2). [31] New York City was, in fact, the center of the heaviest slaveholding region north of the Mason-Dixon line. In the immediate hinterland—Kings and Queens counties on the western end of Long Island, Richmond County on Staten Island, and the portion of Manhattan Island north of the city limits—1,379, or 39.5 percent, of the 3,489 white households owned slaves, and blacks constituted 22.4 percent of the total population. Although the census schedules for New Jersey were destroyed during the War of 1812, the surviving county totals strongly suggest that a similar pattern of slaveowning existed in the portion of New Jersey that came within the orbit of New York. [32] Overall, then, probably about four out of every ten white households within a ten- to twelve-mile radius of New York City owned slaves.

The ratio of slaveholding to nonslaveholding households effectively highlights the striking involvement of whites from this region in the institution of slavery. There were proportionately more households containing slaves in New York's hinterland than in the whole of any southern state. In Maryland 36.5 percent of white households owned slaves, in South Carolina 34.0 percent, and in North Carolina 30.7 percent, but in Kings, Queens, and Richmond counties the figure was 39.5 percent. [33] Of course the labor requirements of these farmers were nowhere near as large as in the plantation South and consequently holdings were much smaller: the average slaveholding in Kings, Queens, and Richmond counties and the northern portion of Manhattan Island was 3.4 slaves. Nevertheless there were still forty-nine owners of ten or more slaves in this region (as opposed to the four who were in this category in New York City). Although the holdings were smaller, the commitment

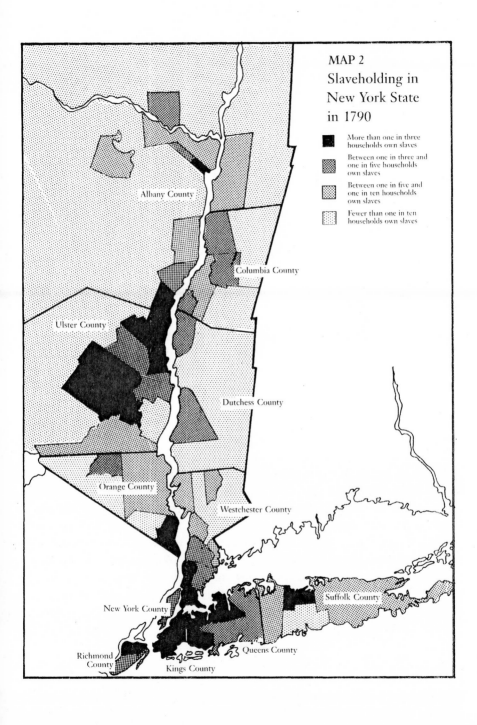

MAP 2

Slaveholding in
New York State
in 1790

■ More than one in three
households own slaves

▨ Between one in three and
one in five households
own slaves

▦ Between one in five and
one in ten households
own slaves

▨ Fewer than one in ten
households own slaves

Albany County

Columbia County

Ulster County

Dutchess County

Orange County

Westchester County

Suffolk County

New York County

Richmond
County

Queens County

Kings County

to and involvement of these farmers in the institution of slavery were comparable with those of the South.

Nowhere was the commitment to slavery more apparent than in Kings County. Strickland commented in his diary on the luxuriant appearance of this area and on the "rustics chiefly of Dutch descent whose chief occupation is that of raising vegitables for the supply of the market of New-York."[34] In Kings, 320 out of the 544 white households, or 58.8 percent, owned slaves in 1790. In some of the towns the rate of slaveownership was remarkable: in New Utrecht three out of every four households owned slaves; in Flatbush the ratio was two out of every three households, and blacks were 41.4 percent of the total population. Not only was a very high proportion of the inhabitants of this area involved in slavery, but the size of their holdings was also very large by northern standards. According to the 1790 census 43.4 percent of Kings County slaveholders owned five or more slaves, and 8.3 percent, or about one in twelve, possessed ten or more slaves.

Strickland's observation points up one of the most intriguing aspects of slavery in New York State—the involvement of the Dutch. At the beginning of this century the Bureau of the Census subjected the surviving (thus excluding New Jersey) manuscript schedules of the 1790 census to close scrutiny and compiled an extensive range of data. The clerks in the bureau placed households into ethnic categories on the basis of the householders' surnames. This material, when combined with the slaveholding figures, made it possible to work out the rate of slaveownership among the different ethnic groups. What such a calculation shows is that of the 9,399 households the Bureau of the Census classified as Dutch, 2,625, or 27.9 percent, owned slaves. This rate was far higher than that for every other major ethnic grouping in the American population— English and Welsh (11.3 percent), Scotch (16.0 percent), and Irish (15.3 percent)—and was surpassed only by the rate among the much smaller number of inhabitants of French origin. This Dutch population was concentrated to an overwhelming extent in New York State, with 96.6 percent of the slaveholders and 90.3 percent of the households that were classified as Dutch residing there.[35]

Contemporary observers of the New York scene were certainly well aware of the connection between the Dutch and slavery. It became part of the ritual of writing a traveler's account to include a few cruel and cutting comments on the Dutch, who at least in part because of the ancient Anglo-Dutch ethnic rivalry and tension in New York, had one of the worst presses imaginable. On a brief excursion into New Jersey the usually temperate and judicious William Strickland could not resist ending his discussion of the local custom of traveling by cart rather than by horse with the comment "[a] fat Dutchman and his fat wife, and two or three clumsy sons and daughters may frequently be seen thus driven and jolted by a not less fat negroe Slave."[36] The French exile La Rochefoucauld-Liancourt, proceeding through Ulster County in 1796, gratuitously described the locals as "dull torpid Hollanders" before recording that "each of the families, in some instances even the poorest has one or two negroes or negresses; slavery being as strictly maintained in the state of New York as in that of Virginia."[37] Such comments on the propensity of the Dutch, even the very poor, to own slaves were frequent. In 1784 the Spanish traveler Francisco de Miranda, while noting the poverty of the Dutch-speaking inhabitants around Albany (many women were unable even to afford shoes), nevertheless observed that "the number of Negroes is large."[38]

One of the main characteristics of the Dutch, emphasized time and again by travelers, was their conservatism. La Rochefoucauld-Liancourt wrote that the Dutch around Kinderhook were "not hasty to change old habits for new; accordingly they till and cultivate the land in the same manner now as they did a hundred years since." On reaching Albany he discovered that "the Ancient customs and confined views of the timid, yet covetous, Dutchmen have carefully been preserved in this city."[39] William Strickland considered that this conservatism was closely linked to the insularity of the Dutch. His comment is worth quoting at length. "Nothing can exceed the state of indolence and ignorance in which these Dutchmen are described to live. Many of them are supposed to live and die without having been five miles from their own houses, unless compelled at any time to go to Albany or to their county town upon public business. I have several times called at Dutch houses to make enquiries, when the owner, unable, though otherwise willing to give information wanted, has called Con, or Funk his oldest Slave, to answer my questions, or point out the road to the place I was going not perhaps distant more than a very few miles."[40]

In the minds of many visitors such insularity went hand in hand

with a naked possessiveness. Médéric Moreau de St. Méry, one of
the numerous Frenchmen traveling in America in the 1790s, concluded that those "Americans descended from the Dutch combine
to a pronounced degree the indolence of the Americans with the
avarice of the Dutch, thus emphasising the eagerness for gain that
is common to both." They carried "niggardliness so far that it
couldn't possibly go farther. They almost starve themselves, and
treat their slaves miserably."[41] It was left to another Frenchman,
J. P. Brissot de Warville, to appreciate that the implications of the
Dutch involvement in slavery for New York and New Jersey blacks
went well beyond the issue of the blacks' physical condition. The
number of slaves in New York was larger than in New England,
Brissot de Warville noted, "because the base of the population is
made up of Dutch, that is, of a people less willing than others to part
with property."[42] Consequently, he was less than sanguine about
the prospects for slaves in both New Jersey and New York.

Opposition to freeing slaves coalesced around the enclaves of
Dutch slaveholders in rural New York. Edward Countryman, after
a close and systematic scrutiny of roll calls in the assembly during the 1780s, concluded that the abolition of slavery was the only
issue on which, over a series of votes, the elected representatives
assumed a stance that was not congruent with their overall political
positions. When it came to that vexed subject the radicals split, and
there was no clear distinction between this group and the conser-
vatives, highlighting the fact that "country members," if not slaveholders themselves, were representatives of slaveholders.[43] In 1790,
John Murray, Jr., writing on behalf of the New York Manumission
Society and attempting to account for the failure of New York to
pass an abolition measure, made essentially the same point about
the country interest. Murray claimed that the major obstacle was "a
great body of Dutch, who hold Slaves in this government," and who
responded with alarm to any suggestion that slavery should end.
Furthermore, there was little hope of change, "as I expect a large
proportion of the Assembly, is constituted of Dutch Men."[44] More
than fifty years later, Erastus Root, reflecting on the attempts to
pass an abolition measure, agreed that the opposition derived from
the "chiefly Dutch" slaveholders. These men, he vividly declared,
"raved and swore by *dunder* and *blitzen* that we were robbing them
of their property," although in the end "we passed the law."[45]

The Dutch population of New York was distributed throughout the state. There were, as we have seen, many Dutch living in
Albany and Ulster counties, but one of the most important con-
centrations was around New York City, particularly on the western
end of Long Island. According to Isaac Weld, yet another traveler
with an acid observation about the Dutch, the inhabitants of this
region were "chiefly of Dutch extraction and they seemed to have
inherited all the coldness, reserve and covetousness of their ances-
tors."[46] A glance at the 1790 census schedule for Kings County
quickly confirms the heavy involvement of the Dutch farmers in
slavery. Though the classifying of individuals into ethnic groups by
their surnames is a process fraught with difficulties, it appears that
about one in every two of the slaveholders in Kings County was
of Dutch origin. This concentration is even more evident among
the larger slaveholders—twenty-two out of the twenty-seven slaveholders who owned ten or more slaves, that is, over 80 percent, had
Dutch surnames.

There is no doubt that the vast majority of slaves in the hinterland
of New York City were employed in agriculture. Information about
them is, of course, hard to come by. The small farmers of New
York's hinterland were not prone to self-reflection and generally
had neither the time nor the inclination to keep detailed records.
But there was at least one exception: during the first decade of the
nineteenth century Dr. Samuel Thompson of Setauket on Long
Island kept a diary. Entries in it refer regularly to his slaves Cuff,
Robin, Sharper, and Franklin attending to the round of chores—
weeding and tending crops, plowing fields, mowing hay, and treat-
ing flax—and convey a sense of the texture of agricultural life on
the small farms servicing the metropolis.[47] On a journey through
northern New Jersey in 1813, Elbridge Gerry, Jr., remarked on the
richness of the area and the six or seven slaves at every cottage,
who "assisted in tilling the ground, but did the most laborious part.
Some were employed with clearing the fields of the lesser rocks.
Others were entrusted with greater power." Gerry went on to describe the valley, with the sun setting on the toiling workers, as
"the most beautiful scene, that the pencil of a Raphael could imitate
and embellish, or the genius of a Scott could describe." Alexander
Coventry's comment that blacks around New York labored at the
"drudgery" may seem more realistic to the modern reader.[48]

Contemporary runaway advertisements provide further detail about the "drudgery" that was the lot of rural blacks. Bill, a fifty-year-old slave who had been brought up near Hempstead on Long Island and who absconded in 1789, was "acquainted with farming in every branch to a nicety." Many of the blacks were highly skilled. One H. Hughes of Westchester County went so far as to advertise that there were "very few hardier fellows at farming in general and none better at the plow" than Pro, his aptly named thirty-year-old runaway. Plato, another runaway from the same area, was intriguingly described as "very conceited respecting farming business; affects to mow after the English system having the last year resided with some English farmers on Throg's Neck." Country blacks were also trained as artisans to help meet the demand for skilled labor. Japhet, an escaped slave from Newark, was a cooper by trade, and Jim, also from the area around Newark, "understands the Coopers trade and all kinds of farming work."[49]

The persistence of and support for slavery in New York and its hinterland is in almost complete contrast with the situation in the Philadelphia area. Gary Nash has shown that in the last years of the colonial period slaveowning in Pennsylvania was predominantly an urban phenomenon: Philadelphians were about four times more likely to own slaves than were the inhabitants of Lancaster, Chester, and Philadelphia counties in the neighboring countryside. Further, the few slaveowners in these rural counties were very heavily drawn from the top stratum of the wealth distribution.[50] In New York, however, not only was the incidence of slaveholding higher but also the positions of the city and the country were reversed: the farmers in the hinterland were about twice as likely as were the inhabitants of the city to own slaves. Slavery had a more tenacious grip on the New York City system and played a more significant role in its economy than it did in Philadelphia, where the inhabitants tended to turn to slavery only when there was a disruption to the flow of indentured servants from Europe.

SLAVERY IN NEW YORK CITY easily weathered the storm of revolution. The agonizing by prominent citizens over the inconsistencies involved in fighting an oppressive Great Britain while still holding blacks in bondage had little discernible impact. By 1790 the inci-

dence of slaveholding in the area clearly distinguished it from any
other northern region and, in this respect at least, aligned it more
closely with the South. Nor was slaveholding tied closely to wealth.
La Rochefoucauld-Liancourt, in attempting to explain why the state
legislature had rejected various abolition measures, noted that the
greater part of the inhabitants of New York did not own slaves, but
that those who did were "the richest and greatest proprietors; and
in the State of New York, as elsewhere, such persons have the principal influence." [51] But La Rochefoucauld-Liancourt, in allowing his
antislavery opinions to cloud his customary perspicacity, had seriously misread the situation. It was true that many of the "richest
and greatest proprietors" owned slaves, but the practice was hardly
confined to the elite. Slavery in New York had penetrated not only
the middling but also the lower levels of society. And far from being
a moribund institution, in this rapidly developing New World economy slavery was poised for one last significant period of change and
expansion.

2

The Decline of Slavery in New York City, 1790–1810

THE NEW YORK that William Strickland observed in 1794 had already begun the dramatic growth that would soon make it the most important city in the United States. With its splendid harbor (open, unlike Philadelphia's, for virtually all of the year), a rapidly developing agricultural hinterland, and easy access to the increasingly important upstate frontier, the city had begun to outstrip both Boston and Philadelphia, its main eighteenth-century rivals. The state's speedily growing population—up 356 percent between 1780 and 1810 compared with Pennsylvania's rise of 148 percent—continually boosted the amount of trade passing through its major commercial center. Scarcely a traveler who visited New York in these years could refrain from commenting, as had Strickland, on the volume of shipping in the harbor and the busy activity on the wharves. In the late 1790s the city nosed ahead of its competitors in the value of exports and imports passing through its port; by the early years of the nineteenth century it had achieved clear economic primacy. For the period 1803–1810 exports leaving Philadelphia, previously the most important port in America, were worth only 68 percent of those leaving New York. In the quarter-century after the British evacuation the city handled fully one-third of the new nation's foreign commerce.[1]

This sharp rise in the volume of trade brought with it a fundamental restructuring of the New York economy, a process that

Thomas Cochran has called the "business revolution." As the scale of mercantile operations increased, business became more specialized. The New York Stock Exchange was founded and the Bank of New York incorporated in the 1790s. Investment bankers, brokers, and lawyers who specialized in various aspects of the increasingly complex financial transactions began to appear.[2] This tendency toward more specialization was not confined to the mercantile community. Related changes in the methods of production in the last years of the eighteenth century were ushering in the process that Sean Wilentz has labeled "metropolitan industrialization." Driven by the imperatives of expanding local and national markets, merchants and some of the more entrepreneurially minded craftsmen were initiating changes in the methods of production that, over the following half-century, would see the traditional world of artisan labor replaced by the new capitalist order of sweated labor and laborsaving machinery.[3] These changes occurred in a halting and uneven fashion and varied from trade to trade, but collectively they signaled the ascendancy of the capitalist mode of production. In the half-century after the Revolution, to put the matter more crudely, New York City made the quantum leap from a premodern to a modern economy.

These economic changes quickly altered the landscape of the city and the lives of its people. Large numbers of migrants, of internal as well as external origin, crowded into the metropolis whose population between 1790 and 1810 almost trebled to more than ninety thousand inhabitants (see table 4). The growth of Boston and Philadelphia, New York's main eighteenth-century rivals, barely matched that of the nation as a whole, but New York doubled the national rate. Such a rapid expansion in both numbers and size greatly strained the city's infrastructure. In these years municipal officials adopted a new system of street numbering, with the odds on one side and the evens on the other, and David Longworth commenced the annual publication of city directories, measures that demonstrated both the practical problems of this newfound magnitude and the increasing obsolescence of the old ways of the "walking city."[4] As migrants continued to arrive, housing became more and more difficult to find and the numbers of the poor and the destitute, dependent for their survival in Manhattan's unforgiving winters on the meager resources of charitable institutions and the municipal

TABLE 4
New York City Population, 1790–1810

Year	Free Blacks	Slaves	Total Black Population	Enslaved % of Black Population	Total Population	Black % of Total Population
1790	1,036	2,056	3,092	66.5	31,225	9.9
1800	3,333	2,534	5,867	43.2	57,663	10.2
1810	7,470	1,446	8,916	16.2	91,659	9.7

Sources: U.S. Bureau of the Census, *Heads of Families at the First Census of the United States Taken in the Year 1790: New York* (Washington, D.C., 1909); U.S. Bureau of the Census, Second Census of the United States, 1800, M32, Record Group 29, National Archives, Washington, D.C.; U.S. Bureau of the Census, Third Census of the United States, 1810, M252, Record Group 29, National Archives. For an account of the origins of these figures, see A Note to the Reader.

government, rose sharply.[5] The economic transformation accompanying this population growth altered the city in other ways. As Hendrik Hartog has shown in his study of the corporation of the city of New York, it was in the years after the Revolution that the city government changed. From being an institution relying on its property holdings as a source of power it became a public body financed largely by taxation and devoting its energies to distinctly public concerns. This separation of public and private spheres was characterized, above all, by "a fairly unambiguous acceptance of the primacy of a market economy."[6] It was, however, in the lives of individuals rather than institutions that the most momentous changes occurred. As Sean Wilentz has so ably demonstrated, the ascendancy of the new capitalist order led to the development of new forms of class relations and social consciousness that affected virtually every facet of life.[7] Few groups would feel the impact of these changes as fully as New York's blacks.

William Strickland's feeling of déjà vu as he set down his impressions of New York probably stemmed from an unspecified and unrealistic idea of what a New World city should look like and how it would function. What he was shrewd enough to appreciate quickly, however, was that the city was largely the product of factors common to all such commercial centers.[8] The particulars may have varied from place to place, but much the same process of economic change had occurred many times before and with similar results. Yet, intentionally or not, Strickland had put his finger on the one important anomaly exhibited by New York: the presence in a commercial urban environment of a substantial minority of blacks and the continued existence of slavery. Throughout the 1790s and for the first decade of the nineteenth century the city's blacks would maintain their share of the population at about 10 percent, a remarkable performance in the context of a rapid demographic expansion (see table 4). It is to the role of slavery and black labor in this rapidly changing economy that we shall now turn.

THE FEW HISTORIANS who have considered slavery in New York in this period have generally concluded that the institution was rapidly disappearing even before the passage of the 1799 Gradual Manumission Act. Such conclusions are largely attributable to ideological preconceptions about the influence of the American Revolution and to a refusal to examine in anything but the most cursory fashion the patterns of slaveholding exhibited in the various census figures. One historian has claimed that "justification and support of slavery in New York dwindled rapidly after 1775" under the impact of the ideology of the Revolution, the tumult of war, and the work of the New York Manumission Society and, further, that slavery was virtually extinct after 1790.[9] Others with a similarly whiggish view have chosen to emphasize the role of the Manumission Society. Another historian cites the gross figures from 1790 and 1800, claiming that they demonstrate the "rapid strides that the movement for emancipation had made by the turn of the century."[10] Although slaves did make up a smaller share of New York's population in the 1790s than they had before the Revolution, this was a product of the city's rapid population growth. Had these authors examined the census figures more closely, they would have realized that the fall in the enslaved percentage of the black population from 66.5 percent in 1790 to 43.2 percent in 1800 (see table 4) resulted not from a decline in the institution but from an increase in the total black population caused largely by black migration to the city and, probably, a rising birthrate. Between 1790 and 1800 there was actually a 22 percent increase in the number of slaves in New York and a 33 percent increase in the number of slaveholders. These figures, which probably

TABLE 5
Manumissions in New York City Wills, 1783–1800

Years	Number of Wills	Wills Mentioning Slaves	Wills Manumitting Slaves
1783–1789	262	31	8
1790–1795	159	18	9
1796–1800	364	40	18
	785	89	35

Source: *Abstracts of Wills on File in the Surrogate's Office, New York City, 1665–1800*, 17 vols. (New York, 1892–1909). This table is based on all New York County wills from 1783 to 1800 included in these volumes.

represent one of the largest increases in any decade of the city's history, are not suggestive either of the extinction of slavery or of great strides being made by the emancipation movement.

What is, in fact, most striking about New York City in this period is the strength of the interest in slavery and the paucity of manumissions. Table 5 sets out all the manumissions in the wills probated between 1783 and 1800, and table 6 includes all those recorded by the Office of the Register for New York County and in the papers of the New York Manumission Society. There were probably other slaves who were not included in these records, but even so the total from these sources—seventy-six manumissions between 1783 and 1800—does not suggest a particularly rich harvest for the New York Manumission Society.[11] Further, these manumissions generally resulted not from the success of antislavery advocates in convincing slaveowners of the error of their ways, but from an extension of the benevolence that New York slaveowners had long associated with their form of slavery. In 1786 Francis Lewis, "Gentleman," rewarded his slave King for "the fidelity, integrity and sobriety ever manifested" toward his master "in the course of a long service" by providing for his freedom.[12] The same attitude is particularly noticeable in manumissions in wills, where freedom was frequently not given immediately but was conditional on good behavior. George Gunn, a silk dyer, directed in his 1797 will that his "black boy" Jack should be entitled to his freedom at the age of thirty provided he was "obedient and faithful." Other owners discriminated very carefully between their slaves, freeing favorites and

TABLE 6
Recorded Manumissions in
New York City, 1783–1810

Years	Number of Manumissions
1783–1790	5
1791–1795	7
1796–1800	29
1801–1805	68
1806–1810	192
	301

Sources: This table is based on the manumissions from the Office of the Register, New York County, and those in the Papers of the New York Manumission Society, New-York Historical Society. They are collected in Harry B. Yoshpe, "Record of Slave Manumissions in New York During the Colonial and Early National Periods," *Journal of Negro History* 26 (1941): 78–104. There is no overlap (no common manumissions) between tables 5 and 6.

condemning others to continued bondage. In his 1798 will Metcalf Eden, a brewer, gave certain of his slaves — Bill, Peter, Jane, little Hannah, Sal, Isaac, Fortune, and young Jack — to his son. Hannah Palmer, however, was to be set free immediately and Eden's executors were to pay her $100 a year for the rest of her life. Similarly, the "negro boy" Harry was to be set free straight away, but "my negro man" Saul and his wife Dianna were to be freed two years after Eden's death and then given $100. Jane, whom he had given to his son, was to be freed in ten years time and Hannah, also the property of the son, at age twenty-one. Silvey was to be manumitted in five years time, and Hagar was left to Eden's wife but was to be freed when the wife died.[13] Although this was an extreme case (less complex but similar examples, however, were by no means uncommon), it demonstrates that manumission was not necessarily immediate and also that it did not necessarily entail a rejection of slavery.

There is, however, one possible proviso. Although the number of decedents manumitting slaves was very small, there appear to be some grounds for arguing that female and male slaveowners viewed their slaves differently. About one in three (eleven out of thirty-five) of the wills manumitting slaves were written by females, a ratio

that is more than twice as high as the proportion of slaveholding
women. Further, females were less likely to include restrictive conditions and tended simply to free all their slaves immediately. About
the same proportion (slightly less than one in two) of females and
males included in their wills bequests for freed slaves, but there
seems to have been a qualitative difference in the type of legacies
left by women. Men almost invariably left money—sometimes a
lump sum but more commonly a fixed amount every year. Arthur
Helme, a merchant, freed his slave Scipio and left him £7 per annum
for life.[14] Women often left larger sums of money and frequently
included other forms of property. Mary Thomas, a widow, manumitted Jane and gave her all the movable estate and furniture and
£10 per annum for life.[15] Maria Farmer, another widow, freed her
slave Nan along with Nan's sons Rob and Prince and also left them
a lot of land at 7 Franckfort Street and sundry other goods, including kitchen utensils, a pewter basin, a pewter soap dish, and three
cords of wood to be delivered during the next winter.[16] This last
item was a thoughtful touch, as the constant shortage of firewood
was the bane of a woman's life in New York winters, and does hint
at the "personalism" that Suzanne Lebsock found in her study of
the wills of Petersburg women.[17] The evidence is hardly conclusive,
but it does suggest that women slaveholders may have been more
likely than men to question the institution of slavery, if only on an
individual rather than abstract level, and to feel a certain degree
of guilt about their ownership of slaves. The will of Mary Bryant
provides an interesting though undoubtedly extreme example—she
left bequests totaling £390 to several blacks, mostly former slaves,
scattered from Saint Kitts to Albany.[18]

Yet manumissions were to have very little impact on the number of slaves in New York until the early nineteenth century. The
dominant feature of the economically buoyant 1790s was, rather, a
renewed interest in the institution of slavery. The sources of this
increase are partly revealed by tracing the 1800 slaveholders back
to the 1790 census schedule. Such a comparison shows that far from
being a static, unchanging group, New York City slaveholders were
characterized by a very high rate of turnover: only 300 out of the
890 male slaveholders in 1790, or slightly more than one in three,
were still slaveowners in the city in 1800.[19] In part, this low rate of
persistence reflected the high death rate in New York in the 1790s:

the yellow fever epidemics of 1795 and 1798, for example, killed at least two thousand New Yorkers, accelerating the transfer of slave property from one generation to the next. And while it is impossible to measure inheritance of slaves from the census, as none of the dependent members of households were recorded in the schedules of this period, it is nevertheless clear that three out of every four male slaveholders in 1800 had not owned slaves in the city in 1790. A few of these new slaveholders were long-term residents who had acquired slaves during the 1790s: in 1800 there were 104 male slaveholders, or about one in four of those matched with the 1790 census, who were established as a head of household in 1790 but had then owned no slaves. Others had been dependent members of households in 1790 who in the next decade established their own households and either purchased or inherited slaves.

But probably more than one in three of the male slaveholders in 1800 were migrants who arrived in New York City in the 1790s and either brought slaves with them or purchased them in the city. Though some of these migrants came from the American mainland, the most conspicuous group were the French-speaking refugees from the great rebellion in Saint Domingue. By 1793 about ten thousand people had fled the West Indian island and settled in America, and while the majority migrated to the South, a substantial minority, particularly the French Royalists, went to New York and other northern cities, bringing some of their slaves with them. Quite a few are listed in the census schedules. For example, there appears to have been a cluster of French émigrés living in Upper Reed Street between City Hall and the collect (a freshwater pond) many of whom, such as John Dupan and Peter Dispinou, owned slaves. But because the names of such persons were usually anglicized very quickly either by themselves or by the census takers (their treatment of some foreign names has to be seen to be believed, though at times, mercifully, they gave up and entered the figures under the rubric "a French family"), it is impossible to estimate the numbers of such French émigrés from the census schedules.[20]

Despite the paucity of statistical evidence there can be little doubt about the presence of many Frenchmen and their slaves in the city. The slaves themselves, often marked with the ritual scarifications of Africa and mutilated by the brands of their Saint Dominguan masters, presented an alien sight, one not seen in New York for many years. Their owners, too, were rendered highly visible not only by their language and customs, but also by their treatment of their slaves. An incident reported in the *Argus* suggests that the émigrés, accustomed to the practices of Port-au-Prince and Cap Français, had a rather different conception of slavery from that of New Yorkers. Early in June 1795 "A Man" had witnessed "an affray (if that can be called an affray in which one of the parties makes no resistance)" between a Frenchman and a black woman. The master took a three-foot length of pine and brutally beat the woman, whom the observer surmised was the Frenchman's slave.[21] The writer used this incident as the occasion for a disquisition on the impropriety of a true republican depriving fellow creatures of their liberty. Reading the letter, though, it is difficult not to feel that the New Yorker's sensibilities were more offended by the overt violence than by the fact of slavery itself. New Yorkers had difficulty associating their form of slavery, which they considered to be rather benevolent and mild, with the barbarism that antislavery propaganda informed them was a part of everyday life in the South and in the West Indies. The French émigrés, who branded their slaves and exhibited a more exacting version of the master-slave relationship, introduced the unacceptable face of slavery north of the Mason-Dixon line, and in the process probably shook the complacency of not a few New York citizens.

The infusion into the slaveholders' ranks of new blood from outside of the city was only one of a number of changes occurring in the institution of slavery in New York. Such changes are made more apparent by an analysis of the composition of the slaveholders listed in the 1800 census. Although the figures in tables 7 and 8 are not quite as high as those for 1790, I have still managed to match with the directories 1,024, or 85.4 percent, of the 1,198 male slaveowners. The proportion of female slaveholders, 12.4 percent of the total, remained at about the same level as in 1790, and 126 of the 170 female slaveholders in 1800, or 74.1 percent, were identified in the directories.

The increase in slavery in the 1790s and the high turnover of slaveholders meant that the male slaveholders in 1800 were a substantially different group of men from those of 1790. Only one in four of the male slaveholders in 1800 had owned slaves in the city in 1790. A comparison of the 1800 male slaveholders with those of

TABLE 7
Male-Headed White Households Containing Blacks in New York City in 1800

	Slaveowning Households				White Households with Free Blacks				Total White Households Containing Blacks			
	Household		Slaves		Household		Free Blacks		Household		Total Blacks	
	N	%	N	%	N	%	N	%	N	%	N	%
Merchant	365	35.7	724	38.6	256	45.3	398	46.6	522	37.4	1,122	41.1
Retail	131	12.8	202	10.8	49	8.7	59	6.9	165	11.8	261	9.6
Professional	88	8.6	153	8.2	51	9.0	76	8.9	114	8.2	229	8.4
Official	40	3.9	85	4.5	21	3.7	39	4.6	50	3.6	124	4.5
Artisan	206	20.1	339	18.1	89	15.8	128	15.0	279	20.0	467	17.1
Service	33	3.2	59	3.2	22	3.9	30	3.5	53	3.8	89	3.3
Maritime	35	3.4	55	2.9	18	3.2	19	2.2	48	3.4	74	2.7
Miscellaneous	23	2.2	34	1.8	17	3.0	22	2.6	36	2.6	56	2.1
No occupation	103	10.1	223	11.9	42	7.4	83	9.7	128	9.2	306	11.2
	1,024	100.0	1,874	100.0	565	100.0	854	100.0	1,395	100.0	2,728	100.0
Not matched	174		315		107		153		262		468	
	1,198		2,189		672		1,007		1,657		3,196	

Source: U.S. Bureau of the Census, Second Census of the United States, 1800, M32, Record Group 29, National Archives, Washington, D.C.; *Longworth's American Almanack, New-York Register, and City Directory, for the Twenty-Fourth Year of American Independence* (New York, 1799); *Longworth's American Almanack, New-York Register, and City Directory, for the Twenty-Fifth Year of American Independence* (New York, 1800); *Longworth's American Almanack, New-York Register, and City Directory, for the Twenty-Sixth Year of American Independence* (New York, 1801).

TABLE 8
Female-Headed White Households Containing Blacks in New York City in 1800

	Slaveowning Households		White Households with Free Blacks		Total White Households Containing Blacks	
	Household	Slaves	Household	Free Blacks	Household	Total Blacks
Retail	9	15	4	4	10	19
Professional	3	3	5	6	7	9
Skill	6	10	4	4	8	14
Service	16	33	20	32	30	65
Widow	49	82	21	32	64	114
No occupation	43	90	20	25	57	115
	126	233	74	103	176	336
Not matched	44	89	32	42	69	131
	170	322	106	145	245	467

Sources: U.S. Bureau of the Census, Second Census of the United States, 1800, M32, Record Group 29, National Archives, Washington, D.C.; *Longworth's American Almanack, New-York Register, and City Directory, for the Twenty-Fourth Year of American Independence* (New York, 1799); *Longworth's American Almanack, New-York Register, and City Directory, for the Twenty-Fifth Year of American Independence* (New York, 1800); *Longworth's American Almanack, New-York Register, and City Directory, for the Twenty-Sixth Year of American Independence* (New York, 1801).

1790, who were discussed in the last chapter, reveals some other significant developments. By 1800 merchants rather than artisans were easily the most important group of slaveholders in the city. Slaveowning merchants had doubled their numbers in the 1790s, increasing their share of all male slaveholders from 21.9 percent in 1790 to 35.7 percent by 1800. There was also a 50 percent increase in the number of slaveowners classified as professionals, so that by 1800 they constituted 8.6 percent of the total number of owners identified in the directories. The retailers, on the other hand, in spite of the large increase in slaveholding in the city, suffered an absolute decline in their numbers. Their share of all male slave-owners plummeted from 22.0 percent in 1790 to only 12.8 percent a decade later.

The change in composition of slaveowners over the ten-year period from 1790 to 1800 reflected, not surprisingly, the economic developments of that decade. Sustained growth throughout the 1790s attracted many aspiring young men into the mercantile sector. In the 1790 city directory 248 men were listed as merchants, but by 1800 there were 1,102, a fourfold increase. Although such figures are not necessarily an exact measure of the size of the merchant community, they do give a good indication of its dramatic expansion. Many ambitious retailers, attracted by potential profits far exceeding those to be made running a shop, gambled and set up as merchants.[22] Four out of every ten of the merchant slaveowners in 1800 who were traced back to the 1790 census had started out as retailers. Furthermore, one in five of this socially mobile group of retailers had owned no slaves at all in 1790.[23] Clearly, those who prospered in the 1790s—the merchants and also the professionals, the majority of whom were lawyers—spent part of their new wealth buying slaves.

As the number of merchants increased, they branched out into new spheres of enterprise that, with the benefit of hindsight, we can see contributed substantially to the financial modernization of New York. Time and again, however, we find those involved in classic free market institutions such as the stock exchange also owning slaves, that is, bound labor. Of the 177 male stockholders in the Bank of New York at its incorporation in 1791, a minimum of 83, or 46.8 percent, were listed as slaveowners in either the 1790 or 1800 census.[24] The New York Manufacturing Society, advertised in February 1789 as a vehicle for establishing a woolen factory, provides another example. By March 17, 1789, 187 investors had subscribed £2,100. According to the 1790 census at least 108 of these were slaveowners, and by 1800 a further 20, including 11 who had owned no slaves in 1790, had acquired slaves.[25] In effect two out of every three who were financially supporting the society were slaveholders at some time in the 1790s. The enterprise flopped after a few years and the investors lost most of their money, but what is important here is that those involved in what Thomas Doerflinger, writing of Philadelphia, has aptly termed the "entrepreneurial efflorescence" of the early national period were increasingly turning to slavery.[26]

The other significant change in the composition of the slaveowners that occurred in the 1790s was a considerable drop in the number of artisans who owned slaves. Although the number of artisans in New York had more than doubled in this period there was an absolute decline in the number of artisan slaveholders. About one in eight of the 1,620 artisans listed in the 1790 directory owned slaves, but by 1800 this figure had dropped dramatically to about one in seventeen of the 3,460 artisans included in the 1800 direc-

tory. Artisans had also surrendered to the merchants their position
as the largest single group of slaveholders in New York. In 1790 the
225 artisans made up 27.6 percent of all slaveholders, but in 1800
the 206 artisans constituted only 20.1 percent of the total number
of slaveholders.

These statistics reflect the long-term decline in the use of slave
labor by New York artisans, a process that had probably commenced before the Revolution. In relation to this development
Sharon Salinger's work on the decline of indentured servitude in
Philadelphia is quite suggestive. Over the second half of the eighteenth century, and particularly after the Revolution, there was a
gradual transition to a system of capitalist labor relations in Philadelphia. The percentage of bound labor, primarily indentured servants but including some slaves, fell from about 40 percent of the
work force in the mid-eighteenth century to virtually nothing in
1800. Increasingly artisans turned away from the use of bound labor
and drew on the large pool of unemployed recent immigrants to
provide wage labor, a cheaper and more flexible method of satisfying their requirements.[27] A similar process was occurring in New
York, although there it had always been slaves and not indentured
servants that mainly supplied the bound labor. After the Revolution,
New York artisans relied less on slave labor than they had during the
colonial period, and their use of slaves declined even further during the 1790s. Apprentices, journeymen, and slaves were gradually
displaced from integrated household production. In a movement
accelerated by the presence of a large and often impoverished pool
of immigrants, including it should be added many of New York's
emerging free black population, the more entrepreneurially minded
artisans replaced bound laborers, previously housed and fed by their
masters, with workers who sold their labor as a commodity and
were forced to buy housing, fuel, and food.[28]

Not all trades were caught up in this economic transformation.
Baker shops, scattered throughout the city and relying on a regular clientele drawn from a small local area, were restricted by the
assize, a control on the price of bread that dated back to medieval
England.[29] Similarly, butchers operating out of a licensed stall in
one of the city's four major markets participated in a regulated market.[30] In both cases the tradesmen were able to avoid the exigencies

of the free market and carry on running their typically small establishments in much the same manner until well into the nineteenth
century. Interestingly, both trades were also relatively heavy users
of slave labor. According to the 1790 directory there were sixty-
two bakers in the city, and a comparison of the 1790 census with
the directories reveals that sixteen, or about one in four, owned
slaves. In the case of the butchers the figure was a little lower—of
forty-eight butchers, ten owned slaves. Furthermore, the number
of slaveowners in these two trades actually increased, albeit marginally, during the 1790s—seventeen bakers and fifteen butchers
owned slaves in 1800. Four of these bakers and two of the butchers,
who were listed in the 1790 census as owning no slaves, had obviously purchased or inherited their slave labor at some time during
the 1790s. The bakers and butchers managed to maintain their old
labor patterns, and in marked contrast to most other trades, slaveowning remained for many of them a viable, even an attractive,
proposition.

Although the 1790s were a period of expansion for slavery, women
still managed to maintain their proportion of the total number of
slaveholders at about one in eight. There was an even higher rate of
turnover in the female than in the male slaveholders, with only 26,
or one in five, of the 132 female owners in 1790 still heading households and owning slaves in 1800. Almost all of the female heads
of households were widows, and the higher turnover rate partly re-
flects the fact that neither widows remarrying nor males dying and
leaving slaves to their widows can be picked up in the census schedules. Yet what is interesting is the number of women for whom
widowhood was less a temporary hiatus between marriages than a
semipermanent way of organizing their lives. Suzanne Lebsock, in
her study of the women of Petersburg, points out that the most eli-
gible wives among the widows—the young and the wealthy—were
in fact the least likely to remarry.[31] The figures from New York certainly suggest that there were at least some women who preferred to
remain single. In 1800, 33 of the 170 women slaveowners, or about
one in five, had also been listed as a head of household ten years
previously at the time of the first census. Many of these women
not only carried on the same occupation as their deceased husbands
but also assumed control of the business.[32] Of these 33 female slave-

owners 7, or more than one in five, had possessed no slaves in 1790. Consequently they must have purchased their slave property, and not simply inherited it from their husbands.

In 1799 the New York legislature finally assented to the Gradual Manumission Act. Under its terms all children born to slave women in New York after July 4, 1799, were to be free, but males were to remain in the service of their masters until they reached the age of twenty-eight and females until they were twenty-five. The passage of the act may have marginally affected the 1800 figures, as the children of slaves born between July 4, 1799, and the taking of the census should have been included as free blacks, not as slaves. It also appears likely that, in contravention of a 1788 law, some masters may have shipped slaves to the South in order to avoid a financial loss on their slave property, further diminishing the 1800 slave total.[33] It was not, however, until the first decade of the nineteenth century that the full impact of the act was felt in the city (see table 6 for the rise in manumissions after 1799). By 1810 the number of slaveholders listed in the census had fallen to 947, a 25.3 percent drop from the 1800 figures and the lowest number recorded in the city in any of the first three federal censuses. Not only were the ranks of the slaveowners dwindling, but so were their holdings: the average number of slaves per owner dropped from 1.98 in 1800 to 1.5 in 1810.

Although the Gradual Manumission Act had a considerable impact both on the numbers of slaveowners and on the size of their holdings, other characteristics of the slaveholders remained much the same as in 1800. Only 202, or one in four, of the 827 male slaveowners in 1810 had been a slaveowning head of household in New York City in 1800. Of these 202 men, 106 had actually owned slaves at the time of the 1790 census. Thus, as in 1800, the overall impression gained from the 1810 census figures is one not of continuity but of change, a surprising result as one would have imagined that the passage of the Gradual Manumission Act would have dampened interest in the slave market. However, more than one in three of the 311 male slaveowners in 1810 who were traced back to the 1800 census had then owned no slaves. The vast majority of the male slaveowners in 1810 had, like these men, either inherited slaves or decided that it was still worthwhile to invest their money in slavery.

Tables 9 and 10 contain the data from a comparison of the 1810

TABLE 9

Male-Headed White Households Containing Blacks in New York City in 1810

| | Slaveowning Households | | | | White Households with Free Blacks | | | | Total White Households Containing Blacks | | | |
| | Household | | Slaves | | Household | | Free Blacks | | Household | | Total Blacks | |
	N	%	N	%	N	%	N	%	N	%	N	%
Merchant	186	25.9	301	28.1	280	26.1	438	27.3	415	25.7	739	27.6
Retail	99	13.8	125	11.7	113	10.5	151	9.4	195	12.1	276	10.3
Professional	65	9.1	99	9.2	117	10.9	175	10.9	161	9.9	274	10.2
Official	18	2.5	26	2.4	35	3.3	50	3.1	47	2.9	76	2.8
Artisan	157	21.9	215	20.0	225	21.0	307	19.1	353	21.9	522	19.5
Service	32	4.5	61	5.7	53	4.9	99	6.2	74	4.6	160	6.0
Maritime	31	4.3	40	3.7	53	4.9	69	4.3	80	5.0	109	4.1
Miscellaneous	17	2.4	27	2.5	38	3.6	53	3.3	50	3.1	80	3.0
No occupation	112	15.6	179	16.7	159	14.8	263	16.4	239	14.8	442	16.5
	717	100.0	1,073	100.0	1,073	100.0	1,605	100.0	1,614	100.0	2,678	100.0
Not matched	110		180		275		504		367		684	
	827		1,253		1,348		2,109		1,981		3,362	

Sources: U.S. Bureau of the Census, Third Census of the United States, 1810, M252, Record Group 29, National Archives, Washington, D.C.; *Longworth's American Almanack, New-York Register, and City Directory; For the Thirty-Fifth Year of American Independence* (New York, 1810); *Elliot and Crissy's New-York Directory, For the Year 1811, and 36th of the Independence of the United States of America* (New York, 1811). For a more detailed account of the construction of this table, see A Note to the Reader.

TABLE 10
Female-Headed White Households Containing Blacks in New York City in 1810

	Slaveowning Households		White Households with Free Blacks		Total White Households Containing Blacks	
	Household	Slaves	Household	Free Blacks	Household	Total Blacks
Retail	3	3	7	8	10	11
Professional	2	2	3	4	5	6
Skill	5	7	11	11	14	18
Service	15	25	42	101	48	126
Widow	41	71	65	108	91	179
No occupation	20	23	35	57	50	80
	86	131	163	289	218	420
	34	44	59	97	86	141
	120	175	222	386	304	561

Sources: U.S. Bureau of the Census, Third Census of the United States, 1810, M252, Record Group 29, National Archives, Washington, D.C.; *Longworth's American Almanack, New-York Register, and City Directory; For the Thirty-Fifth Year of American Independence* (New York, 1810); *Elliot and Crissy's New-York Directory, For the Year 1811, and 36th of the Independence of the United States of America* (New York, 1811). For a more detailed account of the construction of this table, see A Note to the Reader.

census and the 1810 and 1811 directories. To complete these figures 717, or 86.7 percent, of the 827 male slaveholders and 86, or 71.7 percent, of the 120 female slaveholders were matched with the directories. (Women again maintained their share of all slaveholders at about one in eight.) Although the numbers in each category dropped considerably, the proportions remained roughly the same as in 1800, with most groups changing their share only by one or two percentage points. The exception was the merchants, who registered a decline from 35.7 percent to 25.9 percent, but this fall, which appears to run counter to the argument advanced earlier in the chapter, can, I think, be explained. The rise in the share of the category "No occupation" was probably largely at the expense of the merchants. There were 37 male slaveowners in this category in 1810 who were traced back to the 1800 census, and 18 of these, or about half, had previously been merchants. It seems likely that those merchants who made a lot of money in the boom of the 1790s and early 1800s had retired and consequently were listed in the directories with no occupation next to their name. That two-thirds of those 18 former merchants were old enough to head a household and own slaves in 1790 tends to support this conclusion. However, probably the largest factor in this fall was the economic depression that followed on the Embargo. In these changed circumstances many merchants went bankrupt, and more suffered a drastic reversal in their economic fortunes.[34] Consequently they divested themselves of their slave property.

Even in the early 1790s contemporaries could discern that the spoils of New York's growing prosperity were not being evenly distributed and that, partly as a consequence, the geography of their city was changing. In 1791 "A Citizen" commented in a letter printed in the *Daily Advertiser* that "some wards are composed almost wholly of the wealthier class of citizens; whilst others contain almost exclusively the poorer part of the community."[35] Gradually the old "walking city" of mixed neighborhoods was giving way to the specialized residential districts of the emerging "industrial city." Increasingly New York's laboring population lived not in the households of their masters but in separate accommodation, often boardinghouses or rented dwellings concentrated in what were becoming the working-class wards of the city.[36] These areas were often overcrowded and dirty and always suffered the highest mortality rates during the regular visitations of yellow fever; Timothy Dwight, describing one such area near the East River ("a very great collection of miserable temporary buildings"), noted that such neighborhoods stood "aside from the walks of gentlemen who visit this city."[37] Although the more rigid class divisions of the industrial city were not yet fully apparent, New York in the early years of the nineteenth century would barely have been recognizable to inhabitants of the colonial city.

A close examination of maps 1, 3, and 4 reveals small but significant changes in the spatial distribution of New York slaveholders and helps to bring into focus the shift in their composition. One of the clearest differences between 1790 and 1800 was the movement of slaveholders into the recently rebuilt lower West Side. A very high proportion of the residents of Broadway, the showpiece of the city, were slaveowners. La Rochefoucauld-Liancourt said of this area in the late 1790s that because of its "elevated situation, its position on the river, and the elegance of the buildings, it is naturally the place of residence of the most opulent inhabitants."[38] The mercantile elite of the city increasingly displaced the earlier mélange of

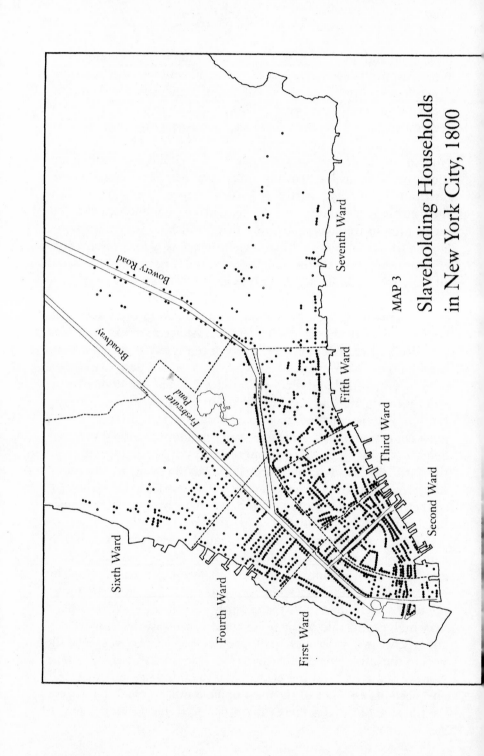

MAP 3

Slaveholding Households
in New York City, 1800

artisans and petty proprietors living in lower Manhattan and clustered on about a dozen streets, all within easy strolling distance of
Wall Street and the stock exchange. In 1800 about one in three, or
480, of the 1,485 white households situated in the First and Second
wards owned slaves.

Another important development occurred at the same time. According to the 1790 directory only a very few of New York's inhabitants did not work and live at the same address.[39] Even merchants
and lawyers, who generally conducted their business in the coffeehouses, the courts, or at the exchange, had small offices in the front
rooms of their dwellings. But during the 1790s this situation began
to change. The mercantile elite commenced building houses, which
though convenient to their place of business were no longer situated within it. By 1800 there were at least ninety-four slaveholders
residing separately from their workplaces.[40] The new dwellings of
this elite, as Betsy Blackmar has noted, emphasized healthfulness
and family comfort,[41] and slaves were acquired to service them—
one reason for the increase in slaveholding in the city in the 1790s.
Writing near the end of the nineteenth century, Charles Haswell
recalled the type of domestic service ("much more onerous than
at this time") that servants were required to perform. Oil lamps
needed to be trimmed and filled, and candlesticks, fenders, and
tongs cleaned. Wood and coal had to be hauled up from the cellars
to the fires that were lit in all the sitting rooms. All water for the
kitchen and baths had to be drawn from the pump in the street and
all refuse water and slops disposed of.[42] It seems probable, too, that
members of the mercantile elite required slaves to perform a further
function: a retinue of liveried servants, like an imposing dwelling
in a superior district, would effectively symbolize their newfound
status. For the genteel or pretentious, slaves could become a form
of conspicuous display.

Further to the north the character of the city changed as the
population became denser and the slaveholders more sparse. By
1808 the broad band across Manhattan through the Fifth, Sixth, and
Seventh wards (see map 4) had the highest proportion of renters,
or nonproperty owners, in the city, a sure sign that the area was
one of artisan and laboring neighborhoods. It was also here, as we
shall see later, that free black households managed to establish a
toehold in the city. In 1800 in the Fifth and Sixth wards there were

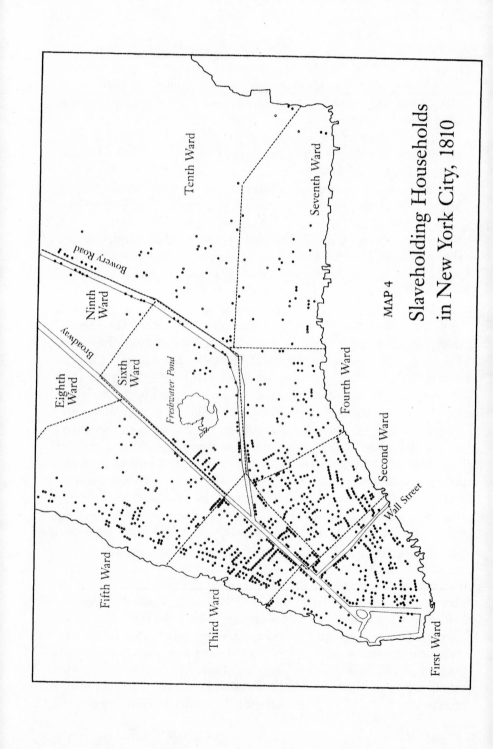

MAP 4

Slaveholding Households
in New York City, 1810

only 324 slaveholders, or about one in thirteen out of the 4,291 white households. The slaveowners in this area tended to reside on the major streets, particularly on Chatham Street and Bowery Lane. On Cherry and the surrounding streets, too, there was a small concentration of slaveowners, most of whom were associated with the shipbuilding industry.[43] Although the artisans as a group were increasingly using wage labor in their workshops, a small group of the more entrepreneurially minded artisans were emulating the mercantile elite and using slaves as servants. Over half of the slaveowners in 1800 who lived apart from their place of work were merchants, but there were also nineteen artisans in this category. The well-known sailmaker Stephen Allen, for example, owned no slaves in 1790, but by the time of the 1800 census he had acquired a slave. At that time he resided at 38 Rutgers Street, but his sail loft was located at Jackson's Wharf.

By 1810 the number of slaveholders had, as a glance at map 4 demonstrates, thinned out in all parts of the city but particularly in the area to the north of Ferry and to the east of Broadway (that is, in the Fourth, Sixth, Seventh, and Tenth wards). Yet even though there was a 25 percent drop in the number of slaveowners, there was a sharp rise in the number of owners with residences separate from their work. In 1810 somewhere between one in five and one in six of the remaining male slaveowners, or 154, fell into this category. The number of merchants involved in this sort of arrangement was almost the same as in 1800, a result of the drop in merchant slaveholding discussed earlier, and the source of the increase was other groups, such as the retailers and the artisans who were following the lead of the merchants. In 1800 nineteen artisans had a separate residence, but by 1810 this number, in spite of the fall in the number of artisan slaveholders, had risen to forty. The early years of the nineteenth century also saw another change in housing preferences. Initially the mercantile elite built their houses at some remove from the unhealthy dock areas but still relatively close to their place of work. In 1800, for example, Isaac Clawson, a merchant who owned two slaves, lived at 61 Broadway, but his store was situated at 26 South Street in a rather less salubrious but not too distant area. The continued ravages of yellow fever epidemics meant that even more emphasis was placed on the "healthfulness" of the location of houses, and increasingly members of the elite built houses farther along the Hudson River out toward Greenwich in the Fifth and the Eighth wards. The Eighth Ward, in particular, was becoming the suburban home of the elite, and by 1808 it ranked only behind the First and Second wards in its overall assessed value in the tax list.[44] Quite a few slaveowners included in the 1810 census lived in the northern half of the Fifth Ward and "commuted" to work somewhere on the southern tip of Manhattan—James Swords, the printer and bookseller, lived at 410 Greenwich but had his shop at 160 Pearl; attorney William Ketteltas lived at 287 Greenwich but used an office at 12 Broad Street; and Isaac Gomez, a merchant, lived at 239 Duane but worked at 109 Water.

What becomes clear, then, is that in the thirty years after the Revolution the institution of slavery was shifting from the center of New York City's economic life to its periphery. In a process that began prior to the Gradual Manumission Act, New York's slaveowners were being drawn increasingly from its economic elite, so that by the early years of the nineteenth century the typical slaveowner was no longer a struggling artisan, small retailer, or ship's captain utilizing slave labor for economic gain, but a merchant, a lawyer, or one of the new breed of entrepreneurial artisans who desired servants. In an ironic twist, the very groups that celebrated and exploited the free market turned to slavery, a form of bound labor, to provide them with servants. For New York's elite slaves were not merely an economic commodity but a form of conspicuous display designed to differentiate their owners from other groups in a city they were so radically changing.

IN THE SOUTH the "peculiar institution" would eventually be ended virtually overnight as a result of the Civil War, but in New York and New Jersey its demise was a more protracted business. The leaders of these states, the last in the North to condemn slavery, moved cautiously, and only after several attempts finally enacted gradual manumission bills in 1799 and 1804.[45] During the debates over these bills the rights of slaveholders—and property rights were at the very core of Revolutionary ideology—were never very far from the legislators' minds. Consequently, only the children of slaves born after July 4, 1799, in New York and July 4, 1804, in New Jersey were affected by the acts, and even they were not freed immediately but were bound to the owner of their mother until they reached their middle twenties. Slaveowners retained the labor of those blacks who were already slaves and secured for a lengthy period the labor of the first generation of free blacks.[46]

Historians who have used only the census totals of blacks in the apparently clear-cut categories of "slave" and "free" have generally ignored these indentured blacks. They have pointed to the rise in the number of free blacks, the drop in the enslaved proportion of the black population through the 1790s, and the passage of the Gradual Manumission Act in 1799 as confirmation of the zeal and effectiveness of the New York Manumission Society. Although these categories of "free" and "slave" were used in the census, an examination of the actual census schedules reveals a more complicated situation. In those schedules, free blacks were divided into two groups, those who were free and lived in black households, and those who lived in white households. The census shows that in 1790 one in three of the city's 1,036 free blacks lived in white households. This was the first time in the history of New York that a census separated free blacks from slaves—the number of free blacks in the colonial city had been so small that *Negro* was virtually synonymous with *slave*. Although this was a notable advance, the origin and exact status of those free blacks living in white households are difficult to establish. Some were genuinely free, as a result of the upheavals of the Revolutionary war or through manumission or self-purchase. But many, although classified as free by the census taker, were probably restricted by some form of indenture. A terse exchange in the *Daily Advertiser* in 1788 points to the existence of such bound forms of labor. On August 5 a short notice reported that Mr. Henry, "a worthy theatric character," had manumitted his three slaves. On August 16, another letter pointed out that Mr. Henry had, in reality, taken out a fourteen-year indenture on each of them, "whereby he has restrained them actually more firmly in his power than before they were bound."[47]

The number of white households containing free blacks more than tripled in the 1790s, from 248 in 1790 to 778 in 1800. In both 1790 and 1800 the occupations of the heads of households with free blacks (see tables 2 and 3 in the previous chapter and tables 7 and 8 in this chapter) were very similar to those of the slaveholders, although compared with their involvement in slavery, merchants were slightly overrepresented and retailers underrepresented among the users of free black labor. There was a high rate of turnover among the users of free blacks, just as there had been among the slaveholders. Of the 534 white households that owned no slaves and solely used free blacks, only 100 can be traced back to the 1790 census, and of these 100 heads of households 55 who had previously owned slaves by 1800 had switched to free labor. What is more interesting, however, is that one in three of these households contained no free blacks and owned no slaves in 1790. Perhaps these men and women discerned the way the wind was blowing in the latter part of the 1790s and deliberately chose to use indentured or free black labor rather than slaves. Yet, although members of this group would later become more important, the correlation between slavery and use of "free" black labor was still the most apparent feature in the 1790s. In both 1790 and 1800 about one in three of the white households that included free blacks also owned slaves, and it is difficult to imagine that the treatment and position of these blacks differed significantly from that of the slaves.

In the first decade of the nineteenth century "free" blacks rather than slaves became the dominant form of black labor in white households. By 1810 there were 1,570 white households that included free blacks in the city. The sort of arrangement organized by Mr. Henry, whereby the master freed the slaves but retained control of their labor, was institutionalized in the provisions of the Gradual Manumission Act that confined the "free" black children of slaves to lengthy periods of servitude. But the impact of the act was wider than this; only after its passage was there a substantial increase in the number of manumissions. In the period from 1783 to 1800 there were just 41 recorded manumissions, but in the next ten years there were 260 (see table 6). Although only 317, or about one in four, of the 1,338 households that contained free blacks but no slaves in 1810 can be traced back to the 1800 census, just under half (145 out of 317) of these households had owned slaves in 1800. It seems clear, therefore, that once it became obvious that slavery would end, New York slaveowners, particularly the merchants (65 out of the 145), became much more inclined to manumit their slaves, whether unconditionally or through some transitional form of bound labor. But not all of the heads of households with free blacks in 1810 were former slaveowners; many had purchased the indentures of blacks from the blacks' previous masters. In August 1800, for example, William W. Gilbert, "gentleman," bound out his twenty-year-old slave Phillis to merchant Samuel Gilford in return for $150. After eight years of service Phillis would be completely free.[48] Of the 317 heads of households containing free blacks traced back from the 1810 census, 115 had no blacks, either slave or free, in their households in 1800. It also seems probable that the vast majority of the heads of households containing free blacks in 1810 who could not be found in the 1800 census had no previous history of owning slaves. In 1810 the demand for free black labor (see tables 9 and 10) was, as it had been in 1790 and in 1800, very similar to that for slaves. It appears, then, that many heads of households who required black labor recognized that slavery must soon end and increasingly preferred to buy the fixed number of years of an indentured black rather than purchase a slave.

Even at this time it would be unwise to attribute the increase in the number of manumissions wholly to a rise in antislavery sentiment. Significantly, the timing of manumissions was closely linked to changes in the economy: throughout the early years of the nineteenth century there were an average of fewer than 20 manumissions a year, but in the economic downturn following the Embargo of December 1807 the number rose to 36 in 1808, 65 in 1809, and then dropped back to 50 in 1810. The role of the slaves in the manumission process, too, should not be forgotten. In New York there had long been a tradition of bargaining between master and slave, and it is likely that a combination of the economic climate and the passage of the Gradual Manumission Act gave many slaves the necessary leverage to negotiate successfully with their owners. Now that slavery was eventually to end, masters were probably more willing to allow slaves to purchase their freedom or to reach an agreement whereby the slave would serve them without trouble for a fixed number of years before being freed. In 1814 George Roper, the slave of Jacob Levy, Jr., "solicited" his master to give him his freedom in return for serving "faithfully" for a three-year period.[49]

As we shall later see, New York's blacks vigorously pursued any opportunity to escape slavery and welcomed the chance to live in the city as free men and women, however unequal their position may in fact have been. However, the characteristic of this transition from slavery to freedom that is most apparent, particularly from the perspective of the white users of black labor, is its continuity. In marked contrast to the disruptions that the post–Civil War South would experience as the users of slave labor initially struggled to reestablish their hegemony over a black labor force, New York City slaveowners adapted to the use of free black labor with remarkable smoothness.[50]

In part this was a consequence of the small number of blacks in the city; even if slaves were a significant part of the work force they were only a minority of the total population. But the most important factor easing the transition was the fact that abolition was legislated for, not imposed, and was gradual. Not only were New York slave-holders subject to virtually no economic loss or questioning of their position in the social hierarchy, but also they were allowed ample time to adjust to the end of slavery.[51] Throughout this period the demand for black labor continued to rise—between 1790 and 1810 the number of white households containing some form of black labor almost doubled—although it lagged behind the increase in the total number of white households, which nearly trebled (see table 11). But over the two decades following the first federal census in 1790 this demand was increasingly met by free blacks rather than slaves. In 1790, 86.3 percent of the households using black labor had contained at least one slave, but by 1810 68.7 percent included one or more free blacks (see table 11). The profile of the users of free black labor was virtually identical to that of slaveowners. In 1810, for example, the occupational distribution was almost the same; the rate of turnover when compared with the previous censuses was similarly high; and an increasing number of users of black labor (173 out of the 1,338 white households containing only free blacks) were even following the new trend of establishing residences sepa-rate from their workplace. By 1810 New York City's free blacks had displaced slaves as the dominant form of labor in white households.

IN THE RURAL SURROUNDS of New York City, however, slavery per-sisted more tenaciously. The frenetic pace of urban development had only a limited impact on the hinterland at this time. To be sure the rapid expansion of the city and the increased demand for foodstuffs must have bound the area even more firmly to the cash economy, but the full effects of the rise of New York City would

TABLE 11
White Households Using Black Labor in New York City, 1790–1810

Year	Total White Households	White Households Using Black Labor		White Households Using Black Labor with Slaves		White Households Using Black Labor with Free Blacks	
		N	%	N	%	N	%
1790	5,590	1,184	21.2	1,022	86.3	248	21.0
1800	10,778	1,902	17.6	1,368	71.9	778	40.9
1810	15,111	2,285	15.1	947	41.4	1,570	68.7

Sources: U.S. Bureau of the Census, *Heads of Families at the First Census of the United States Taken in the Year 1790: New York* (Washington, D.C., U.S. 1909); U.S. Bureau of the Census, Second Census of the United States, 1800, M32, Record Group 29, National Archives, Washington, D.C.; U.S. Bureau of the Census, Third Census of the United States, 1810, M252, Record Group 29, National Archives.

Note: The last two percentage figures in each row do not add up to 100 because of the households containing both slaves *and* free blacks. In 1790 this category included 86, or 7.3 percent, of all white households with blacks. In 1800 the figures were 244 and 12.8 percent, and in 1810, 232 and 10.1 percent.

not be felt until later in the century.[52] In the early years of the nineteenth century the character of Staten Island and of the western end of Long Island remained decidedly rural and rather staid. Leaving aside Brooklyn, which was fast becoming a suburban extension of New York City, population growth was low, lagging far behind the rest of the state.[53] The expanding urban demand for the area's produce kept the price of land high and discouraged migrants from settling there, further accentuating the closed and constricted nature of the largely Dutch-influenced society. As early as 1794 Moreau de St. Méry had commented on the high cost of land in Kings, land that was expensive "because the nearness of New York assures a market for all farm products, and because the Dutch families who form such a large part of the population refuse to sell their holdings."[54]

This refusal to part with property was by no means restricted to land: slavery, too, died hard in New York's hinterland. Ironically, the factors that had combined to push slavery toward the periphery of the city's economy—immigration, the consequent dramatic expansion in the size of the city, and the development of a system of wage labor—made slaves all the more desirable in its hinterland. The farmers of Bergen and Somerset counties in New Jersey and Kings and Richmond in New York wanted slaves not as servants but

TABLE 12

*White Households Using Black Labor in Richmond County
and the Rural Parts of Kings County, 1790–1810*

Year	Total White Households	White Households Using Black Labor		White Households Using Black Labor with Slaves		White Households Using Black Labor with Free Blacks	
		N	%	N	%	N	%
1790	888	505	56.9	456	90.3	112	22.2
1800	1,070	525	49.1	491	93.5	153	29.2
1810	1,251	496	39.6	445	89.7	294	59.3

Sources: U.S. Bureau of the Census, *Heads of Families at the First Census of the United States Taken in the Year 1790: New York* (Washington, D.C., 1909); U.S. Bureau of the Census, Second Census of the United States, 1800, M32, Record Group 29, National Archives, Washington, D.C.; U.S. Bureau of the Census, Third Census of the United States, 1810, M252, Record Group 29, National Archives.

Note: The last two percentage figures in each row do not add up to 100 because of the households containing both slaves *and* free blacks. In 1790 this category included 63, or 12.5 percent, of all white households with blacks. In 1800 the figures were 119 and 22.7 percent, and in 1810, 243 and 49.0 percent.

as agricultural laborers as they sought to profit from feeding the metropolis. Statistics are available that set out the different forms of black labor used by white households in Richmond (Staten Island) and the rural part of Kings (that is, excluding Brooklyn) (table 12). Unfortunately the census schedules for New Jersey no longer exist, preventing similar analysis, but the census totals of free blacks and slaves suggest that a similar pattern occurred in those counties within the economic orbit of Manhattan Island.[55]

Even as late as 1810, over a decade after the passage of the Gradual Manumission Act, more than one in three (445 out of 1,251) of the households in this area still owned slaves. A comparison with Queens, the county on the eastern border of Kings, gives a better sense of the extent of the continued adherence to the institution. Queens, settled from New England, contained very few people of Dutch extraction: the inhabitants were mostly of English origin and included a number of Quakers.[56] Slavery had been well established — in 1790 one in three households owned slaves — although it was never as important as in Kings or Richmond (see table 13). In both Kings and Richmond and in Queens the demand for black labor dropped only marginally between 1790 and 1810 (in Queens from 777 to 718 households and in Kings and Richmond from 505 to 496),

TABLE 13

White Households Using Black Labor in Queens County, 1790–1810

Year	Total White Households	White Households Using Black Labor		White Households Using Black Labor with Slaves		White Households Using Black Labor with Free Blacks	
		N	%	N	%	N	%
1790	2,244	777	34.6	776	99.9	1	0.1
1800	2,680	732	27.3	524	71.6	323	44.1
1810	2,566	718	27.9	363	50.6	619	86.2

Sources: U.S. Bureau of the Census, *Heads of Families at the First Census of the United States Taken in the Year 1790: New York* (Washington, D.C., 1909); U.S. Bureau of the Census, Second Census of the United States, 1800, M32, Record Group 29, National Archives, Washington, D.C.; U.S. Bureau of the Census, Third Census of the United States, 1810, M252, Record Group 29, National Archives.

Note: The last two percentage figures in each row do not add up to 100 because of the households containing both slaves *and* free blacks. In 1800 this category included 115, or 15.7 percent, of all white households with blacks. In 1810 the figures were 264 and 36.8 percent. In 1790 there were no households in this category.

and the average number of blacks (including both slaves and free blacks) in each household stayed at almost the same level (in Queens this figure dropped from 2.97 to 2.79 and in Kings and Richmond from 3.80 to 3.72). Though both areas continued to rely heavily on black labor the position of blacks in them was in almost complete contrast. Whereas in Queens 86.2 percent of households using black labor contained at least one free black, in Kings and Richmond the inhabitants, attempting to delay the inevitable, carried on much as before. Consequently 89.7 percent of the households using black labor still owned one or more slaves. The institution of slavery lingered for a while longer—in 1820 the number of slaves owned by the relatively small population of this area easily exceeded those left in the whole of New York City[57]—but eventually the intention of the legislature was realized and a system of wage labor took its place.

IN HIS MESSAGE to the state legislature in 1817, Governor Daniel D. Tompkins suggested that July 4, 1827, be set as the date on which all remaining slaves in the state—that is, those born before July 4, 1799, who were unaffected by the Gradual Manumission Act—should

finally be freed. There is little doubt that Tompkins in making the
request and the legislature in acceding to it hoped to associate the
end of slavery in New York with the Declaration of Independence,
that most potent symbol of the American Revolution. There can be
little doubt, either, that they realized their aim: historical attention
has focused not on the institution of slavery in New York in the
late eighteenth and early nineteenth centuries, but on the work of
the New York Manumission Society and the passage of the Gradual
Manumission Act, both of which are usually viewed as little more
than products of the Revolution.

Yet a close investigation of the city system of New York in the
1790s and early 1800s shows that the institution of slavery did not
just fade away after and because of the Revolution. Rather it under-
went a number of significant developments that were linked to the
dramatic transformation occurring in New York City in these years.
Slavery did not so much decline in this period as shift from near the
center of the economy to its periphery. As the process of "metropolitan industrialization" began to take effect, blacks living within
white households were no longer viewed as a source of skilled labor.
This change did not occur overnight and trades such as baking and
butchering would maintain the older patterns into the nineteenth
century, but the long-term trend is clear: increasingly these blacks
would be confined to unskilled work and, in particular, to domestic
service. Even the artisan demand for blacks originated largely from
the new breed of entrepreneurs, such as Duncan Phyfe and Stephen
Allen, who like the mercantile and professional elite required domestics to service their residences, now at some remove from the
workplace.

The legislature in Albany may well have laid down in the Gradual
Manumission Act of 1799 that New York slavery would eventually
be abolished, but this hardly ended the demand of white households
for black labor. At the outset, that demand was satisfied by the provisions in the act that confined the children of slaves to the status
of indentured servants until they reached the age of twenty-five
(females) or twenty-eight (males). Respect for the property rights of
slaveholders guaranteed both that slaveholders would not abruptly
be deprived of black labor and that the transition to a wage-labor
system would be smooth and gradual. Slaveowners in New York
City, conceding that the institution's days were numbered, became

more willing to negotiate with their slaves, allowing blacks to pur-chase an early release or manumitting them outright. Slaveowners in the surrounding countryside, on the other hand, and particularly farmers of Dutch origin, maintained the institution of slavery to the bitter end.

3

Impious Prayers

IN A LETTER to Egbert Benson in 1780, John Jay asserted that unless America introduced a gradual abolition measure "her Prayers to Heaven for Liberty will be impious." It was a maxim in God's court as well as in the new nation's own "that those who ask for Equity ought to do it."[1] The seeming paradox of a nation fighting to throw off the "slavery" of England while still holding several hundred thousand blacks in bondage, which had troubled John Jay, continued to perplex many of his contemporaries. The speculation and soul-searching it produced were important factors in the surge of interest in matters pertaining to slavery and to blacks that developed in the years following the Revolution, particularly after 1787. Not only is the sheer quantity of discussion of these matters impressive, but as Winthrop Jordan has pointed out, there is also an "aroma of causality" emanating from the coincidence between this sudden ferment and the formation of the federal Union. Sorting out the role that blacks and slavery would play in the fledgling republic was a crucial component of the search for national self-identity.[2]

Historians have mined this material to produce a rich literature on white ideas about blacks and race and on the nature of the antislavery movement.[3] But there are limitations to this historiography. Scholarly attention has been directed mainly at the discourse of a highly articulate elite, a discourse that was learned, literary, and often international in scope. Winthrop Jordan, for example, in his seminal *White over Black*, centered much of his analysis of the post-Revolutionary period on Thomas Jefferson, the archetypal transatlantic intellectual.[4] Implicit within Jordan's discussion is the assumption that popular attitudes were shaped by this intellectual elite — that elite culture determined the popular response. Such an assumption leads Jordan to miss an interesting facet of white attitudes toward blacks — the way in which elite and popular culture interacted and what this demonstrates about the complexities of white racial opinion.

Of course, "racial opinion" is a slippery and elusive concept at the best of times, and in order to grasp this difficult subject more fully, the scope of this inquiry has been broadened to include all of the Middle Atlantic states. Although a case can clearly be made for the separation of these states from both New England and the South, it would be impractical and would make little sense to extricate New York City from the region in which it was embedded. This chapter, then, contains an analysis of the treatment of blacks and slavery in the magazines, newspapers, and almanacs of the Middle Atlantic states in the quarter-century after the Revolution.[5]

IT WAS NOT until after the Revolution that American magazines firmly established themselves. Many were short-lived, but some, such as the *Columbian Magazine* (1786–1792) and the *American Museum* (1787–1792) of Philadelphia and the *New York Magazine* (1790–1797), were successful and important. The magazines embodied the contradictory currents of the time: they were consciously modeled on renowned English publications such as the *Gentleman's Magazine* and the *London Magazine*, but they also attempted to assert, at times quite vigorously, distinct American values. Their offerings were varied and included history, poetry, fiction, engravings, and articles on such diverse topics as politics, religion, education, the role of women, American manufactures, and antislavery.[6] Frank Luther Mott, in his *History of American Magazines*, estimated that at least three-quarters of the contents of the magazines had already been published in English or American books, pamphlets, newspapers, or other magazines.[7] Mathew Carey frankly admitted in the preface to the fourth volume of the *American Museum* that "this work lays little or no claim to originality." That material often was written and first published elsewhere does not diminish its importance for interpreting eighteenth-century society. In a situation where the printer had at his disposal a vast array of articles from numerous sources the actual process of selection becomes important. The eighteenth-century printer had a good idea of the concerns of his readers. If he did not he quickly went bankrupt. Few circulation figures are available, but clearly sales of individual magazines were numbered in the hundreds, not thousands. Carey, for example, claimed that his *Museum* had 1,250 subscribers; in 1790 the *New York Magazine* had 370 subscribers.[8] But such figures do not tell the full story. The influential readership of the magazines (Carey included George Washington, Timothy Dwight, and John Dickinson among his subscribers) and the fact that readers considerably outnumbered subscribers meant that the magazines were more important than the small circulation figures suggest. They catered to an influential and articulate elite.

In the late 1780s and early 1790s the magazines were the principal forum for an extensive discussion of the origins and distinctiveness of the Negro race. Typically, it was the reprinting in the *Columbian Magazine* of two extracts from Edward Long's *History of Jamaica*, first published anonymously in London in 1774, that set off the debate. In these vitriolic pieces, Long suggested that Negroes constituted a separate race and conjectured that "the ourang-outang and some races of men are very nearly allied."[9] In its next issue, the *Columbian Magazine* printed an extract from the fourteenth query in *Notes on the State of Virginia*, in which Thomas Jefferson stated his suspicion "that the blacks, whether originally a distinct race or made distinct by time and circumstances, are inferior to the whites in the endowments of both body and mind."[10] Attacks on, or in the case of Jefferson, casual indifference to, the biblical doctrine of the unity of mankind did not remain unanswered for long. The most famous defense of the biblical doctrine—Stanhope Smith's *An Essay on the Causes of the Variety of Complexion and Figure in the Human Species*—was reprinted in serial form in the *Museum* in 1789 and 1790. Smith forcefully contended that mankind originated from one source and that racial differences stemmed from the operation of natural causes. More eccentric were the views of Benjamin Rush, who pointed out that many of the traits of the Negro were similar to the symptoms of leprosy, which was probably the original cause of the Negro's black skin. The insight enabled Rush to "add weight to the Christian revelation" and to maintain the prejudice against miscegenation without calling into question "the sameness of descent or natural equality of mankind."[11] For Rush, the metaphor was reality—black skin was a disease.

The debate over racial origins and characteristics involved complex questions inaccessible to nonscientific minds. But the eighteenth-century media popularized these issues by emphasizing the more sensational aspects that were easily illustrated by individual examples. Because environmentalism and the logic of antislavery required proof of an equality of mental characteristics with the Negro race, exceptional blacks who exhibited various "gifts" were grist for the antislavery mill. The best-known example was Benjamin Banneker, a self-educated black who worked out the intricate calculations for an almanac's ephemeris. In a much-reprinted letter, James McHenry, Banneker's mentor, cited this case as "fresh proof that the powers of the mind are disconnected with the colour of the skin." Any system assigning separate origins to blacks would have to be abandoned as "similar instances multiply." [12] The indefatigable Rush helped to publicize the achievements of two other blacks—James Derham, a black doctor from New Orleans, and Thomas Fuller, a seventy-year-old Virginia slave with a "wonderful talent" for arithmetical calculations. [13] Such men were ideal subjects for the antislavery movement to publicize: they were proof of the mental capacity of the blacks and, just as important, they knew their place in a white man's society.

Interest in blacks and slavery ran well beyond the specific issue of race. Another focus of concern was the antislavery movement itself, and to publicize that cause the magazines published a wealth of material in many different forms: poetry, travelers' accounts, articles, letters, fragments, short stories, and even novels. An examination of the totality of this material, as distinct from an attempt to isolate and analyze one specific genre, brings into sharp relief certain aspects of the antislavery movement and certain perceptions that its participants had of themselves and those they sought to help.

Perhaps the most striking characteristic of the antislavery material in the magazines was the emphasis on the slave trade and Africa, and to a lesser extent, slavery in the West Indies, rather than on slavery in America. In part that emphasis mirrored the structure of the magazines. A large proportion of the items in them were of British and French origin and naturally focused on the concerns of those nations. But the concentration on the slave trade reflected the interests of the American movement too, with its strong international links and a domestic situation that made an attack on the institution of slavery itself immensely difficult. Although a few pieces in the magazines directly assailed the South, the general treatment of slavery echoed the reticence of Congress. Being closely associated with Great Britain, rather than with the South, the slave trade was a relatively safe target and much more easily dealt with than the vexed and complicated issue of American abolition.

The Africa of antislavery imagination bore little relation to reality. Benjamin Rush's romantic claim, "I love even the name of Africa," expressed not geographic interest but the symbolic importance of the continent as the home of the "noble savage," unsullied by white ways.[14] The anguish of these literary uncorrupted creatures as they were torn from their homeland and families was easily expressed in the sentimental style of the day.

> "Farewell every pleasure," [he] exclaimed in a voice rendered almost inarticulate by grief. "Adieu, ye native skies! No more shall the unhappy Corymbo rest beneath the spreading arbors of Congo—No more shall the charms of the lovely Yonka give pleasure and delight to a bosom racked with the most excruciating pains; Oh, ye aged parents what were your feelings, how did your bosoms heave." [15]

Typically, the imaginative writers stressed the tropical exuberance and luxuriant vegetation, conjuring up images of a simple and easy life. One writer affirmed that the "Author of Nature" had made Africa "yield almost spontaneously all that is necessary for the subsistence of man." Such idyllic descriptions functioned as a dramatic device heightening the contrast with the life of slavery in the New World. Juxtaposition of elements of the idea of the "noble savage" with the behavior of the slavers revealed starkly the barbarity of the Europeans. Cudjo, an African, exhibited more Christian virtue than the supposed Christians when he protected a white man from the wrath of the village after the Dutch had enslaved many members of their tribe. The callousness of the slavers in their ruthless search for profit was continually emphasized. Ara's parents, distraught with grief, swam after the ship taking their daughter away. The sailors amused themselves for a while by throwing them a rope and dragging them alongside, but finding them too old to be of value, they cut them loose to drown.[16]

Mukhtar Ali Isani has correctly pointed out that in dealing with the subject of slavery the imaginative writers devoted only a limited amount of space to the physical abuse of the blacks. Whippings and cruelty formed the backdrop, but the writers focused on the emotional terrors of the institution.[17] Examination of other material published in the magazines, however, particularly the "factual" descriptions of West Indian slavery contained in extracts from travelers' accounts, reveals a different facet of antislavery concern with the institution. These extracts depict a decadent and depraved society, where horrific physical abuse was part of everyday life. It is impossible to read this material without detecting a libidinous fascination with a West Indian milieu, where the white planter elite broke with impunity the taboos of American society as well as virtually every principle of the antislavery movement. In such accounts, the planters are luxuriously dressed and waited on hand and foot by hordes of black servants. To convey the extent of their power, writers compared the planters to royalty, particularly in matters of sexuality and punishment. In a description of a day in the life of a Surinam planter "His Worship" ends up in bed "in the arms of one or other of his sable sultanas." The planter, in effect a petty monarch, is "as capricious as he is despotic and *despicable*."[18] Few metaphors could have suggested more powerfully to American readers the idea of forbidden fruit.

If the imaginative works passed over the physical abuses of slavery, the travelers' accounts lingered over them. Such narratives were littered with examples of excessive and gratuitous punishments. In an extract from Baron Wimpffen's account of Saint Domingue, to which the *Rural Magazine* gave the interesting title "Refined Cruelty," a domestic slave was thrown into the oven for overcooking the pastry at a dinner party. John Stedman, a traveler to Surinam, gave a list of similarly "detestable examples" that excited the "most heartfelt abhorrence and detestation." When a black who was unfairly whipped retaliated and lunged at the overseer with a knife, he was tied to the boilers and died in excruciating agony. Later on Stedman came across a naked eighteen-year-old black woman being given two hundred lashes and asked that she be spared, but the planter, as was his "policy," immediately doubled the punishment. The crime of the young woman had been to refuse to submit to the "loathsome embraces" of the white.[19]

Themes of planter decadence and the cruelty of slavery were, of course, an integral part of antislavery propaganda, but the excessive

and sensational manner in which literature of this genre dealt with
such issues also pandered to baser desires. This "pious pornography" both titillated its readers and allowed them to feel morally outraged at the cruelty of the hated institution.[20] Occasionally, similar
elements can be found in material produced by American writers.
A fragment written by "Antonetta" for the *New York Magazine,* one
of the very few pieces mentioning slavery in the Middle Atlantic
states, is a good example. The piece begins soberly, mildly disputing
Jefferson's assertion that the blacks were wanting in their finer feelings and claiming that their "sensations, mental and external, are as
acute as those of the people whose skin may be of a different colour."
The author then proceeds to demonstrate the truth of his argument
by recounting the case of Mingo, the slave of a man of property
in upstate New York. The owner tied Mingo up "(as butchers do
sheep intended for slaughter) and after having beaten him till the
blood followed every stroke of the whip, he would retire, leaving
the wretch weltering in his gore, exposed to the burning rays of
summer or the gelid gales of winter." Tiring of this diversion, the
master fastened a length of heavy chain around Mingo's stomach
and neck, leaving four yards trailing behind. This he attached to a
heavy piece of wood, which Mingo was then obliged to drag behind him as he worked. At night the piece of wood was put inside
the house, the chain was passed through a hole cut specially in the
door, and Mingo was forced to sleep on the ground outside.[21]

Many historians have pointed out that the antislavery organizations were concerned not so much with blacks as with the malign
effects of slavery on whites. Few sources make this point as clearly
and effectively as do the imaginative writings. The characters of
the blacks were never developed beyond cursorily sketched stereotypes, while the slaves' actions, whether acquiescing or reacting to
slavery by rebelling or committing suicide, were determined solely
by the oppressive system of slavery. These blacks had no control
over their lives; even the act of speech was usually denied them
by the current sentimental style.[22] But the antislavery movement's
self-image and its relationship with the blacks were most clearly
revealed in those imaginative pieces where the blacks were eman-
cipated. Almost invariably such blacks prostrated themselves, both
literally and symbolically, at the feet of their benefactor. In "The
Slaves" the freed slaves "fell down and embraced the feet of this

'one of a thousand' and sobbed out their thanks. He raised them from their humble situation."[23] The same scene occurred in "The Slave—A Fragment," one of the most commonly reprinted pieces in the 1790s: "'Heaven bless thee, and shower down all its blessings on thee and thine!' said the slave. I had presented him with his liberty. His joy was too great for utterance—and, nature being overpowered, he sunk senseless on the ground."[24] The abundance of such instances in the literature resulted in part from its overblown sentimental style, but it also demonstrated the underlying power relationship between the whites and the blacks. The last-quoted fragment went on to make even more explicit the motivation of the benefactor. "I was amply paid, and felt a more exquisite sensation than if the Indies had been added to my estate." Not only did the emancipator gain his psychic orgasm, but within a few lines, the grateful black had rescued the white man's daughter from a fire, deposited her at his feet, and wordlessly disappeared into the dark.[25]

This emphasis on payment in some form or other permeated the literature. In a fragment entitled "The Paradise of Negro Slaves," the narrator (and it takes little imagination to see that the author, the ubiquitous Benjamin Rush, envisaged himself in the role) dreamed of visiting the Negro paradise. Initially, the blacks reacted with fear and suspicion at the presence of a white man, but the narrator reassured them that "in me—you behold a friend. I have been your advocate—and—Here, he interrupted me, and said, 'Is not your name——.' I answered in the affirmative. Upon this he ran up and embraced me in his arms." The narrator was then escorted to the center of the assembly, seated on a sofa, and introduced to all the principal characters.[26] Similarly, freed blacks who exhibited suitable deference and appreciation toward their benefactors were given a great deal of publicity. Derry, a free black, maintained the widow of his former master for several years by giving her thirty pounds a year. His sole reported comment on learning that he had won ten thousand dollars in the lottery was: "Well, now I will be able to maintain my old mistress generously."[27]

THE EIGHTEENTH-CENTURY NEWSPAPER had a much broader market than the magazines. Frank Luther Mott estimated that in 1765 about 5 percent of white families in the colonies received a newspaper each week.[28] By the end of the eighteenth century, both the number of newspapers and their circulation had mushroomed. In 1793, Noah Webster claimed that of all means of knowledge, "Newspapers are the most eagerly sought after, and the most generally diffused. In no other country on earth, not even in Great-Britain, are Newspapers so generally circulated among the body of the people, as in America."[29] Historians should be wary of such claims. Webster's conception of the "body of the people" was probably rather limited. The contents of the papers suggest that they were directed primarily at the literate "middle classes." The shipping news and long, complicated articles in small smudged print probably had only a limited appeal. Moreover, the "news," frequently made up of extracts from private letters and often reprinted from other newspapers, had a strong overseas bias.

Eighteenth-century newspapers fulfilled a different role from their modern counterparts. As a medium of information they supplemented, but had not yet supplanted, the primacy of the spoken word. Items of local news usually either confirmed or denied rumors and gossip that had penetrated every corner of New York or Philadelphia many hours or even days before. It was not until well into the nineteenth century, when the population reached a size and density large enough to render such a method ineffective, that the newspaper extensively printed local news. The supplementary role of the newspapers is suggested by the fact that the taverns and coffeehouses, important centers for face-to-face contact, frequently held files of newspapers for their customers.

If the portrayal of blacks in magazines was conditioned by antislavery sentiment, their treatment in newspapers reflected more mundane concerns. Little antislavery material appeared. Most frequently, blacks were portrayed in the New York and New Jersey newspapers, where there were still a large number of slaves, as a commodity—either in "for sale" notices or in runaway advertisements. When blacks were featured in the text, it was, not surprisingly, the more sensational aspects of their behavior that were reported. In the imaginative literature in the magazines, violent acts directed at the overseers and planters were often condoned or seen as the inevitable result of the cruel and oppressive institution of slavery. For example, in a fragment set in Virginia, a black killed a planter about to whip another slave and rid the world of a "mon-

ster." But the newspapers, confronted with the reality of black violence, reacted less tolerantly. When Captain Giles of Hudson tried
to correct his slave, he turned with violence upon his master and
committed the "horrid crime of murder."[30]

There is a contrast, too, in the way magazines and newspapers
treated collective black violence. A few writers in the magazines
were prepared to take their antislavery principles to their logical
conclusion and support black rebellion. An article in the *Museum*
claimed that the blacks from Saint Domingue were "asserting those
rights by the sword which it was impossible to secure by mild measures," and that if Americans justified their own Revolution, they
should "justify those who in a cause like ours fight with equal brav-
ery."[31] The turmoil on Saint Domingue received a large amount of
newspaper coverage, but although some reports were vaguely sympathetic to the blacks, the bulk emphasized the mayhem and blood-
shed. Similarly, when there was an outbreak of arson by blacks in
New York and New Jersey in the mid-1790s the newspapers printed
lurid stories of a "combination of incendiaries" who intended to
burn New York to the ground. As we have seen, quite a few Saint
Dominguan planters had fled to the Middle Atlantic states, bringing their slaves with them, and a number of rumors linked these
blacks to the fires in New York City. In an alleged conversation
between two French and three American blacks, rather improbably
overheard on a street in New York, the French blacks said: "Ah,
you Americans are animals; you do not know how to set fire — we
at the Cape know better." Ominously, all those present agreed to
try again when the wind was high. As well as this, L. F. Sonthonax,
a French commissioner sent to Saint Domingue in 1793, was supposed to have rewarded a number of blacks who traveled to America
to fire the cities.[32] Fear of blacks, never too far beneath the surface in the 1790s, was clearly enough expressed in such newspaper
accounts.

The only element of the debate conducted in the magazines
about the origins of the Negro race that received any space in the
newspapers was the issue of albinos. There were accounts of various albinos in the magazines, but it was the case of Henry Moss
that really attracted public attention. Charles Caldwell, a pupil of
Rush's, asserted that the name of Henry Moss "was almost as familiar to readers of newspapers and other periodicals . . . as was that

of John Adams, Thomas Jefferson or James Madison." [33] Though Moss had retained his Negroid features, his skin was gradually becoming white. He aroused considerable curiosity in the scientific community (Rush categorized him as a "spontaneous cure" from leprosy) and even more interest among the general public. His arrival in New York City was greeted with stories in the newspapers under such titles as "Natural Curiosity!" and "Curious Phenomena." The *Minerva* published a letter from a Philadelphian stating that "so wonderful a change ought not to be known to his neighbours only, but the knowledge ought to be diffused and ascertained in a circle as widely extended as possible." In New York, Henry Moss was exhibited to the general public at two shillings for adults and one shilling for children. The combination of a general interest in blacks in the 1790s and curiosity about "freaks" allowed Henry Moss to make a living in this manner. [34]

HISTORIANS WHO HAVE USED the newspapers and magazines have not always acknowledged the limitations of these materials as a source for analyzing eighteenth-century thought. They were printed and read mainly, although not exclusively, in the urban areas — either in New York and Philadelphia or in such larger towns as Albany, Trenton, Hudson, and Lancaster. Printers tried to increase circulation by setting up networks of outriders, but it seems unlikely that the magazines, or even the newspapers, penetrated much beyond the relatively well-to-do rural elite. On the other hand, the almanacs, virtually ignored by historians, were widely disseminated among the lower orders of society, and some, at least, had very large circulations. In the first half of the eighteenth century the almanacs of Nathaniel Ames sold sixty thousand copies, and *Poor Richard* sold ten thousand. [35] Almanacs were read also by members of the elite, but in general they were directed to a less literate and, as the numerous items of agricultural interest suggest, predominantly rural audience. As one almanac maker asserted, "we are read by Multitudes who read nothing else." [36] The word *audience* is used advisedly. The stock in trade of the almanacs — the aphorisms and anecdotes — lent themselves to repetition and being read aloud. The short and simple contents of the almanacs were designed to appeal to, and in some cases possibly originated from, people still firmly rooted in oral traditions.[37]

The topics covered—farming advice, astronomy, "receipts" and cures for illnesses, weather predictions, and anecdotes—merge into folklore, an area that the historical profession has traditionally looked upon with some disdain. The relatively few historians who have used the almanacs have not always been sure of the status of their material. George Lyman Kittredge, in the foreword to his study of Robert Bailey Thomas's *The Farmer's Almanack*, wrote that "some of our subjects demand serious treatment," but others were "beneath the dignity of history."[38] Conceptions of the "dignity of history" have undergone a revolution, particularly in the last twenty-five years, but historians have nevertheless continued to pay little attention to this valuable source for understanding eighteenth-century society.

Like the magazines, the almanacs in the late 1780s and 1790s suddenly focused on blacks—a concentration all the more noticeable because of the absence of such material between 1770 and 1788 and its paucity after 1800. But the interests of the almanacs were fundamentally different from those of the magazines and newspapers, and they printed little antislavery material except for the occasional imaginative piece.[39] The only element of the debate conducted in the magazines over the origins of the Negro race that surfaced in the almanacs was the question of whether blacks could be linked with apes. For example, an item simply entitled "Fable" printed in *Poulson's Town and Country Almanac* featured an ape in what was clearly an allegory of black revolts in general and that in Saint Domingue in particular. An ugly old ape unexpectedly found himself free and sacked his master's house. With "hideous yells and gesticulations" he then dressed and undressed himself in his master's clothes. "Day at last dawned, and every horrid extravagance became fully apparent." When a neighbor's mastiff passed, the ape exclaimed: "Approach and worship Lo! here sit I supreme; I am enlightened; I am free." The mastiff pitied the ape: "Who now shall give thee food? Who now shall shield thee from the sad effects of thine own unruly passions? Free thou art: but how? By violence, by massacre, by conflagration. And for what? To lacerate, to harass, to consume thine own flesh. I cannot, will not respect thee." Although the mastiff was collared, the animal claimed that the collar was a badge of discipline, not of slavery. The mastiff concluded by saying: "Poor maniac! fare thee well!" and walked off.[40] In this fable, one element amenable to popularization was taken out of the complex debate on the origins of the Negro race and applied to a current dilemma, Saint Domingue. Clearly, the ape was equated with the savage and African traits attributed to Saint Dominguan blacks, while the domesticated mastiff represented the supposedly passive American slaves.[41]

Items in the almanacs concerning blacks usually appeared within the traditional format of those publications. African cures for rheumatism and the stone were easily assimilated into the folk medicine that was an important feature of the genre.[42] But blacks were most prominent in the anecdotes that, in this period at least, were one of the almanacs' main characteristics. The anecdotes were short pieces, of up to half a page in length, that relied on humor—a humor, it should be added, that frequently eludes twentieth-century readers. Though most of the anecdotes were clearly British, those of American origin often featured blacks. In complete contrast to the material in the magazines, these anecdotes emphasized dialogue, using a form of black dialect.

In one of the anecdotes imported from England (it is set in Exeter), Pompey, the servant of a captain in the Guinea trade, observed people collecting pies that they had left to be cooked at the bakery. He innocently assumed that the half-penny they paid for baking represented the price of the pie. Pompey obtained a half-penny from his captain, rushed to the shop, and claimed the largest pie: "dis is my pie." On his return to the ship, he shared the pie with his messmates, who were gratified at the repast "procured by untutored simplicity at the expense of some person's hunger."[43] This stilted piece differed markedly from the local anecdotes. In American jokes much more emphasis was placed on dialogue, and the punchline was invariably delivered in black speech. Cato and Caesar got drunk one night at a frolic on Thanksgiving Eve and staggered off home. When Caesar tripped on a post and fell flat on his face he picked himself up and wondered "why de debil de sun no shine in deese dark nights Cato, and not always shining in de dey time, when deres no need of him."[44] Two blacks went into a dram shop and called for a bowl of grog. The first black picked up the drink, con-sumed two-thirds of the contents, and cried "Hem! Hem! Massa, dis here too trong: *do put little more water here*." "Tay mate," says the other black: "no be in sitch dam hurre: *let me cry hem too*."[45]

These jokes involved only blacks and were at their expense. The blacks, particularly in the first one, were depicted as being rather simple. More typically, however, jokes featured dialogue between a black and a white, with the end result being considerably more ambiguous. A captain sailing his ship across the Charleston bar asked the black pilot "what water the ship was in." The black answered, "saltwater Massa." "I know that," replied the captain, "but how much water is there?" "Eh Massa," said the black, "you tink me bring tin pot for measure um?"[46] A gentleman riding from Hanover to Pompton asked an African the way and received the following reply: "Why Masser you must keep right e long. I dont know da be any *wrong* road you be like to miss, ceptin e *right one;* So I dont see how you can possibly get out e way."[47] Although it is possible to view the blacks in both of these anecdotes as being rather simpleminded as well, they ultimately frustrated the intentions of the whites. Similarly, most of the distinctive humor in the anecdotes that featured blacks was dependent on the verbal confrontation between black and white. Interestingly, race, and not slavery, was the source of the humor. In marked contrast to the emphasis on slavery in the magazines, most of the blacks in the anecdotes were either free or their status as slaves was of little importance.

The humor in these anecdotes is remarkably similar to the patterns that Lawrence Levine describes in his analysis of black humor in the late nineteenth and early twentieth centuries.[48] In fact this material from the almanacs appears to be quite authentic, and some of the jokes may be verbatim or slightly embellished accounts of actual conversations.[49] The following anecdote, for example, specifically involved a Mr. Nicholas G. and was set in New Jersey. An old black man approached Mr. G. at Christmas time and begged for some money. Mr. G. knew the black but decided to play him along.

"Who are you?" "Massa no know me? (answered the Negro) My name Harry: Dey call me ole Harry." "Old Harry! (said Mr. G) they call the Devil Old Harry." "Yes Massa (replied the Negro) sometime Ole Harry, sometime Old Nick." Mr G. was so pleased with the repartee, that he gave the Negro a dollar.[50]

Such a conversation could easily have occurred, been repeated by
Mr. G., and eventually entered the written record.

In many of the anecdotes there was no question of ambiguity: the
blacks used their verbal facility, often commented on in runaway
advertisements, to completely outwit the whites.[51] Quash, a black
owned by a clergyman in New Jersey, complained to his master "dat
the poor negar man mus work so hard and massa do noting." The
clergyman patiently explained that his work was more fatiguing:
"I do head work and yours is mere bodily exercise." The next day
Quash was sent to the woods to procure fuel, but as he remained
away for a long time the clergyman went looking for him. He found
the slave sitting pensively on a log. When the clergyman spoke,
Quash started up and rubbed his "midnight brow":

> Oh! massa me — me have been doing head work — Well let me
> hear what your head has done — Suppose Massa, dere be five
> pigeons on dis tree, and you take a gun and soot two of dem,
> how many dere be left? Why three you old sinner — No massa,
> dem toder tree fly away.[52]

Similarly, a blacksmith annoyed at a group of blacks watching him
shoe a horse told them: "I believe hell's broke loose." One of the
blacks replied: "Yes Massa I see de devil got hold of de horse's
foot."[53] In another anecdote a white man boasted of his mathemati-
cal skill to Boston, a black. Boston told the white he "must be a very
good cypher indeed." He then asked the white a question: "Which
can see best, *a mare stone blind, or a horse without eyes?*" The white
man could not answer this or another similar question. "Well! aske
one mo e, *'pose fifty rail make one load, how many he take to make a
d——d great pile?*" The white man could not answer this either and
"retreated from the lists of his African antagonist, with shame and
confusion."[54]

As with most humor, the key element in many of the anecdotes
was the reversal of roles. For a brief moment the blacks outwitted
the whites and made them look foolish. The substitution of a black
man into a given situation perceptively highlighted white attitudes
toward blacks. Two blacks, about to be married, told the justice of
the peace that if he performed the ceremony exactly as he would for
a white couple, they would pay him well; if not, they would pay him

nothing. The justice agreed and after the ceremony reminded the black of his promise.

"Why" said the negro, "you have omitted the essential part." The justice demanded what it was? "Why" answered the negro, "you *forgot to salute the bride*" and bade him good night.[55]

In another anecdote a black on a ship carrying passengers beset with fever was assigned to throw the dead bodies overboard. When the captain observed him about to throw over a body still frantically struggling, he shouted at the black "don't you see that he moves and speaks?" "Why yes Massa. I know he say he no dead; but he always lie so like h-ll nobody nebber know when to believe him." This story assumes rather more bite when it is considered that the definition of *Negro* in the *Encyclopedia* included the following vices — "idleness, treachery, revenge, cruelty, impudence, stealing, lying, profanity, debauchery, nastiness and intemperance."[56]

Religion and the church were the butts of the more pointed anecdotes. A parson who owned a black wench objected to a certain black courting her. The black asked for and received permission from the parson to ask him a question. "Massar, no what the eleventh commament be?" The parson could not answer. "Well," said the black, "me tell wat it be: De eleventh commament is, BES WAY EVERY ONE MINE HIS OWN BISNESS."[57] Another clergyman told his congregation that he was shifting to a different parish. After the service a black went up and asked the clergyman what his motives were. When the clergyman replied that he was answering a call from God Almighty the black was rather skeptical:

"Massa, what you get here?" "I get here 200*l.*" "And what you get toder place?" "Why I am to get 400 *l.*" "I massa, God Almighty call you till he be blind from 400 l to 200 l you no go."[58]

Just as a zealous clergyman was reading out his text for the sermon — "And Satan came also among them" — an old decrepit black walked into the church. Feeling that everyone was pointing at him, the black "with a degree of resentment in his countenance" and looking the priest full in the face asked, "You glad to see your fader?"[59]

The portrayal of blacks in the almanacs was different from the treatment they received in any other form of eighteenth-century literature. Its generally sympathetic nature contrasted sharply with the way the unfortunate Irish were dealt with in the almanacs. The Irish, at least in part because of English traditions, were mercilessly ridiculed as dull, bog-Irish stereotypes. Although the blacks suffered some harsh treatment, particularly in the items that linked them with apes, that treatment lacked the consistency and viciousness of the attacks on the Irish. Further, there was a strand of humor in the anecdotes about the blacks that, largely as a result of the clear delineations of race and power, allowed them to gain a victory, however temporarily, over their supposed racial superiors. It is important to bear in mind at this point that many of the readers of the almanacs were probably from the rural lower orders. The whites outwitted by the blacks in these verbal confrontations were almost invariably the local authority figures of colonial society — gentlemen, and particularly clergymen — who in the last years of the eighteenth century were under attack from Revolutionary egalitarianism. The anecdotes in the almanacs clearly accord with Gordon Wood's suggestion that egalitarian anticlericalism resulted in "fierce expressions of popular hostility to the genteel clergy with their D.D.'s and other aristocratic pretensions."[60]

In the early years of the nineteenth century the almanacs included much less material about blacks. Earlier anecdotes were repeated, but I found only one new one.[61] Although it is similar, its tone distinguishes it from many of those of the 1790s. Its setting was the awakening that accompanied George Whitefield's ministrations in America. Two blacks who had decided to be converted went to a meeting.

> They no sooner, however, saw the preacher than they caught the enthusiasm. They began to weep, sob and blow the nose — and soon rolled themselves in spiritual agony on the ground. In the course of their pious revolutions, they chanced to fall into a heap of cow dung. Upon being told at length, that it was not Mr Whitfield, who was preaching they sprang up, one of them exclaiming, "Gorra dam! no massa Whitfree, Den you see, we b——t ourserf for noting."[62]

This anecdote is concerned not with the clergy, but with evangelical religion. The pun on "b——t" and indeed the whole wording suggest a rather cynical view of the motivation of converts, and the changing of Whitefield's name to Whitfree suggests a connection with the recent Gradual Manumission Act in New York in 1799 (and the one about to pass in New Jersey). Similar material can be found in early nineteenth-century newspapers in which the black is used as a vehicle to criticize such diverse activities as dueling, the behavior of various politicians, and the wearing of corsets.[63] The treatment of blacks in the almanacs—the use of blacks as humorous figures, the use of black dialect, and, particularly, the use of blacks to satirize people and topics of current interest—in many ways foreshadows one of the most important developments in nineteenth-century popular culture, the emergence of the minstrel show.[64]

CLEARLY, THERE WERE common threads linking the treatment of blacks in the different sections of the media. The most obvious was the sudden concentration on blacks in the magazines and almanacs of the late 1780s. Issues raised in the magazines filtered into the newspapers and almanacs and were adapted to their structure. For example, the scientific debate over the origins of the Negro race was converted into stories about Henry Moss and apes. One of the most important common elements, however, was the choice and meaning of words used to describe blacks. Many historians have pointed out that ideas about race tend to be grouped around the polar opposites of "black" and "white," a tendency that clearly parallels, and is often synonymous with, that of traditional oral societies to focus on questions of vice and virtue.[65] Words like *black* and *white* had acquired values and connotations far exceeding those of mere adjectives. When Samuel Magaw preached the first sermon in the African Church in Philadelphia, his text was a verse from Isaiah— "The people that have walked in darkness have seen a great light"— and he rather unnecessarily reminded his predominantly black audience that "the words of Darkness and Light . . . literally denote qualities universally understood as they respect worldly things." [66] By using epithets and puns, the magazines, newspapers, and almanacs further emphasized the dichotomy between blacks and whites: slavery cast a "shade" over America; a black paused to wipe his "midnight brow"; a black stuck in a chimney was extracted from his "sooty" confinement. Washington Irving, always extremely effective at drawing attention to characteristics of his fellow citizens, satirized this by taking it to its rainbowlike extreme in *Salmagundi*. When Tucky Quash entered a ball given by Dessalines in Haiti,

> the yellow beauties blushed blue, and the black ones blushed as red as they could, with pleasure; and there was a universal agitation of fans: every eye brightened and whitened to see Tucky; for he was the pride of the court, the pink of courtesy, the mirror of fashion, the adoration of all the sable fair ones of Hayti.[67]

Yet the patterns exhibited in the media's treatment of the blacks were too complex to be a mere simplification of elite ideas. The central concern of the magazines — antislavery propaganda — rarely surfaced in the newspapers and appears to have been of little interest to readers of the almanacs. Perhaps, as some historians have suggested, there was widespread support for the antislavery cause, but it seems unlikely that the source was the printed word.[68] Both the limited circulation of antislavery material (virtually restricted to the magazines) and the fact that it increasingly became a literary genre somewhat removed from reality, scarcely ever mentioning slavery in New York and New Jersey, make it rather hard to credit it with much direct influence on the Gradual Manumission Acts in those states. The shift toward sentimentalism in antislavery writing marked, as Winthrop Jordan has noted, "a retreat from rational engagement with the ethical problem posed by Negro slavery."[69]

In the case of New York City and its surrounds, this retreat only emphasized the curiously disembodied quality of much of the discussion of the place of blacks and slavery in America. Although slavery had virtually ended in Philadelphia, it had not only survived the Revolution in New York but, also, as we have seen in the previous two chapters, was expanding and would continue to do so until the turn of the century.[70] Similarly, for all his talk of America's need to pass an abolition measure, John Jay still owned slaves in 1800. When it came to slavery, the gap between rhetoric and practice in New York was quite large, a theme that we shall return to in the next chapter.

Newspapers and almanacs, drawing on their own traditions and catering to their own readers, presented an almost completely different portrayal of blacks from that in the magazines. The newspapers highlighted the more sensational aspects of black behavior —

particularly slave runaways and black violence—but the view of blacks emerging from the almanacs is refreshingly different from that which historians usually associate with the lower orders.[71] Anti-slavery sentiment may have rarely surfaced in the almanacs, but the publication and evident popularity of black jokes indicate an identification, even an empathy, with blacks. The portrayal of blacks in the almanacs was neither stylized nor sentimentalized, but matter-of-fact and direct. In contrast to the other genres, the almanacs acknowledged that blacks had a certain amount of control over their speech, their actions, and their lives. Later in the nineteenth century, this tradition would develop a harder, racist edge in the minstrel show, but the treatment of blacks in the late eighteenth-century almanacs was, on the whole, sympathetic and relatively benign.

PART TWO

Blacks

4

A Mild Slavery?

In the 1830s Alexander Coventry, who spent much of his life in the lower Hudson River valley, set down the impressions he had formed in the 1780s and 1790s of the conditions of blacks in that region. Though these blacks were then enslaved the writer felt "warranted in asserting that the laboring class in no country lived more easy, were better clothed and fed, or had more of life."[1] The assessment may have been tinged with nostalgia, but Coventry's judgment merely echoed those of other observers of slavery in New York, and indeed in the North as a whole. Half a century earlier the marquis de Barbé-Marbois had described the area north of Pennsylvania as a "peaceful and happy refuge for negroes." Not only were examples of severity rare, he declared, but the slaves "are here regarded as being part of the family; they are assiduously cared for when sick; they are well fed and well clothed."[2] Just over a decade later, in the 1790s, La Rochefoucauld-Liancourt, a staunch opponent of slavery and probably the most perspicacious of the French travelers, had reached a similar conclusion. Though he deplored the illogical adherence of New Yorkers to slavery La Rochefoucauld-Liancourt still had grudgingly to admit that "slaves are generally treated with greater mildness by their masters in the state of New York, and less oppressed with labour, than they are in the southern states."[3]

These quotes contain essential elements of the myth of the mild nature of the northern slave regime. Like most myths this one was partially based on fact, in this case on real dissimilarities between the slave systems of the North and the South. Northern slavery was neither centered around the growing of staple crops such as tobacco, rice, and cotton nor based on a plantation model. Indeed, the eclectic mix of activities that developed on the patchwork of small farms and urban areas north of the Mason-Dixon line would later be called by Ira Berlin the northern nonplantation system of slavery.[4] In this area slaveholdings were small, typically consisting of one or two slaves, and blacks were often housed under the same roof as their owner. This close physical proximity—on occasion slaves and owners even labored together in the fields or workshops—and the family-based nature of the institution were generally believed to prevent the cruel and violent excesses of slavery that occurred on plantations in other parts of the hemisphere. Certainly, few would have doubted that the northern slave had a better time of it than a slave toiling on a tobacco or rice plantation in the South.

Yet comparative judgments can produce confusion unless what is being compared is precisely defined.[5] Slavery in the northern states was certainly *different* from slavery in the South, but as we shall see it was not necessarily *milder*. Nevertheless, because contemporary material on the day-to-day lives of New York and New Jersey slaves is difficult to come by and because it is almost invariably based on the assumption that slavery was milder in a nonplantation setting, the myth must still provide the starting point for our examination. Unless we can fully understand the basis of these conclusions and their widespread acceptance there is little chance of getting beyond the mainly white sources and reaching the world of the slaves.

THE DEVELOPMENT of the myth that northern slavery was benign was closely associated with the growth of antislavery opinion in the north Atlantic world in the second half of the eighteenth century and particularly in the years after the American Revolution. In the case of New York City and its hinterland the myth functioned as a defense of the institution, deflecting the main thrust of antislavery criticism and almost certainly delaying the passage of an abolition bill. Though the farmers, professionals, artisans, and merchants of this area were the heaviest users of slave labor in the North, New Yorkers simply could not see a connection between their own benevolent version of slavery and the institution excoriated in antislavery tracts. The "pious pornography" discussed in the previous chapter probably reinforced these attitudes. It may have provided a good read, but was hardly a call to action in New York and New Jersey. Slavery north of the Mason-Dixon line was rarely even mentioned, and readers easily managed to dissociate the violence and cruelty graphically depicted in antislavery material from their own experience. New Yorkers condemned the slave trade, slavery in the West Indies, slavery in the South, and even the abstract idea of slavery itself, but convinced of its mildness, they were a good deal more complacent about slavery in their immediate neighborhood.

Even the New York Manumission Society, formed in 1785 for the purpose of giving slaves their liberty "by lawful ways and means," developed only a very limited critique of slavery in New York. Ending slavery was its long-term aim, but the more immediate spur that provoked these New York gentlemen to action was their "outrage" at "violent attempts lately made to seize and export for sale several free Negroes."[6] From its inception the society backed away from confronting the institution head on in New York, being content instead to try and improve the lot of New York free blacks and of slaves within the existing system.

In nothing was this hesitancy about attacking slavery more clearly expressed than in the society's decision, taken within a few months of its founding, to allow slaveowners themselves to become members. It would be "inexpedient" to exclude slaveholders, the Committee of Resolutions Affecting Members of the Society Holding Slaves declared, because those not yet convinced of the correctness of the society's principles "may decline entering into a society the rules of which they may Consider as too severely affecting their present Interest." Moreover, those members who already owned slaves would "gradually withdraw their services," leaving only a rump "who never can be objects of the proposed resolutions."[7]

This curious reasoning allowed slaveowners to constitute a substantial minority of the members of the society, and even of its officeholders. Of the 120 men who had joined the organization by the end of 1790, a minimum of 27 were listed in the 1790 census as owning slaves.[8] Another 8 who either could not be located in the first census or owned no slaves in 1790 had acquired slaves by 1800, as the census of that year showed. Neither the Reverend Abraham Beach nor the Reverend Dr. John Mason, for example, had owned slaves in 1790, but in the 1800 census Beach was listed as having one slave and Mason two. Three out of every ten members who had joined the society in the first six years of its existence were listed as slaveowners in either the 1790 or 1800 census.

Perhaps the best known of these slaveholders was John Jay, chief justice of the United States, governor of New York, and for many years president of the New York Manumission Society. Despite his oft-quoted comment that should America fail to introduce an abolition measure her "Prayers to Heaven for Liberty" during the Revolutionary war would be "impious," Jay was listed in both the 1790 and 1800 censuses as owning five slaves. Expressing "surprise" at this situation, one earlier historian hastened to point out that it would be most unjust "to draw erroneous conclusions from these facts." Had not Jay, in 1784, executed an instrument to free his slave Benoit as soon as the "value of his services amounts to a moderate compensation for the money expended for him"? Having bought the man in 1779, Jay had calculated that by some time in 1787 the benefit from Benoit's labors would have amounted to a sum "sufficient for that purpose."[9] Similarly, George Pellew, in his biography of Jay in the American Statesmen series, noted that Jay was a slaveholder only "in a certain sense." He differentiated his subject from ordinary slaveholders by quoting from a letter to the Albany assessors in which Jay claimed, "I purchase slaves and manumit them when their faithful services shall have afforded a reasonable retribution."[10]

To the modern reader the attitude of Jay and other slaveholders in the New York Manumission Society smacks of little more than hypocrisy. Even if Jay's version of his activities is accepted at face value, all that he was really doing was receiving most of the benefits of slavery while avoiding the moral opprobrium with which transatlantic opinion was increasingly regarding slaveholders. It is doubtful whether Jay's philanthropy caused him any financial inconvenience; indeed, judging from the length of time Benoit was kept enslaved, Jay may well have made a profit. The bottom line, as far as these New York gentlemen were concerned, was that the man made the institution. Not only were their own motives beyond reproach, but slavery, under the firm but caring hand of slaveholders such as themselves, was the most suitable preparation for the eventual freedom of the blacks. Southern or even more particularly West Indian slavery, however, was another matter. There slavery was not going to end in the foreseeable future, and more important, the moral caliber of many slaveholders was, at the very least, question-able. Not for the first time, or for the last, the South was suffering from an image problem in New York. The members of the city's Manumission Society had believed their own propaganda, dissemi-nated so widely in the magazines of the North. For them and other New Yorkers, the urgent problem lay not in their city but farther to the south.

Toleration of slaveholding members in a society ostensibly con-cerned with ending the practice provides a starting point for a re-consideration of the New York Manumission Society's role. Over the years historians have treated the organization very gently: Edgar McManus, for example, concluded that it was "the most effective single agency of antislavery in the State."[11] The reason for such a favorable assessment is the apparently obvious association of the society with the eventual passage of the Gradual Manumission Act in 1799. As a result of the Revolution, so runs the usual story, many New Yorkers realized that slaveholding was immoral, an atti-tude often illustrated by quoting Jay's comment about the "im-pious prayers" of the Revolutionaries. As a consequence the New York Manumission Society was founded. Despite early failures its members persevered, struggling against the entrenched interests of slaveholders, until by the late 1790s they had managed to convince most New Yorkers of the merits of their case—here reference is almost invariably made to William Dunlap's 1797 assertion that "within 20 years the opinion of the injustice of slaveholding has be-come almost universal."[12] In 1799 the act finally went through. In this interpretation, the New York Manumission Society is seen as the instrument of Revolutionary ideology, and one of the few laud-able moments in race relations in the first two and a half centuries of white settlement on the American continent is securely tied to the American Revolution.

Such an interpretation may say more about the mythology of the American Revolution than about the actual course of events in New York. Even a cursory perusal of the New York Manumission Society's papers makes suspect any notion that it was the driving force behind the New York legislation. For a start it was very much a city organization, with little impact in the rest of the state; yet it was not New York City that passed the abolition legislation. In 1799, the legislature did not even meet in the city, assembling in

Albany instead. The attitude of the country, not the city, was crucial in securing the 1799 legislation. Here a number of factors — the
electoral redistribution of 1796 that gave more weight to country
areas,[13] the massive migration of New Englanders into the western parts of the state,[14] and some sort of crisis of identity among
the inhabitants of Dutch origin[15] — appear to have been much more
important than anything the New York Manumission Society did.

What the society's records further show is that the appropriate
context within which to view its activities is not the abolitionist
crusade of the 1830s, but the genteel and paternalistic reform movements of the 1790s and of the early years of the nineteenth century.
Humanitarian and benevolent organizations proliferated in New
York City after the Revolution. In the years to 1825, Raymond A.
Mohl has estimated, over one hundred such groups existed, not
counting the special ad hoc committees set up to combat the regular crises caused by fire, harsh winters, and outbreaks of disease.[16]
The frequently overlapping membership of these organizations was
drawn from a pool of merchants, lawyers, physicians, and other
professionals. Civic-minded, well-to-do, influential, and above all
patrician, these men wished to control and minimize the disruptive
impact of helter-skelter expansion.[17]

Probably the main achievement of the New York Manumission
Society, and certainly the activity that absorbed most of its members' energies in the last decade and a half of the eighteenth century, was the African Free School.[18] Illustrating well the concerns of
these genteel reformers, the school aimed to instill virtue into New
York's free blacks and to prevent them "from running into practices of immorality or Sinking into Habits of Idleness."[19] In this way
the school would help negate the argument that blacks were unfit
for freedom. Yet the African Free School reflected also the more
general desire of the elite involved in this and similar humanitarian
organizations to order the behavior of New York's lower classes.[20]

In the face of strong resistance to emancipation and no doubt
inhibited by the continued presence of slaveholders among its members, the New York Manumission Society scrupulously refrained
from directly attacking slavery in New York. A petition organized
by the society in 1786, a year after its founding, calling on the legislature to prevent the exportation of slaves from New York signaled
the future course of antislavery in the state. In language redolent

of antislavery imaginative literature, the petitioners declared themselves to be "deeply affected" by the nefarious practice of "exporting them like cattle" to the West Indies and the southern states, a practice that frequently resulted in "very affecting instances of husbands being torn from their wives, wives from husbands, parents from their children, children from their parents." But the effect of such language was dissipated by the limited intent of the proposed legislation, which could hardly have offended, let alone threatened, the slaveholders of New York. Although the petition began in a mildly critical vein by affirming that New York blacks were "free by the laws of GOD" even if "held in slavery by the laws of this state," the rest of the document was conciliatory to local slaveholders, agreeing with them that "it is well known that the condition of slaves in this state is *far more tolerable and easy* than in many other countries." [21] The proposed legislation was designed to protect both New York slaves from the slave system thought to exist in the rest of the New World and New York slaveholders from their consciences. In short, the New York Manumission Society was employing the language and rhetoric of antislavery not to end the system itself but to reform it. [22]

To a large extent New Yorkers were successful in maintaining this distance between themselves and other slave societies, although as suggested in an earlier chapter the Saint Dominguan refugees and the branded and mutilated slaves they brought with them introduced an unacceptable face of slavery into the city. The New York Manumission Society was always at its most effective if the quarantine protecting New York from the South and the West Indies was threatened. When suspicious vessels arrived in the harbor, members organized watches and even placed advertisements in the newspapers warning blacks to be wary of kidnappers. [23] Slaveholders who tried to sell slaves to the South were pursued vigorously and brought before the courts. In 1806, for example, the society obtained a court writ to prevent a sloop leaving the port with three free blacks on board. A Frenchman had allegedly gotten them drunk and tricked them into going on to the vessel. [24] Similarly, when characteristics associated with slavery in the South or the West Indies—such as violence and cruelty—surfaced in New York, the society mobilized to try to eradicate them. The standing committee that investigated these incidents became the vehicle by which the members of the

New York Manumission Society sought to impose their own higher standards of behavior on local slaveholders.

The society attempted to regulate and control both the free black population and the local slaveholders and to ensure that the eventual end of slavery occurred with the minimum of disruption. Little wonder, then, that it received substantial encouragement from local slaveowners. An analysis of the 1786 petition to prevent the exportation of New York slaves, the first major activity of the fledgling society, further reveals the conservative nature of the organization. The 132 signatories, a veritable who's who of the city's social, economic, and political elite in the decades following the Revolution, included John Jay, Alexander Hamilton, John Lamb, James Duane, and no fewer than eight Livingstons. A majority were also slaveholders. Although it is not possible to establish how many of these men owned slaves when they signed the petition in 1786, a minimum of 63 out of the 132 possessed slaves at the time of the 1790 census. A further 6, who either owned no slaves in 1790 or could not be found in that census, had acquired slaves by the next census in 1800. Not only did more than one in two of the supporters of the New York Manumission Society's petition of 1786 own slaves at some time in the ensuing decade and a half, but by New York City's standards they were also heavy users of slave labor. The mean slaveholding in the city in 1790 was 2 slaves, but these men owned on average 2.9 slaves each, an increase of almost 50 percent on the city norm. In fact, had the signatories to this document manumitted their own slaves in 1790 they would have freed not far short of one in ten of the slaves in the city.[25]

If even the society ostensibly devoted to the task of ending slavery conceded that the condition of local slaves was "far more tolerable and easy" than elsewhere, it is hardly surprising that most New Yorkers agreed. New Yorkers could fearlessly condemn the barbarities of slavery in the West Indies, or even in the South, yet remain indifferent to the continued existence of the institution in their city. Material from contemporary newspapers illustrates this point well. In 1788, for example, the *Daily Advertiser* reprinted from a British newspaper an account of a number of runaway advertisements presented as evidence before the inquiry into the African slave trade. All the runaways had been scarred by whips and had suffered further mutilation. The piece ended by suggesting that readers could easily confirm such barbarous treatment "by looking over the West Indian newspapers in the city coffee houses."[26] But subscribers to New York's *Daily Advertiser* had no need to consult such a source: over the ensuing two decades their own newspaper printed close to a thousand runaway advertisements, quite a few from Virginia and South Carolina, but the majority of which were from the immediate vicinity. Not a few of the runaways described in them were mutilated in some way or other. In 1802 the slave of a Frenchman temporarily residing in Trenton apparently absconded rather than return with his master to Saint Domingue. When the slave killed himself after being captured, the coroner declared the suicide to have been, "occasioned by dread of slavery."[27] The coroner would more accurately have reflected local opinion had he cited "fear of West Indian slavery," for in the eyes of most New Yorkers, West Indian slavery bore almost no relation to the local benign variety.

Ever willing to differentiate themselves from the South, New Yorkers displayed a remarkable myopia about the continued existence of slavery in and around their city. In the face of ample evidence suggesting that slaveowners in New York were hardly less capable of brutality than were southerners, New Yorkers managed to hold tenaciously to their ideas about the local institution's benevolent nature. Although the sources are far from perfect, the historian of slavery in New York does not have to search very far to find examples of New Yorkers behaving in a cruel and barbarous fashion. In 1792, for example, the *New Jersey Journal*, reporting on the inquest of a female slave who had died a few hours after "a most barbarous and inhuman whipping," quoted the coroner's observation that "a more painful death than she must have suffered can scarcely be possible."[28] Moreau de St. Méry saw an apothecary repeatedly whip a "little mulatto," who was chained in an attic and kept alive on a diet of bread and water for the crime of stealing some drugs.[29] Another traveler, after noting that "shocking cruelties" occurred even in the "enlightened state of New York," recounted the case of a seven-year-old child who was flogged, given salt to make him thirsty, and then confined in a room with nothing to drink.[30] The records of the Standing Committee of the Manumission Society, too, are filled with details of less sensational, almost mundane, cruelties committed by New Yorkers. Assaults, beatings, and attempts to sell slaves illegally to the South occurred with depressing regularity.

Comparisons of the level of physical treatment in different slave regimes are difficult, if not impossible, to make. But if, on the whole, there was some truth in the New Yorkers' assertion that day-to-day living conditions for their slaves were better than those in the South and the West Indies, the distance between slave regimes was less than they cared to admit, and certainly not large enough to justify any claims that theirs was a benevolent regime.[31] The city's slaves, too, rejected any such self-serving comparison. As we shall see in the next chapter, they were probably an even more restive property than their counterparts in the South.

ON ANOTHER LEVEL of treatment, however, New York and New Jersey slaves did not fare nearly so well. In terms of what Eugene Genovese has called the "conditions of life," including family security and opportunities for an independent social and religious life, slaves from around New York were considerably worse off than those in the South.[32] In fact, the ethnocentric assumption that the wholesale adoption of white values and mores was both inevitable and beneficial, a crucial element in the New Yorkers' favorable comparison of themselves with the South, specifically denied the importance of this aspect of black life. The very factors that were believed to promote the well-being of the slaves—in particular, the small holdings and familial nature of slavery—combined to fragment the slave family and to hinder the development of a slave culture.

Recent work on the South, particularly the Chesapeake, has emphasized the crucial importance of the size of slaveholdings and of black to white population ratios in the creation of the Afro-American family and the formation of slave culture.[33] Although New York was the heaviest user of slave labor north of the Mason-Dixon line, slaves were still only about 10 percent of the total population and slaveholdings were almost miniscule by southern standards. In 1790, the year of the first federal census, the average holding in New York City was two slaves. More than half of the city slaveholders owned only one slave, and three out of every four owned either one or two. Consequently, almost one in two of the city slaves either lived by themselves or with only one other slave in the white household. More than eight in every ten slaves were owned by masters with fewer than five slaves. Further, there were only three slave-owners with ten or more slaves, and the largest slaveholding was thirteen.

Although the size of holdings was larger in the city's hinterland— the average in Kings, Queens, Richmond, and Manhattan Island north of the city was 3.4 slaves—contact between slaves on farms was made relatively difficult by the low density of settlement. The greatest concentration of slaves in the North was on the western end of Long Island and on Staten Island. In Richmond County and the rural part of Kings County in 1790 more than a quarter of the total population were slaves, and in marked contrast to the city, only about one in seven of the slaves in this area was owned by a master with either one or two slaves. Conversely, more than six in ten of the slaves lived on farms where there were five or more slaves, and slightly more than 15 percent of the slaves were owned by the one in twenty slaveholders possessing ten or more slaves.

Under these circumstances, the slave family in and around New York was, at best, a fragile creation. Not only was there an unbalanced sex ratio among the slaves in the city, with females significantly outnumbering males, making the search for a sexual partner difficult, but the small size of slaveholdings also resulted in few slave families having the opportunity to live together under the same roof. Furthermore, for some slaveowners living in cramped quarters and with only limited labor requirements a married slave was an unnecessary encumbrance: occasionally buyers of slaves advertising in the papers made it clear that married slaves were unacceptable. In 1798, after Benjamin Moore officiated at the marriage of a black woman he placed a notice in the *Daily Advertiser* explaining that he had thought the woman was free and was unaware that she was the slave of Monson Hayt. Moore willingly conceded that by marrying a slave he had not only inadvertently disturbed Hayt's quiet, but had also "perhaps" injured the value of his property.[34] Although at least some urban slaveowners actively discouraged their slaves from marrying and having children, many New York slaves attempted to overcome the exigencies of their position and establish a family. But the usual result was a split household: typically the male slave was owned by one master and the female and any children by another.

Some owners, however, appear to have been particularly intolerant of the presence of slave children within the confined space of urban housing. "For sale" notices in the press often noted that female slaves were being sold only on account of their children: in 1774, one owner offered to sell his female slave and three children because "it is inconvenient to the owner to keep a breeding wench." A few years later, another grumbled that he was selling his slave wench and her one-year-old male child because the "present proprietor does not like noise." [35] In at least one case the seeming inability to have a child was listed as one of a slave woman's attributes: a twenty-two-year-old "likely handy negro wench" advertised for sale had had "the small pox and measles and has been married several years without having a child." [36]

Even if New York slaves managed to overcome the odds and establish a family the existence of that family was always under threat. As we have seen earlier, slavery in New York City was characterized by a very high rate of turnover among the slaveholders: only a minority of slaveowners in 1800, for example, had been listed in the 1790 census as having slaves. This feature appears to have been particularly disruptive of the slave family, as given labor demands in New York, buyers seldom wanted to purchase families. Although only a fraction of this turnover of slaves is now visible — mainly in wills and for sale notices in the press — what is most striking is the very high number of slaves who were sold or bequeathed as individuals. In the vast majority of cases there is no indication that the slaves were members of a family. [37] Further, when such links clearly did exist, New York and New Jersey slaveowners had little, if any, compunction about sundering them. In 1773, for example, an owner advertised for sale a family consisting of a "very valuable negro man, wench and several children," who were sold for "no fault" and could be bought "either together or separate." [38] Owners were seemingly untroubled by similarly separating very young children from their mothers: in 1772 one owner offered a thirty-year-old female slave for sale either with or without a female child of two years and eight months, and a decade later Samuel Minor of Middlesex County, New Jersey, advertised a twenty-six-year-old woman and her boy of eight and girl of two "either together or separate, as best suits the purchasers." [39] The same pattern continued unabated into the nineteenth century: in 1806, for instance, Lewis Moore of

Hackensack declared his willingness to sell a thirty-four-year-old woman "with one, both or neither" of her two boys of six and four.[40]

Very occasionally slaveowners selling slaves demonstrated a certain amount of concern for the future welfare of their slaves and at least attempted to facilitate the continuance of some semblance of family life. When John Bray of Raritan Landing advertised for sale his thirty-two-year-old male slave, a twenty-four-year-old female slave, and her child of fifteen months, he noted that they "being man and wife would make it most agreeable to sell them together." Nevertheless he ended the notice by commenting that "a few miles separation will not prevent the sale."[41] In 1774 John Broome, a New York merchant, went to considerable trouble in order to help his twenty-nine-year-old slave. Reversing the usual practice, Broome insisted that the reputation of the potential buyer, rather than the slave, should be beyond reproach: the purchaser "must be of known sobriety and good character who lives not above ten miles from Staten Island." Broome went on to explain that his slave's wife "now lives there and after many attempts he has failed in getting her brought nearer to his present residence" in New York City and that offering the slave for sale was "an act of humanity in his master on that account."[42] But even had Broome been successful in finding a suitable purchaser, his slave could probably have visited his wife at most once a week, so that even in such atypical cases mildly concerned masters were able to offer little practical assistance to their slaves.

The characteristics of slavery in and around New York—in particular, small holdings and a high rate of turnover among slave-owners—combined to place severe limits on the establishment of slave families.[43] Undoubtedly, many slaves managed to find a partner and have children, but husband and wife then usually lived apart and the unions themselves were precarious. The reality of life for a slave in a peripheral slave society such as New York was that sooner or later one partner would be sold and moved even farther away. Although the New York Manumission Society managed, at least partially, to prop up the law and prevent many owners from selling slaves to the South or the West Indies, internal sales continued unhindered, inevitably separating husbands from wives and parents from children. William Dunlap, a member of the Manumission Society, witnessed a scene in Perth Amboy in 1797 that must have been repeated frequently: Andrew Bell "seperated a child from its mother, his slave, the Mother by her cries has made the town re-echo & has continued her exclamations for 2 hours incessantly & still continues them." Dunlap recorded in his diary, "I am sick, at oppression," but, of course, he had merely observed the spectacle.[44] It was the slaves and the slave family who took the full brunt of this emotionally devastating feature of New York and New Jersey slave life. Only when slavery ended could the black family establish a firm footing in and around New York.[45]

But in spite of the considerable obstacles in their path, New York slaves were never simply victims of the white institution. Although there were not many slaves in the city and holdings were so small that family life was narrowly circumscribed, New Yorkers still managed to forge a distinctive black culture. In large part this was due to the compact urban environment. Close supervision of slaves in these densely settled areas was almost impossible. On their way to fetch water from the pump or, in the evening, wending their way to the river to dispose of sewage, slaves were able to mix with their compatriots.[46] Furthermore, unlike the situation in southern cities, where the enclosed courtyard style of architecture allowed (theoretically at least) some control of slaves' movements, the design of New York City residences fostered a certain amount of slave autonomy.[47] Typically, slaves lived in cellars or cellar kitchens located partially underground and had separate access to the street, a situation that encouraged the development of networks of kin, friends, and acquaintances among the city blacks. One day in 1804, for example, Jake sought out Ben by going to the cellar kitchen where Ben lived, knocking on the window, and persuading one of the female slaves to pass on the message.[48]

This urban culture can occasionally be glimpsed through the disapproving and distorting prism of white commentary. For example, one detailed advertisement for the sale of a slave in 1775 noted that the man was a very good cook, with "many excellent good qualities and some superlatively bad ones." These detrimental attributes were closely associated with elements of city life that were virtually impossible to regulate and control. In this case an unusual candor compelled the owner "to declare that he is a slave unfit for a town resident but as his vices are chiefly local he would suit a family in the country extremely well." In another advertisement a young slave woman offered for sale in 1770 was described by her owner as having "Foibles that cannot be guarded against in town."[49] Similarly, in 1797 an owner's claim that the female slave he was offering for sale was "no gadder abroad, but behaves herself decently and properly" suggests that such a staid demeanor was not all that common.[50] The extent and importance of New York's flourishing urban black sub-culture, both slave and free, will be considered in more detail in a later chapter. It is sufficient at this stage to point out that, as far as the slaves generally were concerned, these owners were offering the reverse image as reality: "gadding about" and indulging in vices of a "chiefly local" nature were, regardless of white opinion, major attractions of city life for most slaves.

The situation in the surrounding countryside was rather differ-ent. The above-mentioned owner's suggestion that his recalcitrant slave's vices would be controllable in the country hints at the reali-ties of life for rural slaves in New York and New Jersey. Although slaves in this area made up twice as high a proportion of the total population as did slaves in the city and slaveholdings were larger, the low density of rural settlement effectively negated these advan-tages. In their day-to-day lives rural slaves came in contact with a much smaller number of compatriots than did their urban counter-parts, which inevitably limited development of the networks that were so extensive and important for city slaves. While the larger size of rural slaveholdings may have increased marginally the chances of having a spouse resident on the same farm, the problem for the majority who did not live with their sexual partner was only exac-erbated. In New York City couples were unlikely to be separated by more than a fifteen-minute walk, but in rural areas the distance could easily have been many miles.

Occasionally, blacks tried to overcome the tyranny of rural dis-tances by using their master's horse. Sambo, an ingenious slave belonging to a Mount Pleasant doctor, devised his own solution to the problem by constructing a small sled for use in the winter months. His owner's wife noted that the sled "would have Answered to carry a bag of grain to mill & some other little purposes," but Sambo, who had had less utilitarian intentions in mind, converted it into a "pleasure Sled." One evening the restive slave "borrowed" a neighbor's horse, visited friends, and was able to return home by a "desent bed time."[51] Generally, however, rural slaves lived an isolated existence, narrowly bounded by the rigors of work on the small farms that dotted the city's hinterland.

When Philip Morris, a black, testified in court that an event had taken place "last summer, a year ago in water melon time," he was not conforming to a "Sambo" stereotype but merely demonstrating that in a preindustrial era time was measured by the seasons.[52] Similarly, work in New York's rural hinterland was determined by the annual rhythms. Farmers may have lamented that as "soon as ever their master's back is turned, they [slaves] do little or nothing," but the tenacity with which rural slaveholders tried to hold on to their slave labor force well into the nineteenth century certainly suggests that this was not the case.[53] Entries in surviving journals, such as that of Dr. Samuel Thompson, provide further evidence that owners exacted a considerable amount of work from their slaves. In March and April of 1800, Thompson's slaves—Robbin, Sharper, Jack, Cuff, Nan, Franklin, and Ben—worked every day, apart from Sundays, threshing oats, dressing, crackling and swingling flax, sowing clover seed, mending fences, and plowing cornstalks on the forty-acre lot, sowing flax, planting cherry trees, digging up potatoes, and dunging and tending to the vegetable garden.[54] The labor on a mixed farm was probably more varied than the relentless drudgery of tobacco cultivation, but it was still hard work.[55]

In the slack between agricultural tasks complaisant masters allowed their slaves short periods of free time, and some took advantage of this latitude to visit the metropolis. During the day the black population of the city was swelled considerably by slaves from the surrounding area. Some slaves secured their owner's permission: Andrew Powlis, who lived seven miles from the Brooklyn ferry, was allowed by his master to go to New York for a few days to see his friends.[56] Others doubtless slipped away, risking punishment by failing to obtain the required pass. Nor was it uncommon for slaves to make regular trips, either with or without their masters, to the city markets to buy and sell produce. While waiting for the tide to turn, they could often enjoy a few free hours. Jersey masters and their slaves, chiefly from Haverstraw, Hackensack, Bergen, and Communipaw, patronized the Buttermilk Market on the Hudson, while those from Long Island went to Catharine Market on the other side of Manhattan. According to Thomas F. De Voe, the New York antiquarian, on market days after their work was done and on holidays the Jersey blacks would "shin it" across the island to Catharine Slip and engage in breakdown contests with the Long Islanders for money or a "bunch of eels and fish."[57]

Although material on black rural life is extraordinarily hard to come by, it appears that at various times of the year country blacks attended organized gatherings as well. The most important institution here was the church. Slaves generally had Sundays off, and blacks came from miles around to attend religious services. In 1800 Samuel Thompson noted in his diary that "the black man Paul" preached two sermons to a large assembly in the meetinghouse and that a contribution was collected for him.[58] Secular holidays were also observed; Thompson recorded that his slaves had celebrated the new year. Runaway advertisements furnish examples of slaves who had permission to stay away for holidays but did not return. In 1796, for instance, Jack had his master's "consent to keep the late holidays," but "as he has been away for a longer time than he had permission it is supposed that he intends not returning."[59] At various times in the year the rural gentry engaged in a round of "frolics," sledding, and turkey shoots, and to a more limited extent so did the slaves. In June 1803 Thompson allowed his slave Killis to attend a "strawberry frolic."[60] Pierre Van Cortlandt, whose family seat was on the east bank of the Hudson, wrote in 1799 to James Mandiville in nearby Peekskill claiming that "my Negro man Ishmael is one of the Fiddlers that frequents you[r] house at frolicking times." In future, Van Cortlandt intended to "prosicute any person that Encourages, or Suffer him to play the fiddle at Night in their houses."[61]

By far the most significant of these events in the lives of New York and New Jersey slaves, and, I would argue, one of the most important and revealing cultural phenomena in the history of the black experience in America was Pinkster. As this festival is also one of the least well understood aspects of black life in New York we need to consider the wider history of the holiday before attempting to assess its importance in the surrounds of New York City.

Pinkster came across to America with the seventeenth-century Dutch settlers. The term was originally related to the Dutch name for Whitsuntide or Pentecost—*Pfingsten* in German.[62] Initially in New York the holiday was a Dutch and not a black festival, similar in many ways to the English Boxing Day, when the servants were given a day off after the Christmas holiday. By the nineteenth century, however, the holiday was primarily black and associated most closely with Albany, though it was also observed in other places where there was a strong Dutch presence—along the Hudson Valley, on Long Island, and in eastern New Jersey. Historians have previously been forced to rely on antiquarian accounts of Pinkster, written decades after the event and permeated with a sense of the quaintness of things past and no longer relevant.[63] By contrast, the following brief analysis of Pinkster in Albany at the turn of the century is based on the first known contemporaneous description.[64]

In the week preceding the festival there was a gradual buildup "during which, the negroes patrol the streets in the evening more than usual, and begin to practice a little upon the Guinea drum." The slaves also set up an encampment on Pinkster Hill, which was to become the "*theatre of action.*" A series of arbors were constructed by setting stakes in the ground and then weaving through them branches from a shrub growing on the adjoining plain to create a series of "airy cottages" that were "impervious to solar rays." These shelters, arranged to form an amphitheater in front of the royal arbor, were filled with fruit, cakes, beer, and liquor.

On the Monday after Pinkster, which corresponded to the Episcopal Whitsunday, a large part of the Dutch population, even those not normally religiously inclined, attended church. At the same time blacks and whites from miles around formed a "motley group of thousands" on the hill awaiting the appearance of King Charles, the principal character in the festival. He was an "old Guinea Negro" "whose authority is absolute, and whose will is law during the Pinkster holidays." After parading through the town, King Charles arrived on the hill and sat through a welcoming ceremony.[65] He then proceeded around the encampment and collected one shilling from every black man's tent and two shillings from every tent occupied by a white. If any individual refused to pay, the King directed that his tent be "instantly demolished."

For the next three or four days and nights a variety of sports and activities were planned. The most important of these, indeed the apparent highlight of the festival, was Toto, or the Guinea dance. This took place in the amphitheater in front of the royal arbor. There sat the "chief musician dressed in a horrid manner—rolling his eyes and tossing his head with an air of savage wildness; grunting and mumbling out certain inarticulate but hideous sounds" as he beat upon a Guinea drum. On either side of this character were two imps, "decorated with feathers and cow tails," performing similar "uncouth and terrifying grimaces" while playing on smaller drums and imitating "his sounds of frightful dissonance." Meanwhile, males and females danced, but as "there is no regular air in the music, so neither are there any regular movements in this dance." In fact, the dancers placed their bodies "in the most disgusting attitudes" and performed the "most lewd and indecent gesticulation, at the crisis of which the parties meet and embrace in a kind of amorous Indian hug, terminating in a sort of masquerade capture, which must cover even a harlot with blushes to describe."

Unfortunately our observer was silent about the other activities and sports, contenting himself with the tantalizing comment that these were scenes that "Raphael the master of painters could not delineate, not Milton, the biographer of devils, describe." After the final ceremony, in which the King descended into Albany, the festival ended. Slaves spent the rest of the week going home and "in getting sober so that by the beginning of the subsequent week, the city gets composed and business goes on as usual."

Historical accounts of Pinkster that are themselves based on the work of antiquarians writing many years after the Albany Common Council passed an ordinance banning the festival in 1811 are, necessarily, extremely sketchy. Nevertheless, historians have usually categorized Pinkster as clear evidence of the continued importance of African cultural forms in the New World. A. J. Williams-Myers concluded that for two hundred years some forms of Africanisms survived within New York slavery "encapsulated in the Pinkster carnival," and that, although the festival may have had European origins, by the nineteenth century it was "an African celebration." [66] Sterling Stuckey adduces Pinkster, which in spite of white participation was "acknowledged to be African," as evidence in support of his contention that in the North and in the South, both during and after slavery, "black culture was national in scope, the principal forms of cultural expression being essentially the same." Arguing from a black nationalist position, Stuckey insists both on the "oneness" of black culture in the twentieth century and on its origins in Central and West Africa.[67]

In rejecting Stanley Elkins's characterization of imported slaves

as a tabula rasa on which Anglo-America would inscribe its culture
it is too easy to go to the other extreme and discover a slave population of Africans demonstrating a degree of autonomy in their lives
that stretches the bounds of credulity.[68] Africa and the African past
were of great importance in New York, as elsewhere in America,
but to couch the argument merely in terms of African survival is
to evince a static and simplistic understanding of the concept of
culture and, by ignoring the realities of the structure of power,
to misunderstand and slight the achievement of New York slaves.[69]
Clearly, in the case of Pinkster African elements were of great significance, but we have little chance of coming to any understanding
of the festival unless historians acknowledge that it was a complex
syncretization of African and Dutch cultures created within the
context of American slavery as it existed along the Hudson River
valley, on Long Island, and in New Jersey.

Pinkster was one of the many European festivals that celebrated
the change of seasons and the renewal of life associated with spring,
a function it continued to perform in the New World. As a result, various flowers were associated particularly with Pinkster. Alice
Morse Earle recorded that in New York and New Jersey the blue
flag, or iris, was known as the "pinkster bloom." The azalea that
bloomed plentifully throughout New York in May, however, was
most commonly identified as the "pinkster flower," or along the
banks of the Hudson, as the "pinkster blummachee."[70] The first
sentence of our anonymous description, a comment on the "verdant
scenery which begins to display itself from our barren and dusty
hills," also emphasizes the transformation of the upstate countryside that accompanied the "vernal holiday." Similarly, the account of
the encampment details the effect of the wind on the arbors, which
gave the appearance "not of art but nature" and formed a "beautiful
contrast with the forbidding nakedness of the surrounding hills."

Aspects of the rituals that formed an integral part of the festival further establish the European antecedents of Pinkster. On
that Monday, as the King paraded through the streets of Albany on
the way to Pinkster Hill he was preceded by a standard displaying
"significant colours" and a portrait of the King specifying the dura-
tion of his reign. King Charles was mounted on a "superb steed,
of a beautiful cream colour" and followed by a large procession of
the "most distinguished and illustrious characters." Similarly, at the

end of the festival, when the King descended into Albany again, he and his attendants patrolled the streets "calling at one door after another, and demanding tribute, which demand he enforces by such a horrid noise and frightful grimaces, that you are glad to bestow something to get rid of him, especially if you have a delicate wife or timid children."

There can be little doubt that such activities were New World descendants of the rituals associated with the festivals of misrule, or the world turned upside down, analyzed so ably by historians of early modern Europe such as Natalie Zemon Davis.[71] For a short period those at the bottom of the social hierarchy—women, apprentices, the young, and in the case of Albany, the slaves—reversed their lowly status and lack of power. On Pinkster Hill, and immediately preceding and after the festival on the streets of Albany, an African-born slave assumed the position and the authority normally accorded only to the local patroon. The constrictions of an ordered society were temporarily loosened, a transformation all the more striking when the most important divisions in the social structure were racial. During the festivities slaves attained a rough equivalence to their masters, a feature conveyed by our observer's caustic comment, on strolling through the encampment, that "here lies a beastly black and there lies a beastly white sleeping or wallowing in the mud or dirt."

In part Pinkster functioned as a safety valve allowing a cathartic release from the pent-up frustrations both of the long winter and of the institution of slavery. "All restraints are flung off" and "depraved nature" exhibited as "every vice is practised without reproof and without reserve." According to our guide, it was even rumored that "the married negroes consider themselves as absolved, on these occasions, from their matrimonial obligations." However, the point of reference for this brief bacchanalian interlude was always the order and certainty of the "normal" social structure. As Victor Turner has pointed out, the rituals of status reversal both reaffirm the hierarchical principle and underline the reasonableness of everyday culturally predictable behavior between the various levels of society.[72] Significantly the description of Pinkster ends with the remark that, by the following week, "the city gets composed and business goes on as usual." The antiquarian reminiscences similarly emphasized the cyclical nature of the festival: Dr. James Eights, for example, concluded his account of Pinkster in Albany by noting that the city returned to its usual "quietude," properly restored to the "accustomed routine of duty and order."[73]

In this case there was another element that helped to emphasize the functional role the festivities played in reinforcing the social order. As every observer of and participant in the event was well aware, Pinkster Hill was the site of the gallows.[74] Executions and public punishments, rituals that often involved slaves and also drew thousands of spectators from a wide area, occurred on the very same ground as that on which the bulk of Pinkster activities took place. In 1794 the *Albany Register* described the reaction to the postponement of the executions of Bet, Dean, and Pompey, three blacks convicted of starting the fire that nearly burned Albany to the ground in 1793. According to the newspaper the "vast concourse" of people gathered on the hill, some from many miles away, had expected "to have been *entertained* by the *execution* of the *Negro criminals*" and were none too happy at being deprived of the chance to "view the *instructive ceremony*."[75] These spectacles, too, affirmed the status quo, albeit in a less subtle fashion. Ironically, later in the century Pinkster Hill became Capitol Hill.

Yet to categorize Pinkster merely as a prepolitical festive event deflecting attention away from reality and serving as little more than a prop for the existing social order is to ignore the inventiveness of the slaves. Davis, in her study of misrule in sixteenth-century France, was struck "by the social creativity of the so-called inarticulate, by the way in which they seize upon older social forms and change them to fit their needs."[76] The same comment aptly describes, perhaps with even more force, the way Albany slaves transformed and created something new from the detritus of the original Dutch settlement of New York. By the time Pinkster reached its apogee in the early years of the nineteenth century the slaves had infused the European ceremony with cultural memories of Africa. An African-born slave presided over the festival and the music and dancing, so offensive to the sensibilities of our observer, were strongly influenced by African cultural patterns. This provides clear evidence of the way slaves were able to adapt Pinkster to allow the perpetuation of important community values.[77]

To depict Pinkster as an African survival pure and simple, however, is to push this argument to the point of absurdity. One of the most remarkable features of the festival was the variety of artifacts and cultural influences that was absorbed into the ceremony, a feature easily demonstrated by turning to the antiquarian accounts. It appears, then, that the chief character in a ceremony on a Dutch holiday in America was an African-born black wearing a British brigadier's jacket of scarlet, a tricornered cocked hat, and yellow buckskins.[78] Further, although the principal roles were played by blacks, the drama derived much of its meaning from the largely white audience, who at varying points such as in the final ceremony in Albany were also drawn in as participants. Our observer makes it clear that a large number of whites watched the spectacle, and for all we know they may have joined in some of the activities other than Toto, activities that the writer chose not to delineate.

The ability of Pinkster to absorb other cultural forms and influences, demonstrated on an individual level by the accretions to King Charles's ceremonial garb, was also evident in the evolution of the festival as a whole. Later antiquarian accounts suggest that within a very few years the festival developed into a more commercialized entertainment, one that was particularly appealing to young white children. According to Dr. Eights, the area to the rear of the amphitheater was appropriated by exhibitions of wild animals (including a Bengal tiger), ropedancing, and circus riding and became "the playing ground of all simple gaming sports." Someone with an "unpronounceable name" performed wonders on the slack rope; another rode the famous horse Selim and somersaulted through a blazing hoop; Rickett, "the celebrated clown of the day," displayed his stock of buffoonery on horseback as well; and later in the week Jack Van Patten, the city bully, defeated all comers in a boxing competition.[79]

By 1811 the good burghers of Albany considered the festival a menace. In that year the Albany Common Council passed a city ordinance that forbade the erection of booths, tents, or stalls within the city limits for the purpose of selling alcohol or food, collecting together in numbers for gambling or dancing, and marching or parading, with or without any kind of music, during the "days commonly called pinxter."[80] Some historians have hinted darkly at the suppression of African culture, but if the antiquarian accounts are to be believed, it would appear more likely that the ending of the festival is best understood within the context of a broader attempt to eliminate vestiges of an earlier popular culture that had little appeal for an emerging middle class.[81] Regardless of the origin of the law, when the white elite withdrew its sanction, in the area around Albany Pinkster rapidly faded away and within a few years was little more than fodder for the reminiscences of old men.

Pinkster was celebrated elsewhere in New York and New Jersey, although without the spectacular flair and style evident in Albany. The few who have discussed Pinkster in the southern portion of the state have asserted that the festival was centered on New York City. In part this supposition appears to rest on an analogy with the role that the city of Albany played further up the Hudson, but James Fenimore Cooper's novel *Satanstoe* has probably been even more influential. Historians, desperately short of material, have clutched gratefully at Cooper's account of thousands of blacks celebrating Pinkster on the "commons," or City Hall Park, in 1757 and accepted it as evidence of the festival's existence at this date. The fact that Cooper was born in 1789 and the novel published in 1845 appears not to have worried anyone unduly.[82]

Thus far I have examined Pinkster in Albany only during its peak period in the early years of the nineteenth century. What is also important in any assessment of its significance is the chronology of the festival. The first known usage of the word in America was in a book of sermons written by Adrian Fischer and printed in 1667.[83] The next is in 1789. Some authors have attributed the absence of references to Pinkster in the intervening years to the tendency of "social historians," as they call contemporary observers, to be "highly arbitrary in their choice of material" and to "skip over commonplace things" if they saw fit to do so. It is almost beyond belief that at least a few fleeting references to an event supposedly involving thousands of blacks, and one that could hardly be described as "commonplace," have not survived.[84] Had the festival assumed even minor importance for the black population some slaves must surely have been arrested for being drunk or disorderly and made their mark in the court records or newspapers; likewise, a diarist or a traveler would certainly have recorded a brief observation about the event.

Although disproving the existence of something is always difficult and seldom sounds convincing, I am extremely skeptical that Pinkster was of much importance for New York and New Jersey slaves throughout the eighteenth century.[85] Consequently, I would like to suggest an alternative explanation, one that can accommodate this extraordinary 120-year silence. Pinkster indeed persisted throughout these years, but it was primarily a holiday for the Dutch. Although the slaves owned by the Dutch probably were involved to a minor extent, the festival was celebrated in a relatively low-key fashion. Around New York the holiday was little more than a week in which farmers engaged in a round of "visits," but in the surrounds of Albany, where Dutch cultural patterns were much more important, some of the other more boisterous rituals were probably continued.[86] After the Revolution, however, many of the younger Dutch began to question seriously the relevance of the old ways for life in the new nation, a crisis most clearly revealed in the often bitter disputes up and down the Hudson Valley that resulted in the dropping of the Dutch language from religious services. As part of the ensuing process of Americanization stimulated by the Revolution the Dutch community increasingly abandoned their older customs.

Gradually, in the early years of the American nation, blacks played an increasing role in Pinkster while that of the Dutch diminished. As one would expect, the higher profile resulted in a few references to Pinkster actually surviving. The first cited in the *Dictionary of Americanisms* is from 1797, but I have found one from a few years earlier.[87] In 1789 Alexander Coventry recorded in his diary that Cuff, his slave, was "keeping Pinkster, a festival or feast among the Dutch."[88] In 1797 William Dunlap, traveling from the city to Passaic Falls in New Jersey, noted that "the settlements along the river are Dutch, it is the holiday they call pinkster & every public house is crowded with merry makers." Further, the "blacks as well as their masters were frolicking."[89] In both cases Pinkster was clearly a biracial event.

The only surviving piece of contemporaneous evidence specifically commenting on the chronology of Pinkster helps clarify events. When in 1803 the editor of the *Daily Advertiser* reprinted from the *Albany Centinel* the description of Pinkster extensively referred to above, he appended a short note claiming that this account "will convey to our readers a faint idea of a festival, formerly universally celebrated, and still in the recollection of our ancient inhabitants, but which a change of manners has *entirely abolished* in this city." From this it is clear that even in 1803 the festival was of

little significance in New York City. In the surrounding countryside, however, Dutch customs were always more important than in
the metropolis. They had been maintained throughout the eighteenth century and now, in the case of Pinkster, were being taken
over by the slaves.

The renewal of the Pinkster festival coincided with an influx of
recently freed blacks from the surrounding countryside into New
York City, a migration that contributed toward the revival of other
Dutch traditions among city blacks. In 1801, for example, when
John Sipson "lost" his watch a black named Thomas Jackson sent
Sipson to a "high Dutch fortune teller" who correctly divined the
whereabouts of the watch. The fortune-teller's apparent success had
little effect on the court — Jackson was found guilty of the theft of
the watch — but what is interesting about this case is that a black
was involved with a "high Dutch fortune teller." [90]

The revival of Pinkster and the way in which New York blacks
had infused new life into this Old World relic began to attract
attention from a variety of sources at precisely this time. In 1803,
the same year that the *Albany Centinel* published its account of the
ceremony, a pamphlet entitled *A Pinkster Ode For the Year 1803.*
Most Respectfully Dedicated To Carolus Africanus, Rex: Thus Rendered
in English: King Charles, Captain-General and Commander in Chief of
the Pinkster Boys, written by "Absalom Aimwell," was published in
Albany. [91] Similarly, in New York the reprinting of the *Albany Cen-*
tinel article was followed the next year by a special performance at
the theater on Pinkster Monday. That night the evening's entertainment was capped off by a "pantomime interlude" under the
direction of one Signor Bologna entitled "Pinxter Monday or Harlequin's Frolics." [92] Judging from the publicity blurb for the show
printed in the *New York Evening Post*, which announced that the pantomime had already been received with "unbounded applause" at
Covent Garden, there was probably little influence from the slaves.
(Given the usual stereotypes of blacks, the structure of the pantomime with a harlequin and the "irresistible comic humour" of
the clown were no doubt susceptible to the injection of a little ad-
libbed local content.) [93] Nevertheless, it is still a significant indicator
of the increasing acceptance of the holiday that the theater should
appropriate that title on Pinkster Monday. Interestingly, the different expressions — in a newspaper, a poem, and a pantomime — of this

renewed curiosity reflected nicely one of Pinkster's main characteristics: it seems only fitting that a festival that absorbed a variety of
cultural influences should itself be incorporated into a number of
different genres.

Gabriel Furman, a nineteenth-century historian of Long Island,
provides support for these speculations about the chronology of
Pinkster. According to Furman, the festival, which by the 1870s had
"sunk lamentably low, and without any apparent reason," had from
the first settlement of the country been a holiday among the Dutch
inhabitants. Although Pinkster had also been a "species" of black
festivity on Long Island at the same time that it was observed by
the whites, from the commencement of the nineteenth century the
day "became entirely left to the former."[94] In the end what is most
striking about Pinkster is that well after a century of silence the historical record suddenly contains quite detailed information about
the holiday. The publication of Aimwell's poem, the description in
the *Albany Centinel*, Signor Bologna's pantomime, and even the date
of the antiquarian observations of Pinkster in Albany all coincided
in the early years of the nineteenth century. Pinkster itself had a
history that stretched back to seventeenth-century Holland, but the
black version of the carnival was of much more recent origin and
was yet one more example of the invention of tradition.[95] Drawing on both their African past and their position as slaves in the
early years of the Republic, New York and New Jersey blacks had
seized a custom the Dutch were in the process of discarding and
created a new cultural event, whose brief history is one of the more
intriguing episodes in the story of blacks in America.

For New York slaves in the rural areas surrounding the city, Pinkster became the most important break from the rigors of farm life.
Initially, in the period after the Revolution, the holiday was celebrated in the countryside, but from the early years of the nineteenth
century, no doubt stimulated by the steady stream of free black
migrants from rural areas to the city, signs of Pinkster were apparent in New York City. Furman relates that Long Island blacks
came across with their sassafras and swingled tow for sale in order
to raise money to keep the holiday.[96] De Voe similarly details slaves
selling roots, berries, oysters, and clams that they had collected on
Long Island and brought across in their skiffs. Most of his account,
however, is devoted to an oft-quoted description of a jig or break-

down, where famed dancers such as Ned, Jack, and Bobolink Bob displayed, for a share of a collection, their acrobatic dancing skills on a raised board.[97]

It would be a distortion to make too much of the revival of Pinkster: the reality of life for rural slaves was still one of hard work, a fragmented family life, and relative isolation. Pinkster, watermelon frolics, and the occasional visit to the city (the pull of the city for rural slaves appears to reflect more than just a bias in the sources) may have provided a few days respite for slaves, but were meager compensation for everything else they had to endure. Although the slave appropriation of Pinkster testifies to an imaginative syncretization of important traditions from Africa with those of their white owners, the vigor of slave culture should not be allowed to mask behind some romantic haze the adverse conditions under which that culture was created. New York slaves were certainly under no such illusions. In the final analysis, perhaps the most telling fact about slave life in these rural areas was the speed with which, when freed, blacks left their former owners and headed for the city.

OVER THE LAST FEW YEARS historians closely examining slavery at the local level have demonstrated that, far from being monolithic, the institution developed a number of mutations that impinged significantly on the master-slave relationship. Undoubtedly the most striking of these was the task system that emerged in the South Carolina and Georgia lowcountry.[98] On a more limited scale, a practice that appears to have been associated particularly with slavery in New York and New Jersey differentiated the institution there from that in the South. Though scarce, the material on slavery in the area around New York does contain a surprising number of references to slaves voicing opinions about their future, bargaining with their masters over the conditions of their enslavement, and even negotiating with third parties to buy them from their owners. As with the task system, the origins of these local practices remain obscure, but by the time of the Revolution such modifications had allowed some slaves a greater measure of control over their lives and helped, if only marginally, to ameliorate the rigors of slavery.

At least from the 1770s a number of owners advertising their slaves in New York newspapers included the information that the sale was at the instigation of the slaves themselves. In 1781, for example, a black woman was being "sold for no fault but at her own desire."[99] Typically, such slaves were attracted by the allure of city life: a likely young negro fellow" was "sold for no fault, but as he inclines to live in the city, as he was always brought up in one."[100] The imminent departure of an owner for the country threatened considerable disruption to slaves' lives, and many were, at the very least, reluctant to leave the metropolis: a female was being sold as a result of her "not chusing to go into the country where her masters family has lately removed"; another woman had "an aversion to living in the country"; and an even more insistent black was "sold for no fault only he will not live in the country."[101] The twenty-two-year-old woman who had "no objections to living in the country" was indeed unusual.[102] Twenty-five years later, rural life was an equally unappealing prospect for most city slaves. The owner of a slave woman was "about to remove into the country with his family," but the slave was not "willing to go."[103] Similarly, in 1802 a purchaser was sought for an eighteen-year-old slave who was being sold because of his "unwillingness to remain with the family lately removed into the country," a displacement that had apparently led to unpleasantness and "disagreements with the rest of the servants."[104] Although many descriptions from vendors were obviously self-interested, tempting one to regard them with some skepticism, there is enough evidence from other sources to suggest that the advertisements may be taken at face value in these cases.

The diary of Alexander Coventry, for instance, contains a couple of examples from the lower Hudson in the late 1780s, where the wishes of the slave were in fact paramount. On one occasion Coventry crossed over to the west bank with the intention of buying a particular slave, notorious for being "very proud" and for his "haughty mien," only to discover that the slave "preferred not to leave his old mistress, and so she would not sell him." A few months later Jack, the slave of a neighbor called Van Alstine, approached Coventry and asked Coventry to purchase him from his owner. Jack claimed that "his mother and he could not agree; he had told his master he must have another house to live in, and he sent him to me."[105]

Although in the last example the owner had suggested to the slave a possible purchaser, it appears more commonly to have been the case that slaves were given a pass for a few days in order to find a new master themselves. Runaway advertisements provide a number of instances where slaves took advantage of such passes and absconded. As William Wykham had given his slave Will "a permit some time since to seek a master, it is probable he may make use of it to favor his elopement."[106] Similarly, Lydia's owner mentioned that he had given her a pass "for one day last week to get a new master, but this is out of date."[107] A few years earlier Charles Arding had allowed his slave Flummary "permission for a few days to look for a master," but Flummary had not returned.[108]

While some slaves absconded, many others must have used the passes for their intended function. Dr. Samuel Thompson, approached by a slave named Killis, later bought him from his owner for £108/12/6.[109] Another Long Islander, John Baxter, recorded in his diary that in May 1808 a slave named Nero came "looking for a master." In this case negotiations must have taken quite some time, for it was not until August 1809 that Baxter noted that he had offered John W. Stoothoff, Nero's owner, £130 for the slave.[110] In neither of these cases do we have any idea of the motivation of the slaves: Killis and Nero may have wished to move closer to kin and family or, perhaps, just to acquire a less irascible master. But what is clear is that such negotiations allowed a few fortunate slaves the opportunity to take a little of the keenness off slavery's edge.

This practice assumed an even more important function for New York blacks toward the end of the century. If slaves could find a buyer willing to allow them to purchase their own freedom over a number of years, they could free themselves from the hated institution. Interestingly, the two surviving letters from New York slaves in this period both involve attempts to maneuver themselves into just such a situation. In 1807, General Peter Gansevoort purchased Gustus from Benjamin Van Loon, but the slave soon informed his new owner that he wished to "change his situation on account of his dislike of doing housework." Gustus already had a new owner in mind, one Judge William Walker, a man whom he had met some time previously. Gansevoort wrote Walker offering to sell Gustus for the $287.56 that he had paid for him. Gustus also wrote, in a clear but painstaking script, asking Walker whether he was still interested in acquiring him, and if not, whether he would notify Gustus "so that I can look for another master." Gustus ended his letter by declaring that should Walker buy him "you

will not find me lacking in the promise I made you when I was
at your house." Although Gansevoort delayed the negotiations "in
hopes that Gustus might become more reconciled to his situation,"
the deal eventually went through. The details of the arrangement
strongly suggest, however, that it was not merely his desire to avoid
housework that had encouraged Gustus to make the change: Gansevoort agreed to manumit the slave, after which Gustus was voluntarily to indenture himself to Walker and his heirs for seven years.
After that, he would be free. Walker's amendment to his letter, in
which he inserted the word "faithfully" in the margin in front of
"seven years," intimated that he expected a return on his money. But
what emerges most clearly from this incident is the skill of Gustus.
Neither Gansevoort, who was reluctant to part with Gustus but
unwilling to risk owning a disgruntled slave, nor Walker appeared
enthusiastic about the arrangement. Yet Gustus had seized on a
conversation with Walker of at least some months earlier, managed
a complex set of negotiations, and in the end apparently achieved
his ambition — the promise of freedom.[111]

The other surviving letter is from Caesar Brown, a Long Island
slave, to his new owner, Mrs. Sophia Brown. Penned in an assured
and confident hand, the letter reveals Brown as an articulate and
resourceful individual. The slave begins by pointing out that the
death of his late mistress, which he regretted "most sincerely," had
left him "your slave, notwithstanding the constant assurances of
Mr. Brown my former Master & his wife to the contrary, who really
did promise to make me free at their death." All of Brown's slaves
were either to be sold or sent to Mrs. Sophia Brown, and all had
been appraised "at a proper valuation, except me, on whom they
have fixed the immoderate price of 500 Dollars." Caesar Brown
then reminded his new mistress of the "zeal & fidelity" with which
he had served his old master and of his attachment to "my young
master & you." He hoped that she and her husband would help
"to make my Situation Somewhat more independent than it has
been hitherto." If they desired him to go to New York "I will with
pleasure go there and serve you forever," but if he was to be sold,
Caesar Brown asked her to "indulge" him by lowering the price so
he could attempt, with the aid of some friends, to purchase his freedom. Brown ended the letter with "I have the Honor to be, Dear
Madam, Your Faithful Slave, Caesar Brown."[112]

Clearly there were limits to this practice. First, it did not apply to all. As we saw earlier many slaveowners disposed of their human property with no thought for the slaves' wishes. Second, not only was it necessary to have a complaisant master, but the slaves also had to find someone willing both to buy them and to pay a price that was acceptable to their owner. In 1786 Jack, the slave of a Mrs. Upham, approached Alexander Coventry seeking a new master and claiming that he thought he could be bought for about £40. However, Mrs. Upham related, Jack "had got drunk twice, and in his frolic would have a bill of sale." Nevertheless, she was willing to sell Jack for £70 and his wife for £50, prices that were too high for Coventry.[113] Failure to reach agreement undoubtedly led in many cases to disillusionment and friction with the owner. In 1809 John Baxter laconically recorded that his slave Hannah was looking for a master. In June of the next year he commented that "Hannah the Negro wench came back having found a master as she says." However, the diary entry for two days later, noting that Baxter had given "my wench Hannah a Small Dressing for her good language," and the lack of any subsequent details about her sale suggest that there was some dispute about whether Baxter would actually part with her when the time came.[114]

Furthermore, slaves had virtually no legal rights or chance of redress in the courts if their owner reneged. In practical terms they had little more to rely on than the goodwill of their owners. In 1805 Caty, an indentured black girl, won agreement from her master, a Mr. Videll, to end her servitude. The subsequent details of this case are far from clear from the court records, but the result is not—Caty ended up pleading guilty to a charge of stealing from the Vidells. Outraged at her treatment, Caty made an impassioned, if futile, address to the courtroom, and even the dry-as-dust style of the clerk cannot conceal the defendant's sense of harsh usage. Once convicted, Caty claimed that "if ever she comes out of the State Prison She will do that which is ten times worse (meaning ten times worse than what she had already Done to the said Mrs. Videll) and you (addressing herself to Mrs. Videll) had therefore [better] try and keep me there."[115]

In spite of such caveats there can be little doubt that the practice of bargaining for a new master blunted the rigors of slavery for

many blacks and accelerated its demise in New York. As it became
clear after 1799 that slavery was to end, slaves were able to exploit
this tradition either by making a deal with their own master or by
securing a new master willing to let them attain freedom. Sometimes freedom was achieved through self-purchase; in other cases
slaves were let go after providing their owners with a few years of
trouble-free service. But regardless of the method, the result was
the same — slaves in New York, largely through their own efforts,
hastened the death of slavery, broadening the scope of the emancipation program and moving forward by a number of years the
more limited and leisurely timetable put in place by the state legislature. Although under the New York legislation slaves born before
1799 were not to be freed until July 4, 1827, all but the most recalcitrant slaveowners had come to some sort of arrangement with
their slaves well before this date. Again, one is impressed with the
ability of these slaves to sense the indecisiveness of their masters
and to convert a local practice into an effective vehicle for attaining
freedom.

AN ANALYSIS OF AN INCIDENT from the life of one slave helps to
bring together some of the disparate strands of slave life considered
in this chapter. On September 2, 1805, in the presence of two witnesses John S. Glen and his daughter Sarah Glen signed a written
agreement with their slave Yat, promising him freedom in six years
if he adhered to certain conditions.[116] Those conditions make explicit many of the constraints imposed on slaves in a society where
holdings were small and owners were a continuing presence.

Yat had to promise to serve his owners faithfully. He was not
allowed to absent himself, day or night, without permission, except
on specified holidays. He was permitted three days for Christmas,
two days for the New Year's celebration, two for Easter, and three
for Pinkster. Once every three weeks Yat was released at two hours
before sunset on Saturday and allowed to visit his wife, who lived
some distance from Schenectady. He had to return by ten o'clock
on the Monday morning. Yat also had to agree not to take any more
wives, not to commit adultery, and to attend church at least once
every four weeks. In the same clause the Glens specified that, ex-

cept on holidays, the slave was not to "go a Fidling" without their permission, a provision that was to be enforced by having Yat turn his fiddle over to his owners for safekeeping.

Failure by Yat to perform any of the covenants rendered the agreement null and void. Additionally, the penalties for any misdemeanor were stringent. If he ran away he would again become a slave in perpetuity, his master having the right to sell him. If Yat broke a hogshead of spirits or caused any damage by neglect, he would be condemned to servitude and subject to sale for the rest of his life. At the end of what promised to be, for Yat, a very taxing and arduous six years, there was one final obstacle — the newly freed slave had to give his note for $90 payable one year later. Magnanimously, the Glens waived any interest on the note.

One gloss on this contract already exists: it is provided by Cornelius Van Horne, who early this century rescued the agreement from what he termed "utter oblivion" and wrote in a letter in 1913 that he "pictured Yat as a jolly, good-natured darkey." Van Horne went on to speculate that the restrictive clauses would have weighed very little with Yat, who "when their [his owners'] backs were turned . . . made faces at them, and rolled his eyes, and his ivory teeth has shown, and with a sly grin and a chuckle he has made his mark." [117] Yet in allowing his racist imagination to run riot, Van Horne had missed completely the significance of this possibly unique document. Yat lived in a peripheral slave society at a time when the institution was winding down. As a consequence, he was able to reach an agreement with his master and gain his freedom. But this was no act of charity. Not only did his owners secure "faithful" and continuous service at a time when, as we shall see, slaves were becoming more and more restive, but they had also, assuming that Yat managed to avoid falling foul of all the penalty clauses, extracted a large sum in cash from their property.

Paradoxically, the very factors that gave Yat and thousands of other New York slaves a chance to free themselves, a chance denied the vast majority of their southern compatriots for another half a century, undermined the slave family and impeded the growth of a slave culture. In this peripheral slave society with its small holdings the scope for white intervention in black lives was much greater than in the plantation South: Yat, for example, was limited to periodic visits to his family and even deprived of his fiddle (music, along with dance, was probably the most-valued medium of self-expression for slaves throughout America) except on a few specified holidays.[118]

When Alexander Coventry asserted that slaves had "more of life" than any other laboring class, he was no doubt referring to such activities as the "frolics," or Pinkster, or other occasions on which he had observed slaves singing and dancing. Yet the ability of New York and New Jersey slaves to adapt to their unpromising environ-ment and create a dynamic and sustaining culture cannot conceal the cruel reality of their situation. The idea of a benevolent slave society was a chimera, a self-deceiving myth propagated by New Yorkers in a vain attempt to distinguish themselves from the evil that they perceived to exist in the South. Certainly, there were sig-nificant differences between slave life in the South and in New York, but they were not of the kind New Yorkers chose to believe existed. New York slavery may have been small-scale and centered on the family rather than the plantation, but it was also implacable, bru-tal, and little short of devastating in its impact on the black family. If white New Yorkers congratulated themselves on the relative be-nevolence of their slave system, their black counterparts had few such illusions. As we shall see in the next chapter, they demonstrated their contempt for such self-serving notions about the mildness of the regime that held them by the frequency and tenacity with which they struggled to free themselves from it.

5

Running Away

IN EARLY JULY 1787 two Schenectady slaves fetching their master's cows came upon a pocket book lying on the ground. Later, another black was able to identify the five notes inside the pocket book as ten-pound bills, but the three were given little time to enjoy their good fortune. Before long they had been charged with passing counterfeit notes and committed to jail in nearby Albany.

Newspapers throughout the state reported the incident, in part because forged currency was a matter of concern to the business community, but also because the story provided ground for risible speculation concerning black behavior. The *New York Journal*, after noting that it had not yet been able to ascertain how readers could detect the false bills, pointed out that it was "shrewdly suspected that there are also *white* villains in this counterfeiting business," villains who had employed the "*sable* boys" to pass the currency. The *Hudson Weekly Gazette* explained more fully how it had reached the same conclusion. Any story about blacks happening upon money was inherently implausible, for if one black had found such a large sum of money and was honest, he would immediately have informed his master. On the other hand, were the black "rogue enough to keep the money, he would have little thought of dividing it with two others." It was only sensible to conclude, therefore, that "infamous persons" had used the blacks to circulate the bills. The last surviving piece of information about the case, contained in a letter from a gentleman in Albany to the *Daily Advertiser*, suggested, however, that the earlier comment was baseless and that the charges would not be made good. Interviewed in separate rooms, the two blacks who had discovered the money had given evidence "exactly concurring with the defence the other had made." Apparently, the writer was suggesting, blacks were incapable of concocting and sticking to a plausible alibi and must have been telling the truth.[1]

Whether readers of these newspapers viewed such accounts as warnings against the circulation of forged notes, or as amusing anecdotes about the behavior of blacks, all but a very few undoubtedly saw in the incident further evidence of black simplicity. In practice it made little difference whether the slaves were innocent or the dupes of white villains: in either case they had been incapable of acting without the guiding hand of a white, even if that hand belonged to a forger. Yet anyone attempting to unravel the dense skein created by assumptions of racial inferiority might have picked up a half sentence, buried deep inside the *Daily Advertiser*'s version of events, that did not fit. As soon as the black who had found the money had appreciated its value he had "endeavoured to purchase his wife's freedom." A windfall had given this black, a slave and undoubtedly an illiterate as well, the opportunity to rescue his wife from bondage, and he had seized it eagerly. On his own ground he was attempting to shape both his own and his wife's lives, and that ground eloquently challenges any easy white assumptions about both the resignation or docility of blacks and the benevolence of slavery in New York.

Although direct black testimony on slavery in New York is relatively scarce — after all, the vast majority of blacks could neither read nor write — fragments such as the above incident allow the historian to reconstruct, if only in a limited fashion, the world of the slaves.[2] Newspapers from the New York area are a rich and largely untapped source of such evidence, much of it contained in runaway advertisements scattered in the eighteenth-century equivalent of the classified columns, where it lies buried between advertisements for the sale of dry goods and the shipping news. Collected and analyzed as a whole this evidence shows slaves not in a position of weakness, as mere passive recipients of white paternalism or the butt of white racism, but in one of strength as they to a surprising extent resisted physically as well as culturally the institution of slavery.

FROM AT LEAST THE TIME that Samuel Coleridge penned his acerbic comment, "What a History! Horses and Negroes! Negroes and Horses!" various writers have exploited the advertisements for runaway slaves in order to stigmatize the peculiar institution.[3] In the nineteenth century American abolitionists drew on this source to publicize their cause. In the first half of the present century historians began to examine the advertisements in the course of their inquiries into the institution of slavery itself, but it was not until 1972, with the publication of Gerald Mullin's quantitative study of Virginia runaways, that they were analyzed extensively and used for other than illustrative purposes. Since that time the analysis of these advertisements has become the standard coin of works on eighteenth-century slavery.[4]

Although interpretations of the contents of the advertisements and of the act of running away have reached high levels of sophistication, historians have paid insufficient attention to the original context within which the advertisements appeared. That context — namely, their publication in newspapers — raises a number of interesting questions about the role of print, and more generally of writing, in the subjugation of blacks, questions that are of some importance in decoding this type of material.[5] While a few slaves in New York at the end of the eighteenth century could read and write, literate slaves were still a very small minority of the population. Blacks possessing these abilities were thought worthy of remark and even evoked surprise. Whites attempted to use their near monopoly of the skills of literacy in the policing of black behavior: for instance, slaves needing to travel or wishing to find a new master were supposed to carry written permission from their owner.[6] Thus, for many slaves, writing must have been closely linked to white authority, the authority of their owner who granted them a pass, or of the magistrate's clerk who recorded the inevitable whippings. Small wonder then that New York's slaves and free blacks, recognizing the power of literacy, flocked to the African School in the 1790s and early nineteenth century. In 1793 the *Daily Advertiser* claimed that 160 had enrolled since the founding of the school in 1789. By 1796, however, the numbers appear to have increased dramatically: in that year, according to the *American Minerva*, there were 140 students of both sexes at the public examination.[7]

The same strictures applied even more strongly to the printed word. Social power depends on the ability to define and impose meaning, and the whites' almost complete monopoly on space in the press considerably facilitated their dominance. The very occasional black incursions into the newspapers usually brought forth a quick response: this form of "public" discourse was regarded as the preserve of white males.[8] In 1788 "Humanio," almost certainly a black, complained in the *Daily Advertiser* of grave robbers forcibly removing the body of a young child from the black cemetery in Gold Street. Two days later the newspaper published a derisive rejoinder analyzing not the substance of "Humanio"'s letter but his writing style. "A Student of Physic" took "Humanio" "to be some *manumitted slave*" and questioned his ability even to participate in such a discussion "without first applying for another quarters tuition at the *free negro school;* that he may thereby be enabled to carry his meanings at least in good if not in elegant language."[9]

White dominance over blacks through the monopoly of the print media was illustrated in other ways. Whites classified blacks in runaway advertisements and "for sale" notices as inferior beings, grouping them, as Coleridge pointed out, with the livestock. The implicit power relationship underpinning such labeling is brought to the surface in an extraordinary series of advertisements from New Jersey in the 1780s, in which one black challenged that relationship by responding in print. In a January notice in the *New Jersey Gazette* David Cowell, a doctor from Trenton, offered to sell or exchange an able-bodied Negro man, who understood farming and "the care and management of horses equal to any in the country." In the next issue of the *Gazette* the "able-bodied Negro man" in question replied: since Cowell "has no legal right to any such Negro Man, nor pretensions to claim any but myself" his "duty to the publick" required him to inform them that the writer had a contract for his freedom "written and executed by his [Cowell's] own hand, which he has often attempted and still persists in endeavouring to violate, although I have very sufficient proof that the said consideration is fully paid him." Further, the black expected to receive "that freedom, justice and protection, which I am entitled to by the laws of the state, although I am a Negro." The notice was signed simply "Adam." On February 23 Cowell placed another advertisement in the *Gazette* denying that he had ever promised Adam freedom. In fact, he said, Adam had proved very unfaithful, attempting to run away to New York the previous summer, an escapade that not only cost Cowell great expense in jail fees and money paid to the guards but also caused him the considerable inconvenience of having to ride more than two hundred miles to fetch his human property. Cowell also stated his belief that Nathan Beaks and Stacy Potts were the instigators of Adam's recalcitrance. Consequently he had brought an action in the Supreme Court, "as soon as I found an attorney who had not received a retaining fee against me."

The following week Adam replied once again. He would, he declared, welcome the chance to place his case before the "impartial tribunal of the publick." The two gentlemen mentioned by Cowell would not "descend to take notice of his *notable* performance," but Adam had no such scruples. Cowell's attempt to violate their "solemn engagement" was, he asserted, the least exceptionable part of his master's behavior: Cowell was "notorious for having defrauded his [Cowell's] father, [and] robbed his brothers and sisters of their patrimony" as well as for the venality and debauchery that had rendered "his person as nauseous as his character is contemptible." As if this were not enough, Adam also impugned his master's reputation as a doctor by claiming that through Cowell's "negligence and misconduct numbers of brave soldiers have been sent to eternity, at a time when their services were most necessary." Adam ended by praying "for the prosperity of that government which protects the rights of a poor Negro." Cowell appears to have wilted somewhat in the face of this onslaught, but he managed to retaliate the following week, albeit rather weakly, asserting that the "three quaking authors of the two illiberal pieces of calumny signed ADAM" were traitors and that the character and cause of the whites involved was "blacker than the slave they want to keep in their debt." He also cited a recommendation from the "Head of the Department" in which it was detailed that Cowell was not only an "industrious, humane and skilfull Senior Physician and Surgeon" but also that he had "manifested great zeal to the American cause." Here the exchange ended, but one final advertisement placed by Cowell appeared three years later. Adam's faith in the Jersey government had apparently been misplaced, for the justices of the Supreme Court had publicly declared him to be Cowell's property. But Adam was still at large, and Cowell persisted in his belief that the "same evil minded advisers as formerly" were responsible for his successful evasion of the constables. Just before Christmas 1783 a very brief notice informed the *Gazette* readers of Cowell's death.[10]

Even in this unusual affair there is an assumption that Adam was incapable of behaving in this presumptuous fashion on his own. Cowell, at least, was certain that his slave was not playing an active role in the affair, but was merely the tool of the "quaking authors" who were using Adam to malign him. But what is more remarkable about the episode is that such aggressive advertisements were ever published under a slave's name.[11] The exceptional, perhaps even unique, nature of Adam's public defiance, his contesting of whites' monopoly of the printed word, and his open repudiation of the master's claims on him do emphasize the point that in more normal circumstances the power of labeling and classifying blacks resided firmly with the whites and, further, that the printed word was one of the means of enforcing the slave system.[12]

In *Flight and Rebellion*, a pioneering study of slave resistance in eighteenth-century Virginia, Gerald Mullin places runaway advertisements in a different context. To him they belong to the category of what Marc Bloch called "witnesses in spite of themselves" — items such as wills, ledgers, and court records that were not created with an eye to posterity or for the benefit of historians. Mullin argues that unlike more traditional narratives, which are inevitably distorted by authorial bias, such "unconscious evidence" provides a "fairly objective" source for looking at those who left little direct testimony.[13] Yet such a formulation ignores the role that language plays in linking both types of evidence, the inadvertent and the direct. After all, both incidental evidence and narrative accounts are conveyed through the English language, and that language itself is anything but objective. Consider, for example, the accounts of the physical appearance of blacks contained in the runaway advertisements. Such descriptions appear to be dispassionate, illustrating well the "objectivity" of the advertisements, but we need to understand that the language used in them was loaded with meanings not always accessible to modern readers. Many of the Americans who read these advertisements believed, for example, that there was a direct and readily discernible link between appearance on the one hand and character and intellect on the other. Thus "Africanus," in an article entitled "Negroes inferior to Whites" published in the *New York Journal*, drew on the "science of physiogomy" to bolster his argument: "who would look for marks of genius and penetration in the countenances composed of dull and heavy eyes, flat noses and blubber lips — yet these are characteristic features of the

negro nations." [14] Increasingly in the period after the Revolution
such ideas, which were clearly related to the widespread interest in
and debate over the origin of the Negro race, permeated the runaway advertisements: Paris's "lips are thick and he has an African
face"; Lindor had an "African nose and lips." [15] Other blacks had
features that varied from what was considered to be the norm. The
twenty-six-year-old runaway Will was described as having a "nose
differing from the rest of his complexion, [as it] is projective and
of the Roman kind." At times masters were even more explicit: a
fifteen-year-old mulatto who ran away in 1795 had a face that was
"not unpleasant though expressive of the worst character." [16] Even
ostensibly objective descriptions of "thick lips" or "flat noses," then,
are freighted with cultural meaning, referring back to a whole body
of "scientific" speculation about the physical origins and intellectual
capacity of blacks. In reality the difference between runaway advertisements and narratives is one of degree rather than kind. The
truncated format of the advertisements resulted not in a more objective depiction of the runaways but in the slaveowners' recourse to
a series of abbreviations, a type of shorthand, to convey their meaning. [17] Although the significance of these codes was readily apparent
to eighteenth-century New Yorkers, twentieth-century historians
have more difficulty in deciphering them. Certainly runaway advertisements contain a wealth of information about blacks, and in
this chapter and in chapter 7 I try to use them to reveal as much
as possible of black life, but it is important to remember that we
discern these slaves through the eyes and, most important, through
the language of their owners.

The runaway advertisements analyzed in this study were compiled from a selection of New York and New Jersey newspapers
published between 1771 and 1805. [18] In order to concentrate on the
role of New York City, all runaways from the area of New York
State to the north and west of Ulster and Dutchess counties have
been excluded. In addition, all advertisements in the press describing slaves who had decamped from their owners in Connecticut,
Pennsylvania, and the southern states were discarded. In fact, most
of the runaways came from New York City and the surrounding
counties of Kings, Queens, Westchester, and Richmond and from
Bergen and Somerset in New Jersey. In all, the collected advertisements give details concerning 1,232 runaway slaves. [19]

TABLE 14
*Origins of New York and New Jersey
Runaways, 1771–1805*

	N	%
America	73	20.5
West Indies	70	19.7
Africa	45	12.6
Mulatto	168	47.2
	356	100.0

Note: Origin was specified in 28.9 percent (356 out of 1,232) of cases.

The most immediately striking feature of the slaves described in these runaway advertisements is their immense variety. For instance, Strickland's comment that New York blacks "may be seen of all shades till the stain is entirely worne out" is amply borne out.[20] Slaves ranged in color from jet black through all manner of lighter hues — Grotis was a "sambo color," James was rather cruelly depicted by his owner as having the complexion of a "mongrel," the mulatto John Wagon was "so remarkably white that he might possibly pass for a white man."[21] There was a similar diversity in physical size: the obviously formidable fifty-six-year-old Jane Miers was "large and corpulent" and about six feet tall, whereas a Guinea-born "boy" who spoke a little English and a little French was, according to his owner, about three and a half feet tall.[22]

Unfortunately, the owners of such slaves were not as forthcoming as their southern counterparts: the advertisements from New York and New Jersey were usually much less detailed, and for every variable — place of birth, skill, or ability to speak English — there is a much higher percentage of "unknowns" than in comparable compilations for the South. Nevertheless, for all their shortcomings the figures do suggest some characteristics of the runaway population and, if used sensibly, can provide a foundation for understanding this facet of slave life.

Although the origins of the runaways are indicated in only just over one-quarter of the advertisements, the statistics in table 14 further illustrate the heterogeneity of the runaway population. The categories in the table are those used by the owners of the slaves, but unfortunately they are not discrete: mulattoes obviously were born in the New World, but a sizable share of the mulattoes included in table 14 were born not in America, but in the West Indies. Similarly, a proportion of the blacks described as coming from the West Indies were undoubtedly African born. In spite of this blurring of the classifications it is clear that more than one in three of the runaways where origin was indicated, and probably closer to four in ten, were originally from the West Indies or Africa. My impression is that were we to possess full details for all of the advertised runaways this ratio would drop, but not by that much.

It is hardly surprising that the runaways were not a homogeneous group. New York was a port city, and many of the fugitive slaves were sailors who had jumped ship. Furthermore, refugees who flocked to New York from the two great upheavals in this period frequently brought slaves with them. During British occupation in the Revolution loyalists from all over America descended on the city, and many of their slaves ran away. Similarly in the 1790s and the early years of the nineteenth century, slaves owned by Saint Dominguan refugees fled in significant numbers. Although a few of the Africans listed in table 14 were undoubtedly brought over by slave traders in the last years of the colonial period, the majority came indirectly, often with French émigrés, via the West Indies.[23] The ability of the runaways to speak the English language, a detail included in about one in four cases, gives another indication of the provenance of these slaves. Of the 316 runaways whose linguistic ability was described, 87, or 27.5 percent, were either unable to speak the English language at all or spoke it very badly.

In four out of five cases the owners specified the age of the runaways. Although the precise age may well have been incorrect—undoubtedly many of the slaves were themselves uncertain of their age—the errors were unlikely to be so serious as to invalidate the use of this information as a rough guide to how old these slaves were. Only 16 of the 986 fugitives whose ages were given were fifty or older, Jane Miers at fifty-six being the eldest. The majority of runaways were in their late teens or early twenties, and three out of every four were under the age of twenty-six.

Most runaways in other states were also in their late teens and early twenties, but the number of even younger slaves who absconded from the New York region seems greater than was usual.[24] These slaves, it should be emphasized, were running away independently and not in some family group. Consider the case of York, a slave who fled from his master, Peter Creighton, several times in the early 1780s. York had only recently arrived from Jamaica, and whenever he slipped away he headed for one of the Royal Navy's frigates in the harbor. His master described him in one advertisement as "very artful" and in another as being "much addicted to drinking and lying, very talkative and very subtle for his age." That age was only thirteen.[25] York was by no means unusual: nearly one in six of the runaways was under the age of sixteen.

Even very young slaves appeared to have learned already that survival depended on their ability to dissemble and to deceive whites. In January 1797 Israel Duree placed a notice in the *Argus* giving details of a "lost" black he had apprehended on New Year's Eve: the slave was a six- or seven-year-old mulatto, who had told Duree that his name was George, that his master's name was M'Lary, and that they had both lately arrived from Charleston. Two months later Jacob Ten Eyck of Vesey Street inserted a similar notice in the *Argus:* a likely mulatto had come to his door claiming that he was from Charleston, that his master's name was M'Lary, and that he had lost his way. At this point the lad appears as the lost waif, adrift in the big city, and if only he could have changed his color, the potential protagonist of a sentimental novel about the vicissitudes of life in the metropolis. "George," however, was less the helpless victim than these descriptions might suggest. In July 1797 an advertisement appeared in the *Daily Advertiser* describing a mulatto who had run away on May 10. His name was Jo, but when questioned he "calls himself George and says he came from Charleston and that he was left on shore and is lost." From the owner's account it appears that Duree had underestimated the slave's age in the first notice — Jo was in fact about ten years old.[26] What is plain, however, is that Jo had played both on his youthful appearance and on the gullibility of white householders in order to absent himself from his master's service for quite lengthy periods of time. Similar instances were hardly unusual. In 1795 one New Yorker advertised that he had taken up an eight-year-old and was skeptical of this slave's claim that his master and mistress were dead. The next year a runaway advertisement in the *Argus* detailed the case of an eleven-year-old French mulatto named Catharine, who was telling people around the city that her master had gone away to Santo Domingo.[27]

Overall, then, several characteristics of the advertised runaway population in the New York region are now apparent. Probably in excess of one in three escaped slaves were born either in the West Indies or in Africa and generally the fugitives were young, with three in every four under the age of twenty-six. In addition, the runaways were predominantly male. Proportionately, women made up a larger share of the runaways than in the southern states, but it is still the case that only slightly more than one in five (267 out of 1,232) of the fugitives was female.[28] Finally, about one in six (209 out of 1,232) of the runaways was described as skilled.[29]

How representative of the broader slave population were the runaway slaves recorded in the New York and New Jersey newspapers? This is difficult to determine because of the paucity of our knowledge about the demographic structure of the slave population. Nevertheless, in two areas it is possible to make a rough assessment of the relationship. Although the sex ratio in the slave population of New York City was heavily skewed toward females, that of the region as a whole tended to be more evenly balanced. According to the New York census of 1786 there were 7,178 black males and 7,006 black females in the New York portion of the region under consideration here.[30] Unfortunately there are no figures for New Jersey, but it is unlikely that slaves from this region exhibited a divergent pattern. Thus it would appear that the preponderance of males among the runaways only slightly paralleled the slave population as a whole. Similarly, mulattoes were quite a significant minority in the slave population, but it is extremely improbable that they constituted anything like 47.2 percent (see table 14).[31] As a precise measure of the demographic features of the slave population as a whole, the statistics from the runaway advertisements are of little use, but as we shall later see they can still help delineate the influences that shaped black culture and provide some indication of the complexity of the cultural interaction that occurred in this region.[32]

VARIETY ALSO CHARACTERIZED the physical act of running away. Some elopements were almost spur-of-the-moment decisions, with the slaves getting away with the clothes on their backs and little else. One black was last seen marching off with a bridle in his hand, muttering something about a lost horse.[33] Other escapes were more carefully planned, as evidenced by the fact that the runaways carried off changes of clothing and a variety of other items. Yaff left Gravesend on Long Island in a skiff "with a couple of live sheep and a beehive full of honey."[34] In another case, a future stock image of Hollywood and of the miniseries was unwittingly subverted when two slaves decamped, only to be followed by two bloodhounds, which also failed to return.[35] Other runaways stole money or easily transportable goods: M. Burot's slave, for instance, left with his master's gold watch and half of his linen.[36] Yet for a meticulously orchestrated departure incorporating more than a modicum of revenge few could rival that of Ruth, a slave from near Perth Amboy. Ruth waited until her master, Nicholas Fletcher, was away and then let a number of accomplices into his residence. They beat up Ruth's mistress, tied her to the bed, and sacked the house before departing in a waiting boat with the plate, clothes, and an iron chest containing money and papers. Given these circumstances Fletcher's depiction of the runaway appears less an objective description than a statement from behind clenched teeth: Ruth was a "stout masculine wench" of a "yellowish cast" who possessed a "coarse rough voice."[37]

The intentions of the runaways can sometimes be inferred from the style of their departure. Clearly Ruth did not anticipate returning to her master's house in the foreseeable future, but other slaves obviously did mean to slip away for only a short time. Andrew Caldwell's advertisement for Jack suggests that some blacks viewed running away as a temporary expedient: Caldwell would have posted his slave as a runaway sooner, but as Jack "had a trick of absenting himself for two to three weeks at a time and returning home it was thought he might do the same now."[38] Some of the owners, surmising that their slaves fell within the same category, included in their advertisements appeals to the slaves themselves, hopeful that even if they could not read, word would still reach them. The usual inducement for return was an offer to waive punishment, but the tone in which this offer was couched varied considerably. Sometimes it was patronizing and condescending: John Jackson's owner promised that if "he voluntarily returns to his master, asks his pardon, and promises never to leave him again, he will be forgiven, and no notice taken of his ungrateful behaviour." [39] Other masters, obviously accustomed to having their slaves abscond, presented a more world-weary persona: James Thompson advertised that if his runaway Jim came back of his own accord and behaved, "he will once more be forgiven." [40] At times, and particularly toward the end of the period under consideration, the enticement was more substantial: in 1800 a female slaveowner offered a runaway family the "privilege of working themselves free" should they return. [41]

Some slaveholders found the motivations and actions of their runaways utterly perplexing. In their own way such owners were concerned with the welfare of their blacks and considered slavery, particularly under their firm but caring hand, as being in the best interests of the slaves. Although few were as explicit as the owner of a fifteen-year-old mulatto, who thought that his runaway "ought to be considered as a lost child, whom the greatest misfortunes await if he is not set again under the benevolent authority, the care and watchful eye of his master," many would have found the sentiment unexceptionable. [42] In addition, such owners often believed that the slaves recognized their good intentions and reciprocated with feelings of affection. Some owners refused to accept that their slaves fled voluntarily and conjectured about third parties detaining the runaways against their will. [43] Others, when they discovered that slaves did not necessarily share their own benign view of slavery, exhibited wounded pride. One runaway had slipped away the previous fall, "for which he never received the least correction." Now, by running away again, "he has shewed his gratitude." [44] Bet, who absconded in 1798, had "been treated and indulged more like an equal than a servant." [45] Reactions such as these anticipate those of many southern planters when, during the Civil War, favorite slaves bolted at the first chance. [46] They also provide yet more evidence of the yawning chasm between black and white perceptions of slavery, even under the supposedly mild regime that existed in New York.

Some slaveholders were able to include more precise information about the intentions and whereabouts of their runaways. In one in five cases (257 out of 1,232) owners offered a specific motive for the departure, and in one in four instances (326 out of 1,232) they ventured an opinion about the destination of the runaway (see table 15). [47] The immediate question, of course, is how accurate this in-

TABLE 15
*Motives and Destinations of New York and
New Jersey Runaways, 1771–1805*

Motive	N	%
To visit	50	20.2
To pass as free	183	74.1
To avoid or because of punishment	14	5.7
	247	100.0

Destination	N	%
Countryside	72	22.0
New York City	120	36.8
Outside New York and New Jersey	92	28.3
Army	42	12.9
	326	100.0

Note: Owners offered an opinion on motivation for 20.0 percent of the 1,232 runaways and on the destination in 26.5 percent of cases.

formation was likely to be. There is no real way of checking, but we can at least say that in many instances the source of the owner's estimate is readily apparent.[48] At times the information originated from conversations with the slaves themselves. It appeared likely that Joshua Blue, who ran away in 1800, would go to sea, as he had often mentioned that "if free, he should prefer that mode of life."[49] Similarly, Duke was notorious for talking "much of Philadelphia and Rhode Island," so there seemed to be little doubt when he ran away in 1779 that he would attempt to leave the colony.[50] In other cases runaways were expected to repeat previous escape attempts: the last time Jack, from Rocky Hill Mills near Princeton, had eloped he had been caught ten miles short of Boston, and his owner suspected that he would try the same route again.[51] But the most frequent basis for opinions as to the likely destinations of escaped slaves was a sighting of the runaways. Fifteen-year-old David, who escaped in 1801, had been "seen that evening at the theatre and since in several parts of the city."[52] Pro, who had escaped from his master in Westchester, was observed in the week previous to the placing of the advertisement in Fairfield, Connecticut, where he was "standing for Boston." [53] Owners' estimates were certainly not infallible, but taken as a whole they offer some guide to black intentions. What is certain is that they are all we have.

In three out of every four cases where the owner did suggest an explanation for a slave's departure, the fugitives were expected to attempt to break completely from the institution of slavery by passing as free men or women. For such slaves, New York City acted as a magnet. More than one in three of all the runaways were anticipated to be heading there. For owners of runaways the city was a frustrating environment, small enough to allow sightings of slaves but large enough to make recapturing them very difficult. In 1795 eighteen-year-old Calypso was "seen running with a bundle of cloaths and her shoes in her hand through Pearl and Cherry Streets, then turning into Oliver, then into Rutgers, and finally into Roosevelt Street on the left hand; here were lost her tracts." [54] For the slaves the city provided not only anonymity but also ample opportunities for work: Sharp's owner suspected that he was in New York and "probably will get employ at some building as a laborer." [55] Usually, too, there was employment to be had on the large number of ships in the harbor, and most important for the typically impecunious runaways, it was traditional to pay a portion of wages in advance as a signing-on fee. In 1802, for instance, Stephen Morell advertised that his runaway slave James Alexander was rumored to have received a new set of clothing from the master of a vessel "as his month's advance." [56]

New York in the late eighteenth and early nineteenth centuries was a bustling and dynamic city offering many of the advantages usually associated with urban life. Even Polly, an apparently aptly named male runaway who according to his owner Alexander McKenzie "will endeavour to pass for a woman though he wears mens clothing," could expect to find an amenable environment in the metropolis. [57] Most important, though, the city offered slaves the possibility of sanctuary among the relatively concentrated black population. The considerable growth in the numbers of free blacks in the years after the Revolution gave rise to suspicion, much of it probably justified, that this group played an important role in harboring and aiding runaways. [58] In particular, the "French negroes" from the West Indies, who were often isolated by language and who appear to have congregated in the city, posed such a threat. Telmaque, Alcindor, and Calypso, the three "French negroes" of one B. Darracq, spent a relatively enjoyable time from May to October

1794 in New York before traveling with their master to a farm in Rahway, New Jersey. But evidently life on the farm suffered by comparison, for in early December they ran away and Darracq expected them to return to the city as "they are displeased with the country." [59] Slaves such as these, or the mulatto runaway who deserted the brig *Philanthropist* and who spoke a little English but "tolerable good French," could find, at the very least, companionship from other French blacks in the city. [60]

Heading for New York City was not restricted to the acculturated blacks: African-born slaves who could barely speak English fled there regularly. In 1792, for example, the fifty-year-old African slave Cook, who "talks bad English," ran away from Flatbush on Long Island and was rumored to be living in the metropolis, where he "pretends to be free." According to Mullin such behavior would have been unusual in Virginia among the American-born unacculturated slaves, let alone the African born. [61] Runaways, whether of African, West Indian, or American origin, could merge into the urban background and pass as free blacks with comparative ease. Regrettably, however, we hear only of those who were caught. Phillis White, who was convicted of stealing six pounds of cheese, told the court that she was the slave of a Mr. Lewis Lopez of Elizabeth, but that she had "ran away from him a Considerable time ago." Phillis was now "married to a free man, and kept House in Division Street." [62]

It was also anticipated by owners that a substantial proportion of the runaways who attempted to pass as free would leave the New York and New Jersey region. More than one in four of all the fugitives for whom the owner listed a destination fell into this category (see table 15). A few were supposed to be heading for relatively surprising places: in 1773, Bret was endeavoring to get to the Mississippi; thirteen years later a mulatto was expected to try and board a vessel bound for the West Indies "as he ran away once before and went there." [63] But generally the favored destinations were Philadelphia or, even more commonly, the New England states. In 1785, Joseph Ellis of Gloucester, New Jersey, advertised that his slave Samuel, who "was used to driving a team and is remarkably fond of talking of horses," had been seen at the "Black Horse" traveling eastward and doubtless would try to obtain work driving a team. [64]

The escape of slaves such as Samuel was potentially a substantial financial loss for their owners. Consequently, it is not surprising

that in the "entrepreneurial efflorescence"[65] of the 1790s a few individuals recognized an unfulfilled demand and sought to profit from
it. In 1799 John Colter advertised his services as a slave catcher.
Colter pointed out that as a result of emancipation in Massachusetts many gentlemen in New York and New Jersey had suffered the
loss of their slaves. According to Colter these runaways "principally
take up their residence in the town of Boston." For the modest fee
of at least fifty dollars Colter would catch the fugitives and send
them on the packet to the New York jail. However, the note attached to the end of the advertisement stating that Colter would not
be "accountable for property the slave may possess when detected"
suggests that there were opportunities for greater financial gain.[66]
There are occasional hints that Colter and those of his ilk may have
met with some success. In 1797 a runaway named Sam was supposed
to have traveled from Flatbush to New York City and then on to
Boston "as he ran away last May, a year since to that place but was
apprehended and brought back with six other negroes."[67] It should
be added that there are also occasional suggestions that runaways
managed to organize themselves as well: in 1798 the twenty-two-
year-old Abraham, who spoke broken English and creole French,
had fled from his owner, who subsequently heard that his slave had
lurked around Bunker Hill on the fringe of the city before heading off for Philadelphia "along with a number of negroes, who have
lately run away from their masters in this city."[68]

Some owners went to considerable lengths to pursue their valuable property. In 1802 the owner of Will, who ran away in 1799,
placed a new advertisement in the paper, detailing that his slave
had been seen in Providence "but on being pursued left that and is
now supposed to be in some other part of the Eastern States." The
record for persistence, however, must go to the owner of Daniel:
according to an advertisement in 1789 Daniel had been absent for
eleven years, during which time he had been to Nova Scotia, but the
previous spring he had been taken up in the city while visiting his
wife in the Bowery.[69] The advertisement was occasioned by Daniel
slipping away yet again.

There was one other important destination for slaves who were
attempting to sever ties with slavery and pass as free. Although the
Revolutionary war lasted for only a fifth of the period under consideration here, it was still the case that about one in eight fugitives
listed with a destination were believed to be fleeing to the military

forces (see table 15). Many found that either the army or the an-
cillary forces offered a refuge beyond the reach of their masters:
in 1777 George Shaw claimed that his two slaves had "entered into
his Majesty's service as waggon drivers & their names are on the
Commissary's books," but he staunchly maintained that they "are
my property."[70] Others were drawn by the excitement and possible financial gain of life on one of the privateers operating out of
New York harbor: Cato, for instance, "designed to go a privateer-
ing."[71] In addition, a further group were expected by their owners
to swell the camp followers and hangers-on attracted to any army.
In 1778 the mulatto slave Sarah, who was pregnant and had a six-
year-old son in tow, was expected to return to the "1st. Maryland
Regiment where she pretends to have a husband, with who she has
been the principal part of this campaign and passed herself as a
free woman."[72]

In the vast majority of cases in which an explanation for the departure was included in the advertisement the slaves were expected
to pass as free. There was, however, a smaller group of such cases—
about one in five (see table 15)—where the owner suggested that
the reason for elopement was to seek out friends or relatives. Such
a motive did not necessarily, of course, preclude a desire on the
part of the slave to be free, and this category of fugitive must have
blurred into those "passing as free." Suke, for example, who ran
away in 1801, had a "numerous acquaintance of her own color in
George Street" in the city.[73] Although she may have slipped away
simply to visit her friends, it is also probable that she would have
sought help from such friends had she intended to sever all ties
with the institution of slavery. Nevertheless it seems that owners
believed the primary motivation of this group was something other
than a desire to leave slavery permanently. While some of these
slaves headed, as did Suke, for the city, most were expected to travel
to the countryside. Rutger Van Brunt's slave left his master's farm
in New Utrecht on Long Island in a skiff and was "supposed to be
gone up the North River as he is acquainted at Claverack at which
place he was taken up about two years since."[74] Often the slave's
attachment to a particular place was based on previous residence in
the area. In 1801, when Margaret and her two-month-old mulatto
child absconded "without the smallest provocation," her master pre-
sumed she would travel to Long Island, the region in which he had
originally purchased her.[75]

In about one in every twenty cases owners claimed that their slaves absconded either to avoid retribution for some recently discovered crime or in response to punishment already meted out. Primus was "guilty of stealing some money, which is the only reason of his absenting himself."[76] York, suspected of maliciously burning down a barn and killing several horses and cattle in the process, fled in May 1800 because, his owner concluded, new evidence linked him to the fire.[77] Occasionally the crime was more exotic. One morning in late April 1794, having been caught in bed in her owner's house with "[t]wo low-live *white* scoundrels, dressed [sic] like *gentlemen*," Jude, encumbered with an iron collar and with the threat of a whipping hanging over her head, quite sensibly departed. Secure in his rectitude and using more italics to demonstrate the strength of his moral outrage, her owner continued: "[l]etting into a house at midnight, thieves, robbers, murderers, drunkards, (alias *whoremasters*) would be considered *alarming* by every good citizen." What made the whole affair even worse was that it "was intended that this Girl should have had her *freedom* at a certain age."[78]

Direct evidence from blacks as to why they ran away is very rare. One scrap that has survived, however, illustrates that slaves were sometimes motivated not by the threat of correction but by resentment at what had already occurred. In 1804 Toby was charged with stealing two coats and three pairs of pantaloons. In court, Toby related that he and his master "about three or four months ago had a falling out whereupon his master whiped him as he supposed unjustly—That immediately after his said Master had whiped him he went away from him." Intriguingly, even though he had been apprehended, Toby now described himself as "formerly was a Slave to Doctor Coventry."[79] By both word and action the slave had indicated that, as far as he was concerned, Coventry had transgressed his code of acceptable behavior and that therefore Coventry no longer owned him.

Examination of the owners' estimation of the intention of runaways from the region around New York demonstrates that, by a ratio of almost four to one, the fugitives were considered to be more likely to try to pass as free than to visit friends or relatives. Variations from this general pattern as a result of particular factors or by certain groups within the slave community reveal even more about the texture of black life in this area (tables 16, 17, and 18).

TABLE 16

Motives and Destinations of Runaways from New York City and Environs, 1771–1806 – Influence of Skill, Linguistic Ability, and Sex

	Skilled Slave	Not Known	Speaks Well	Speaks Badly	Not Known	Male	Female	Total
To visit	4 (8.0) (8.0)	46 (92.0) (23.5)	10 (20.0) (15.1)	1 (2.0) (6.7)	39 (78.0) (23.5)	32 (64.0) (16.2)	18 (36.0) (36.8)	50 (100.0) (20.2)
To pass as free	44 (24.0) (88.0)	139 (76.0) (70.6)	50 (27.3) (75.8)	14 (7.7) (93.3)	119 (65.0) (71.7)	155 (84.7) (70.6)	28 (15.3) (57.1)	183 (100.0) (74.1)
To avoid punishment	2 (14.3) (4.0)	12 (85.7) (6.1)	6 (42.9) (9.1)	0	8 (57.1) (4.8)	11 (78.6) (5.5)	3 (21.4) (6.1)	14 (100.0) (5.7)
Total	50 (20.2) (100.0)	197 (79.8) (100.0)	66 (26.7) (100.0)	15 (6.1) (100.0)	166 (67.2) (100.0)	198 (80.2) (100.0)	49 (19.8) (100.0)	247 (100.0) (100.0)
Countryside	7 (9.7) (13.7)	65 (90.3) (23.6)	12 (16.7) (18.2)	2 (2.8) (11.8)	58 (80.5) (23.9)	48 (66.7) (19.0)	24 (33.3) (32.4)	72 (100.0) (22.0)
New York City	12 (10.0) (23.5)	108 (90.0) (39.3)	22 (18.3) (33.3)	5 (4.2) (29.4)	93 (77.5) (38.3)	90 (75.0) (35.7)	30 (25.0) (40.6)	120 (100.0) (36.8)
Outside N.Y. and N.J.	28 (30.4) (54.9)	64 (69.6) (23.3)	23 (25.0) (34.9)	9 (9.8) (52.9)	60 (65.2) (24.7)	78 (84.8) (31.0)	14 (15.2) (18.9)	92 (100.0) (28.3)
Army	4 (9.5) (7.9)	38 (90.5) (13.8)	9 (21.4) (13.6)	1 (2.4) (5.9)	32 (76.2) (13.1)	36 (85.7) (14.3)	6 (14.3) (8.1)	42 (100.0) (12.9)
Total	51 (15.6) (100.0)	275 (84.4) (100.0)	66 (20.3) (100.0)	17 (5.2) (100.0)	243 (74.5) (100.0)	252 (77.3) (100.0)	74 (22.7) (100.0)	326 (100.0) (100.0)

Note: Figures in parentheses are percentages.

One factor that affected slave behavior was skill. Slaves to whom owners attributed a skill were more likely than unskilled slaves to try and pass as free, with almost nine out of ten skilled blacks falling into this category (see table 16). Similarly, skilled blacks demonstrated less interest than other slaves in heading for the countryside, for New York City, or even in fleeing to one of the armies during the Revolution, but the skilled were more than twice as likely as the unskilled to attempt to leave the state. In fact, more than one in two of the skilled slaves were expected to abscond out of the New York and New Jersey area.

Another variable of some importance was the ability of the runaways to speak the English language (see table 16). Although the behavior of those classified as able to speak well differed by only a few percentage points from the general pattern, that of the group who could either not utter a word of English or spoke it badly diverged considerably. The numbers are relatively small, but it is significant that in fourteen out of the fifteen cases in which the owner attributed a reason for the elopement the fugitives were expected to try and pass as free. In 1779 the owner of Grace, a thirty-year-old "Coromantee wench" who had country marks on her face and spoke broken English, had heard that "she tells people that she is free." Another slave told his Trenton jailers through an interpreter that he was "a free man and was on his way to Guinea."[80] Most in this category were recent arrivals from Africa or the West Indies and consequently had not been in the area long enough to develop networks of kin and friends who could help them when they fled. More than one in two were expected to leave the New York and New Jersey region.

But the most important factor affecting slave behavior was the sex of the runaway (see table 16). Although the majority of females were expected to pass as free, the proportion behaving in this fashion was less than that for males. Further, females were more than twice as likely as males to run away for the purpose of visiting. There was also a higher probability that females intending to pass as free would run to New York than was the case with males, no doubt reflecting the greater opportunities for women to pick up work in the city. As a result males outnumbered females by a ratio of almost six to one in the category of runaways leaving the state.

TABLE 17

Motives and Destinations of Runaways from New York City and Environs, 1771–1805 — Influence of Birthplace

	Mulatto	West Indian	American	African	Not Known	Total
To visit	1 (2.0) (3.0)	2 (4.0) (16.7)	3 (6.0) (20.0)	1 (2.0) (12.5)	43 (86.0) (24.0)	50 (100.0)
To pass as free	29 (15.8) (87.9)	10 (5.5) (83.3)	12 (6.6) (80.0)	7 (3.8) (87.5)	125 (68.3) (69.8)	183 (100.0)
To avoid punishment	3 (21.4) (9.1)	0	0	0	11 (78.6) (6.2)	14 (100.0)
Total	33 (13.4) (100.0)	12 (4.8) (100.0)	15 (6.1) (100.0)	8 (3.2) (100.0)	179 (72.5) (100.0)	247 (100.0)
Countryside	4 (5.6) (11.4)	2 (2.8) (11.1)	6 (8.3) (27.3)	1 (1.4) (8.3)	59 (81.9) (24.7)	72 (100.0)
New York City	14 (11.7) (40.0)	8 (6.7) (44.5)	7 (5.8) (31.8)	6 (5.0) (50.0)	85 (70.8) (35.6)	120 (100.0)
Outside N.Y. and N.J.	15 (16.3) (42.9)	6 (6.6) (33.3)	5 (5.4) (22.7)	5 (5.4) (41.7)	61 (66.3) (25.5)	92 (100.0)
Army	2 (4.8) (5.7)	2 (4.8) (11.1)	4 (9.5) (18.2)	0	34 (80.9) (14.2)	42 (100.0)
Total	35 (10.7) (100.0)	18 (5.5) (100.0)	22 (6.8) (100.0)	12 (3.7) (100.0)	239 (73.3) (100.0)	326 (100.0)

Note: Figures in parentheses are percentages.

TABLE 18

Motives and Destinations of New York and New Jersey Runaways, 1771–1805 — Influence of Age

	0–15	16–25	26–35	36+	Not Known	Total
To visit	2 (4.0) (10.0)	17 (34.0) (14.7)	14 (28.0) (26.9)	2 (4.0) (16.7)	15 (30.0) (31.9)	50 (100.0)
To pass as free	17 (9.3) (85.0)	94 (51.4) (81.0)	34 (18.5) (65.4)	8 (4.4) (66.6)	30 (16.4) (63.8)	183 (100.0)
To avoid punishment	1 (7.1) (5.0)	5 (35.7) (4.3)	4 (28.6) (7.7)	2 (14.3) (16.7)	2 (14.3) (4.3)	14 (100.0)
Total	20 (8.1) (100.0)	116 (47.0) (100.0)	52 (21.1) (100.0)	12 (4.8) (100.0)	47 (19.0) (100.0)	247 (100.0)
Countryside	4 (5.6) (15.4)	30 (41.7) (18.9)	13 (18.0) (24.1)	5 (6.9) (26.3)	20 (27.8) (29.4)	72 (100.0)
New York City	9 (7.5) (34.6)	58 (48.4) (36.5)	19 (15.8) (35.2)	9 (7.5) (47.4)	25 (20.8) (36.8)	120 (100.0)
Outside N.Y. and N.J.	8 (8.7) (30.8)	50 (54.3) (31.4)	12 (13.1) (22.2)	5 (5.4) (26.3)	17 (18.5) (25.0)	92 (100.0)
Army	5 (11.9) (19.2)	21 (50.0) (13.2)	10 (23.8) (18.5)	0	6 (14.3) (8.8)	42 (100.0)
Total	26 (8.0) (100.0)	159 (48.8) (100.0)	54 (16.5) (100.0)	19 (5.8) (100.0)	68 (20.9) (100.0)	326 (100.0)

Note: Figures in parentheses are percentages.

These differences were to a large extent the product of the distinctive nature of the black female experience in New York and
New Jersey. As we have seen in the previous chapter, a slave society
where the average holding was only about two slaves severely limited the opportunities for conducting anything but a fragmented
family life. In such a situation the responsibilities for looking after
young children almost invariably devolved on the mother, a factor
that must have inhibited many women from even attempting to run
away. Occasionally women solved this problem by abandoning their
children: in 1792 Mary, a sixteen-year-old runaway, "left her suck-
ling child behind."[81] Others took their children with them, but the
practical problems of this course of action were substantial. Consider, for example, the difficulties Constance must have confronted
when she decided to abscond in 1800: not only did she have her two
children—a three-year-old and a seven-year-old—to worry about,
but Constance was also African born and spoke very little English.[82]
However, quite a few females were resilient enough to run away
carrying (often literally) young children with them. Almost one in
seven (37 out of 267) of all the female runaways were accompanied
by at least one child. In eleven of these cases the females ran off
with a male as well, but in the majority of instances (in fact slightly
more than 70 percent) they had to manage on their own.

Not only did the responsibility of looking after children undoubtedly prevent many young women from absconding, but it also affected the behavior of those daring enough to attempt escape with
their children. Such females were much more likely to run away to
visit than to try and pass as free—in six out of the ten cases where
owners gave details of motivation they classified the fugitives in the
former category. In 1777 nineteen-year-old Charity and her two-
year-old child, Peter, were expected to flee to White Plains as "she
was bought from Dr. Graham about 10 months hence and seemed
anxious to get back." Similarly, twenty years later Margaret and her
four-year-old bandy-legged child named John or Jack were supposed to have gone to the area near Cowneck and Cedar Swamp
on Long Island "as her friends are there."[83] Possibly these women
were seeking out their husbands or sexual partners, although this
is seldom mentioned as a factor by the owners. Clearly, this was
the one group of runaways who most nearly conformed to the pat-

terns of the fugitive slaves in the South. Consequently, they were more reliant on support from networks of kin and friends than were other slaves from the New York region. There was only one male single parent among the runaways, and significantly his behavior was similar to that of the females: in 1789 Esmal and his three children—thirteen-year-old Pantes, six-year-old Sill, and nineteen-month-old Ann—were thought to have gone either to Long Island or Morrisania, "where he formerly lived." [84]

One in three (6 out of 18) of all the women categorized as visiting and nearly one in three of the females (7 out of 24) expected to travel to the countryside in fact had children in tow (see table 16). A smaller proportion of women heading for New York City (5 out of 30) were in the same situation. However, no women accompanied by children were expected to leave the state. As far as the advertisements reveal, the only female slave still living with her children who attempted to flee out of the New York region had to abandon them: in 1797 twenty-eight-year-old Mink and twenty-six-year-old Rose left behind five children, including one still at Rose's breast, when they headed off for New England and freedom. [85]

The relationship between place of birth and the behavior of the runaways is set out in table 17. Although the number of unknowns is very high, the statistics do suggest that the American born were more likely to visit and head for the country than were the Africans, who in eleven out of twelve cases proceeded for either New York City or out of the state (see table 17). Mulattoes, however, were a divergent group, as they appear to have been in every state: they were the least likely to run away for the purpose of visiting (1 out of 33) and the most likely to attempt to leave the state (15 out of 35). [86] Age was another factor that influenced the conduct of the runaways (see table 18). The young, particularly those under the age of twenty-six, were less likely than their elders to be classified as visiting or heading for the countryside; the young were more likely to try to break out of the institution of slavery and pass as free or attempt to leave the state.

It is still the case that the majority of runaways in every category deserted their masters with the intention of passing as free, but there were some significant variations in the behavior of some groups of runaways. Admittedly, the analysis of the effect of variables such as place of birth and skill is made more difficult because of the incompleteness of the data and the resulting large number of unknowns, but this material does hint at a further pattern of behavior, a pattern rooted in the fragmented family life of New York and New Jersey slaves. It appears that there were two contrasting types most likely to attempt permanently to escape the institution of slavery: the highly acculturated, such as the mulattoes, who were often skilled; and the least acculturated, or most recent arrivals in the area. The common features exhibited by both these groups were their youth (and here the figures are most complete) and, closely allied to this, a paucity of ties to the slave society. On the other hand, those slaves who had developed networks of kin and acquaintances in the area—the American born, women with children, and those in the older age brackets—were the most likely to run away for the purpose of visiting. This kind of runaway was, in effect, taking a leave of absence rather than trying to sever the bonds of slavery.

The fragmented family life of New York and New Jersey blacks and the small holdings in this area were also reflected in the small number of runaways absconding in groups. There were 87 groups of two or more runaways, totaling 194 slaves, or 15.7 percent of all the fugitives.[87] Of these 87 groups more than four in five (72) consisted of only two slaves, and only one group comprised as many as five slaves. The vast majority consisted of slaves of the same sex (5 were all female and 54 all male), and of the 28 groups with both males and females only 13, according to the advertisements, included a husband and wife. The most common combination was two young black males. Occasionally there were hints of ethnic ties—three black males in one group had the same country marks (African ritual scarifications) on the sides of their temples[88]—but the vast majority of groups were work, not family, related. Running away in New York and New Jersey was essentially an individual act, and the statistics show little evidence of the supportive and cooperative arrangements historians have uncovered in the South.[89]

The general pattern of running away in the New York region, particularly the high proportion of runaways expected to attempt permanent escape and the low number involved in visiting, is at marked variance with that in the southern states. Historians ana-

lyzing runaway advertisements from that region have come up with
a variety of explanations for black behavior. Gerald Mullin argued
that in Virginia the aspirations and hopes of unacculturated slaves
were bound up within the context of the plantation, and that runaways from this group tended either to visit relatives or "lurk"
about their owner's or neighboring plantations. Acculturated slaves,
on the other hand, had broader horizons; they were more likely
to break out of this relatively closed world by fleeing to towns or
even out of the colony and trying to pass as free. In another study,
which looked at a small number of runaways in North Carolina, the
authors concluded that the slaves were defending a "moral economy." But by far the most convincing account of the phenomenon
of running away is Philip Morgan's subtle rendering of black behavior in South Carolina. After a prodigious amount of research,
Morgan eschewed any simple interpretation that equates running
away with resistance. Instead, he located slave actions within the
complex context of a developing black culture. Such an approach
reveals, among other things, that by a ratio of four to one South
Carolinian blacks were more likely to abscond for the purpose of
visiting relatives and friends than to attempt permanent escape.[90]

An analysis of the intentions of runaways from the area around
New York requires much less subtlety. Here, as we have seen, the
simple interpretation will suffice: overwhelmingly blacks were running away with the intention of effecting a permanent escape from
slavery. Yet it was not just intention that separated these runaways
from those in the South. It is also clear that, allowing for population
differences, slaves from the New York region absconded in greater
numbers than their southern compatriots. Although the entire slave
population of this region was fewer than 25,000 in 1790, over the
thirty-five-year period from 1771 to 1805 1,232 slaves, or on average
thirty-five a year, were advertised as runaways. Attempts to compare
this figure with those for other states encounter many difficulties:
does a higher number of notices from one area tell us something
about black behavior, or does it merely indicate a higher propensity
among owners to advertise for runaways, as a result, for example,
of a greater acceptance and usage of newspapers? Nevertheless, and
even keeping these issues in mind, the contrasts with Virginia and
South Carolina are instructive. Gerald Mullin's research on Virginia for the period 1736 to 1801 uncovered 1,280 runaways, or an

FIGURE 1

Distribution of New York and New Jersey Runaways, 1771–1805

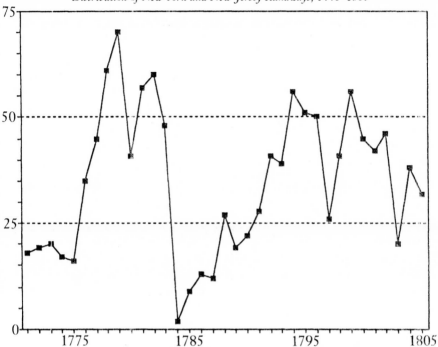

average of 19.7 a year, and Philip Morgan, in his analysis of South Carolina from 1732 to 1782, collected advertisements describing 3,558 slaves, or about 69.8 per year. Not only did these historians use *all* extant newspapers (in the present study only a sample of an admittedly much larger number of newspapers could be examined),[91] but the slave populations of Virginia (188,000 in 1770) and South Carolina (57,000 in 1760) were, of course, considerably larger.[92]

The relatively high number of New York and New Jersey runaways can, perhaps, be explained within the specific historical context of physical resistance by blacks in the last decades of the eighteenth century. The distribution of the runaways over the thirty-five-year period demonstrates clearly that there were two peaks of runaway activity—one during the Revolution and the other in the late 1790s and early 1800s (see figure 1).

In August 1776, when Caster absconded, his master commented

TABLE 19
Sex of New York and New Jersey Runaways, 1771–1805

	1771–1775		1776–1785		1786–1795		1796–1805		Total	
	N	%	N	%	N	%	N	%	N	%
Male	87	96.7	329	76.9	248	80.5	301	74.1	965	78.3
Female	3	3.3	99	23.1	60	19.5	105	25.9	267	21.7
	90	100.0	428	100.0	308	100.0	406	100.0	1,232	100.0

in the runaway advertisement that his slave was "well pleased and elevated when anyone speaks to him about war."[93] Perhaps Caster was just bloodthirsty, but particularly given his subsequent desertion from his master, it is more likely that he recognized that war would provide many opportunities for slaves to improve their lot. Even if Caster failed to appreciate this, thousands of other slaves in the American colonies were certainly quick to take advantage of the conflict. Estimates of the loss of slaves in the southern colonies range as high as fifty thousand and up.[94] In the New York area, losses were obviously considerably smaller, but they were substantial nonetheless.[95]

Advertised runaways were only a small proportion of the slaves lost to their owners, but as figure 1 demonstrates, even here the numbers rose dramatically by comparison with those of the prewar period. What is more interesting, however, is that the type of slave absconding also changed. Tables 19 and 20 give a breakdown by sex and age of the advertised runaways over time. Although the figures for the prewar period are perhaps a bit thin, the increase in the numbers of women and the young running away is still dramatic. Before the Revolution there were a miniscule number of advertised female runaways, but in the decade commencing in 1776 females constituted almost one in four of the escaped slaves. Similarly, the age of runaways dropped suddenly with the onset of the Revolution: in the period 1771–1775 less than one in two of the fugitives were under the age of twenty-six, but in the Revolutionary years more than three in four were in this age bracket. These years also saw the emergence of a new element among the runaways—the very young—one in five of the runaways in that decade were under the

TABLE 20
Age of New York and New Jersey Runaways, 1771–1805

Age	1771–1775 N	%	1776–1785 N	%	1786–1795 N	%	1796–1805 N	%	Total N	%
0–15	0		65	20.3	33	13.1	63	18.3	161	16.3
16–25	32	45.7	181	56.4	152	60.6	206	59.9	571	57.9
26–35	30	42.9	56	17.4	39	15.5	56	16.3	181	18.4
36+	8	11.4	19	5.9	27	10.8	19	5.5	73	7.4
	70	100.0	321	100.0	251	100.0	344	100.0	986	100.0

Note: The age of the runaways was specified in 80.0 percent of cases.

age of sixteen. The considerable disruption and dislocation in this area caused by the war, combined with promises of freedom (particularly from the British), gave these slaves, for the first time, a realistic chance of liberty. It was a chance that large numbers of men, women, and children obviously tried to exploit.

Although historians have traditionally linked the demise of northern slavery to the American Revolution, this relationship certainly did not hold in either New York or New Jersey. Slavery here was quickly reestablished, and as we have seen earlier the slave populations of these states continued to increase, reaching a peak at the turn of the century. With the return of stability to the embattled war zone around New York City, the number of fugitive slaves sharply declined, but beginning in the late 1780s (see figure 1) the incidence of running away rose steeply, both reflecting and contributing to the restive mood of the black population in the postwar years.

This more assertive, even aggressive, demeanor exhibited by blacks had a number of causes. The West Indian slaves brought into New York in the 1790s came from a society where violent resistance to slavery was almost a commonplace. Many must have brought with them firsthand knowledge of the latest conflagration, the great slave rebellion on Saint Domingue.[96] "French Negroes" maintained a high profile throughout the 1790s and early 1800s, involving themselves in most of the black unrest in the city, and had a substantial impact on the mood and orientation of the black population. The troubles of white New Yorkers, however, were hardly imported:

news of Saint Domingue and the arrival of West Indian blacks
merely exacerbated an already volatile situation. Although slavery
had resumed after the Revolution, circumstances had changed considerably from the colonial years: slavery had ended in New England and was dying quickly in Pennsylvania, and the population
of free blacks in New York City itself was increasing rapidly. The
growing proportion of New York blacks living as free persons must
have made bondage all the more distasteful for those still enslaved.
Further, in both New Jersey and New York various proposals for
ending slavery were debated by the legislatures and discussed in the
press. It seemed inevitable that sooner or later these states would
follow the rest of the North and introduce some form of abolition
measure. Thus, for New York and New Jersey slaves it was no longer
certain that they would spend the rest of their lives in bondage, and
many showed a marked disinclination to wait passively for the white
elite to make up its mind about their future.

A mosaic of incidents — some minor, others more significant —
that took place in the 1790s and early 1800s suggests a new mood of
assertiveness among blacks and, consequently, an increased tension
in race relations. In 1798, for example, when Sally Gale stole some
items from a store, she was chased by Finch, a white man, to a cellar
in Hague Street. But here a "Mulatto Man Stood at the Door with
some kind of weapon in his hand and Declared he would knock the
said Finch's Brains out if Offered to Come in." [97] In 1801 Christopher Prill, a gardener at Corlear's Hook, was so tormented and
threatened by three black boys that he sought a court order for his
own protection. Not only had these blacks set their dog at his cows,
but when Prill attempted to stop them they responded by throwing
stones at him and one "Swore most wickedly & profanely that he
would kill the Deponent." [98] Material such as this — and there are
other examples in the court records and newspapers — is very difficult to assess, but the unconcealed belligerence of these blacks certainly appears to be a development new to the post-Revolutionary
period.

The impact of this type of behavior was clearer when it took the
form of collective action. Individual blacks had occasionally joined
New York mobs, though they were usually only a small minority
of those involved. But in 1801 the first full-blown black riot occurred. Rumors swept the city that a Madame Jeanne Mathusine

Droibillan Volunbrun was preparing illegally to ship twenty slaves to the southern states, and a group of "French negroes" gathered outside the woman's house on Eagle Street to protest. That evening the crowd, swelled now to 250, threatened to "burn the said Volunbrun's house, murder all the white people in it and take away a number of Black Slaves." The mob was dispersed only by the forcible action of fifty members of the watch.[99] Such direct action by blacks and the involvement of the ubiquitous "French Negroes" in the affray immediately raised the specter of Saint Domingue, an event seldom far from the minds of whites along the entire Atlantic seaboard at this time.

Although there was no attempt at a full-scale revolt, in the 1790s blacks were involved in several outbreaks of arson. However, it should be remembered that fires were usually seen as the precursors of a black revolt. This connection would have been particularly strong in New York, where black arsonists would immediately bring to mind memories of the 1741 conspiracy.[100] In his 1793 tract on capital punishment, William Bradford had classified arson as the "crime of slaves and children." Almost invariably, according to Bradford, the motive for incendiarism was revenge, and "to a free mind the pleasure of revenge is lost when its object is ignorant of the hand that inflicts the blow."[101] Periodically throughout the eighteenth century recalcitrant slaves had indulged themselves in such anonymous pleasures, burning down the odd haystack or barn, but in the 1790s there was a more serious turn of events: blacks made several attempts to fire the principally wooden and immensely combustible buildings in urban areas of the state.

In November 1793 two young black girls, Bet and Dean, incited by a third slave, Pomp, were prevented from burning the city of Albany to the ground only by a heavy fall of sleet. Twenty-six houses were destroyed and an estimated £100,000 damage inflicted. The white population was further disconcerted by a rash of copycat fires that occurred over the next fortnight, though these were quickly extinguished.[102] Three years later a similar outbreak occurred in New York City. In November 1796, several fires were started when unknown blacks tossed burning coals wrapped in oiled paper into open cellars. Notwithstanding the strengthening of the watch and a rash of newspaper articles, which not only implicated the "French Negroes" but also warned citizens to keep their eyes open, there were at least half a dozen more attempts in December.[103] William Bradford's suggestion that arson be removed from the list of capital crimes doubtless received short shrift in such an atmosphere. In a letter to his son, Lewis Morris lamented that New York had had "a most terrible time lately" because of the fires. Much property had been damaged, and "all exclaim loudly now against the freedom of Negroes it has been a fatal stab to that Business." Morris also told of New York gentlemen serving on the watch every night, evidently with some success: they had secured some blacks while others had been "shot down owing to their not answering quick." [104]

Morris was writing from Morrisania, not New York City, and the contents of his letter are almost certainly more useful as an indicator of white concern and of the rumors that were circulating than of the situation in the city itself.[105] What is significant about the letter, however, is the connection drawn immediately between the violence and the protracted debate over ending slavery, a connection that was inevitable in the shadow of Saint Domingue. Although those opposed to manumission never fully articulated a proslavery argument—as defenders of the status quo they could afford to let the advocates of antislavery make the running and then mire them down in a bog of procedural detail[106]—there were several thinly veiled references in the press to the possible consequences of abolition. In 1796, for example, the editor of the *American Minerva* directed readers to "pay particular attention" to the declarations of the grand jury in Edenton, North Carolina, as they were of a "serious nature." What had alarmed the jurors was the combination of Quaker activism and emancipation sentiment, which had "greatly corrupted" the minds of the slaves and, they believed, led to the encouragement of arson, running away, and other acts it was thought better not to specify. Nevertheless they could not help but reflect upon the "miserable havock and massacres" that were occurring in the West Indies "in consequence of emancipation." [107] In similar fashion, in 1797 the editor of the *Minerva* appended a note to a report from Baltimore of a slave woman who poisoned her owner's family, suggesting that this action should "serve as a solemn warning to those who are disposed to testamentary liberation of their slaves." [108] As we saw earlier there was hardly a flood of testamentary manumissions in the 1790s.

The sharp rise in runaways in the 1790s is best understood in this context. From the mid-1790s on there was talk of abolition, talk that inevitably reached the slaves and led to a considerable amount of unrest. Probably the clearest evidence comes from the Dutch stronghold of Ulster County, where in the wake of the defeat of the abolition bill in 1796 a group of predominantly Dutch slaveholders formed the Slave Aprehending Society of Shawangunk. According to the preamble of the society's constitution, "a Suspicion seems to prevail among many of the Negro Slaves that the Legislature of the State has liberated them and that they are now held in servitude by the arbitrary power of their Masters." The "uneasiness and disquietude" of the blacks in the area was being played upon, they claimed, by white agitators who were encouraging the slaves to abscond, a course of action that the society intended to prevent.[109] Little more is known of the history or effectiveness of the society, but its aims, and its very existence, point to the problems of controlling impatient slaves in a context of uncertainty about the future of slavery.

Although there is no evidence of the formation of other similar societies, the material from the runaway advertisements suggests a widespread pattern of struggle between owners and slaves in and around New York City. By the 1790s the prospects for successful escape from the institution had been increased immeasurably by the gradual abolition of slavery in Pennsylvania and New England and the consequent rapid expansion of free black communities in Philadelphia, Boston, New Haven, and New York. Increasingly from the mid-1790s blacks who were tired of delays in the passage of an abolition bill, or who, like the slaves in Ulster County, were convinced that they were already free but still illegally detained in bondage, decided to take their chances and flee slavery.

The incidence of slaves running away abated only marginally after the passage, in 1799, of New York's Gradual Manumission Act. New Jersey blacks were still enslaved, although it seemed likely that the legislature there would be influenced by the example of New York. But the New York measure promised gradual freedom, affecting only future generations of blacks; those already enslaved would have to spend the rest of their lives in bondage. The young were the most adversely affected by this legislation, and as in the Revolutionary period, those in the lower age brackets formed an increasing proportion of the runaways. In the decade after 1795, almost four in every five of the advertised runaways were under the age of twenty-six (see table 20), the age cohort most likely to try and break free of the institution when they absconded. In cases where the motive is known, more than four in five of the fugitives under the age of twenty-six were expected to try and pass as free, but among those twenty-six and older the figure dropped sharply to about 65 percent (see table 18). By the turn of the century the great majority of runaways had been born either during or after the Revolution, had been raised in close proximity to a growing population of free blacks, and were part of a generation for whom freedom was an achievable goal. Denied their chance by white legislatures, many simply took matters into their own hands.

From the time of the Revolution, then, but even more noticeably in the 1790s, there is strong evidence that blacks in and around New York City vigorously resisted slavery. Isolated acts of running away might be overlooked, but the spectacle of hundreds of slaves absconding was obviously more telling. This was particularly so because a high proportion of New York's runaways, unlike most in the South, were seeking to flee from their owners permanently. But running away was hardly the limit of black action. Blacks were becoming generally more assertive, challenging white authority in ways that ranged from the placing by Adam, the New Jersey slave, of the advertisement that denied his owner's right to sell him, to the attempt by a group of slaves to burn the city down. At a time of uncertainty about the future of slavery in New York, this surge of black activism placed pressure on an increasingly apprehensive white population.[110]

This activism should not surprise us. In spite of their relatively small numbers, New York blacks had established a tradition of opposition to slavery that few, if any, states could equal. Both the 1712 revolt and the 1741 conspiracy figure prominently in the story of slave resistance in America, but it is likely that the activities of blacks in the years after the Revolution, while less spectacular than those earlier occurrences, were more effective. Of course, the nexus between black resistance and white political action is very difficult to discern, but the sequence of events in New York is suggestive.[111] The immediate reaction of Lewis Morris to the fires in the city was to suggest that this outbreak of arson would kill off any attempt to end slavery, yet the fact remains that within three years a gradual abolition measure finally passed. A few months before the fires similar legislation had failed. Historians' accounts of the end of slavery in the North have invariably focused on the development of white opposition to the institution, relegating slaves to a minor role, but the evidence in this chapter suggests that if black resistance was not strong enough in itself to bring about the end of slavery, it must surely have hastened its demise.

In the end, though, it may be that the real significance of black resistance does not lie in such institutional changes. Perhaps the most remarkable development in the area in and around New York City, and indeed in the entire North, was the speed with which slavery disintegrated once the Gradual Manumission Act had passed. To be sure, some slaveholders—particularly those of Dutch extraction on Long Island, in New Jersey, and on the west bank of the Hudson—held on to the bitter end, but many more either freed their slaves (though not legally obliged to do so) or allowed them to negotiate some sort of self-purchase arrangement. To a large extent, then, the details of the demise of slavery were worked out on an individual basis rather than by legislative fiat. Here it is appropriate to recall the story that began this chapter, the story of the black who attempted to buy his wife's freedom, for what that story illustrates well is the determination of slaves to attain liberty, even under the supposedly benevolent regime existing in New York. In this case the slave failed, but increasingly through the 1790s, and particularly after 1799, more and more blacks would succeed. The willingness of slaveowners to enter into such negotiations is not difficult to understand. Once it had become certain that slavery would eventually end, it must have seemed easier for many owners to secure several years of trouble-free service, or a cash payment from their slaves, rather than face the risk of losing both their slaves and any possible recompense when their increasingly restive human property decided to abscond. Negotiations of this type were conducted against a background of challenges by slaves to white authority and an increasing incidence of running away, and it is in this sense that the history of black resistance from the Revolution on enabled many New York and New Jersey slaves to win their freedom. What they made of that freedom is the subject of the rest of this book.

6

Free Blacks

IN AUGUST 1814, as the British naval blockade of New York tightened, the "free people of color" called a public meeting and resolved to offer their services to the city's Committee of Defense. To this end, a notice was inserted in the *New York Evening Post* instructing the blacks to assemble in the Park at five o'clock on Monday morning and then to proceed to Brooklyn Heights to assist in erecting fortifications. The subsequent labors of this group were of little practical value, as the expected attack did not materialize; later that week the British forces sailed up the Potomac and burned the Capitol and the White House. But the symbolic importance of the involvement of New York's free blacks in the defense of their city was considerable. The vast majority of those who crossed the East River to help fortify Brooklyn Heights were either former slaves or the sons of slaves. The looming crisis threatened to bring down a regime that so recently had enslaved them and that still held many of their compatriots in bondage. But instead of showing hostility or indifference, New York's free blacks publicly had seized the opportunity to demonstrate their allegiance to the city.

A letter from a "Citizen of Color" printed in the *Evening Post* under the caption "A Test of Patriotism" made this very point. It was, he declared, the "duty of every colored man resident in this city to volunteer." Under New York's liberal laws, the writer continued, "we dwell in safety and pursue our honest callings, none daring to molest us, whatever his complexion or circumstances."[1] Such statements were probably dictated as much by pragmatism as by patriotism, by blacks' desire to convince white New Yorkers of their civic worth, and thus to win better treatment. Hindsight has shown, of course, that such hopes would eventually prove to be naive. Leon Litwack and others have demonstrated that free blacks were not in the end able to live as independent and equal citizens in a society paying no heed to "complexion or circumstances."[2] But in 1814 this was by no means clear. The later emphasis of historians on white discrimination has imbued the story with an air of inevitability and diverted attention away from the achievements and experiences of the first generation of free blacks in New York. Overly optimistic though they may appear from our perspective, the claims of the "Citizen of Color" provide a starting point for reassessing the formation of the free black community in New York City during the three decades following the Revolution.

Shifting the focus from the whites to the blacks reveals, as it has elsewhere, that blacks were not passive ciphers, helplessly swept along by currents of repression and discrimination and controlled solely by whites. The recently freed slaves, in particular, were exceptional men and women. The story of their emancipation illustrates their ingenuity and strength. In marked contrast to southern slavery, slavery in New York City and the surrounding countryside ended gradually, over several decades, and the slaves themselves played a role in determining just when they would become free. The case of John Moranda illustrates well how, even before any antislavery measure passed through the legislature, some New York blacks were able to capitalize on the tradition of negotiating over the conditions of slavery discussed in earlier chapters and achieve freedom. John Moranda was the slave of John De Baan, but on October 29, 1795, De Baan freed Moranda after Samuel Jones, Jr., an attorney-at-law and well-known New York political figure, had paid him the sum of $200. Within a few months Moranda had managed to scrape together $50, which he used to purchase the freedom of his four-year-old daughter Susan, who was the slave of John Haring, Esq., of Bergen County, New Jersey. Three years later in May 1798 John Moranda paid $160 to Gardner Jones, a prominent physician, and liberated his thirty-three-year-old wife, Susan Moranda, and his son, John.[3] At the beginning of the 1790s Moranda had been a slave; by the end of the decade he had managed to purchase his freedom, support himself, and free the rest of his family. At the time of both the 1800 and 1810 censuses Moranda and his family were living in Warren Street, probably in the same house, a degree of residential stability that, as we shall see, was unusual for free blacks.

Even in the 1790s a case such as John Moranda's was not that unusual, but in the early years of the nineteenth century more and more New York blacks, in effect given a negotiating edge by the state legislature, were able to achieve similar results. New York's Gradual Manumission Act of 1799 compelled slaveowners to free any children born to slaves after July 4, 1799; New Jersey passed similar legislation in 1804. Slaves born in New York before 1799 were eventually set free on July 4, 1827, under the provisions of an act passed in 1817, while in New Jersey there were still a handful of slaves at the time of the Civil War. But this is not the whole story. Although some slaveowners held on to their slaves as long as they possibly could, many others, though not legally obliged to do so, freed their slaves. Once it was certain slavery would eventually end, slaveowners became more susceptible to pressure from their slaves and often agreed to arrangements whereby slaves were liberated in consideration of a number of years of trouble-free service or cash or both. In 1805, for example, Elizabeth Fine certified that she would free her slave Margaret if she remained for eight years and behaved "as she always has done in an orderly manner as a servant ought to do." Failure to fulfill this condition would render the agreement "void and of no effect." John Blauvelt of Bergen County, New Jersey, agreed in 1809 that if his slave Sam made payments of $50 a year over four years, he would be freed.[4] To a large extent, then, the details of the end of slavery in New York and New Jersey were worked out on an individual basis, by bargaining between slave and owner, rather than by legislative fiat. Success in such negotiations and an early release from slavery were partly the result of luck, but the process also favored the most industrious, tenacious, and skilled of the slaves. Having gained for the first time, and largely through their own efforts, substantial control over their lives, many New York and New Jersey blacks exercised their newfound power by leaving the place where they had been slaves and starting new lives in New York City. The years of slavery's slow demise fell well short of being a golden age for those blacks, but that brief period in the city's history was characterized not so much by discrimination and repression (although they were present) as by the sense of optimism and hope captured in the words of the "Citizen of Color." My purpose in this and the next chapter, then, is to analyze this group as they made the difficult transition from slavery to freedom and to try and understand what it meant to be a black in New York City in the 1790s and early 1800s.

ALTHOUGH THERE WERE some free blacks in New York in the seventeenth and eighteenth centuries, they were of little significance. Even the census takers failed to differentiate them from slaves, using the category "Negro" for both. Probably there were never more than 100 free blacks in New York City during the colonial period. But in the years after the Revolution the free black population expanded rapidly, and by 1810 there were 7,470 blacks in this category, making up 8.1 percent of New York's population (see table 4). The 1790s and early 1800s saw the genesis, therefore, of the most important urban black center in nineteenth- and twentieth-century America.

From where had these free blacks come? The sources of this sharp rise in population were diverse. Although the enslaved percentage of the black population dropped from 66.5 percent in 1790 to 43.2 percent in 1800, the increase in the number of free blacks cannot be attributed simply to the activities of New York City slaveholders who, swayed by the egalitarian rhetoric of the Revolution and influenced by the New York Manumission Society, dutifully freed their slaves. The decline in the enslaved percentage of the black population was caused not by a drop in the number of slaves, but by a sharp increase in the number of free blacks. Slavery did not simply fade away in these years. On the contrary, there was a 23 percent increase in the number of slaves in the 1790s and a massive 33 percent increase in the number of slaveholders — probably one of the largest decadal increases in the history of the city. Individual manumissions did occur, but as we saw earlier they had little impact on the total slave population until the nineteenth century.

The reasons for the growth of the free black population can be understood only by examining the larger context. In the years after the Revolution, New York, overtaking both Boston and Philadelphia, emerged as the biggest and most important city in the United States. Its population nearly doubled between 1790 and 1800. Even

TABLE 21

Population in Richmond County and the Rural Part of Kings County, 1790–1810

Year	Free Blacks in Black Households	Free Blacks in White Households	Slaves	Blacks in White Households	Total Blacks	Total Whites
1790	21 (6)	138	1,782	1,920	1,941	4,782
1800	11 (3)	208	1,736	1,944	1,955	5,998
1810	48 (8)	681	1,167	1,848	1,896	7,352

Sources: U.S. Bureau of the Census, *Heads of Families at the First Census of the United States Taken in the Year 1790: New York* (Washington, D.C., 1909); U.S. Bureau of the Census, Second Census of the United States, 1800, M32, Record Group 29, National Archives, Washington, D.C.; U.S. Bureau of the Census, Third Census of the United States, 1810, M252, Record Group 29, National Archives.

Note: Brooklyn has been excluded from the Kings County figures. The figures in parentheses are the number of black households.

more remarkable was the increase in the black population, both slave and free. Not only did that population keep up with the city's very high rate of demographic growth, but also blacks increased marginally their share of the population, from 9.9 percent to 10.2 percent. The main factors in black population growth are similar to those influencing white population—migration from the surrounding countryside and from overseas.[5]

In 1803 an irate "Citizen" wrote to the *New York Gazette and General Advertiser* objecting to the "whole host of Africans that now deluge our city."[6] Census records are not nearly detailed enough to allow us to disaggregate this influx of blacks with any precision, but the gross figures do give us some idea of what had happened. Throughout the colonial and early national periods the hinterland of New York City had the heaviest concentration of slaveholding north of the Mason-Dixon line. For example, in 1790 more than one in every two households on Staten Island and in the rural parts of Kings County contained slaves.[7] Slavery died hard in this area, but by 1810 the Gradual Manumission Act was beginning to have an effect and the number of blacks living in white households was diminishing (see table 21). Newly freed blacks did not, however, settle in this area: in 1810 there were only eight free black households, an increase of two from 1790. In fact, far from expanding with natural growth, the total black population was shrinking in these years. In a pattern repeated all across New York State and New Jersey, those blacks who were able to do so left the areas where they had been held as slaves. Probably they did so for many related reasons—the unavailability and high cost of land in slaveholding areas, the hostility of former owners, and the desire to escape from a constrictive rural society in which they would always be stamped as slaves. The city of New York was a magnet for many such blacks, offering them not only work but also anonymity.[8]

The other major source of migration to New York was Saint Domingue. Although historians have recognized the importance of black immigration in the 1790s from Saint Domingue to the American South, particularly to Charleston and New Orleans, the impact on New York of those refugees has gone relatively unnoticed.[9] By 1793 about ten thousand people had fled the great slave rebellion in the French West Indian colony and had settled in America.[10] Although the majority migrated to the South, a substantial minority, particularly the French Royalists, went to New York after 1793 and among them were many blacks—either free mulattoes or slaves who came with their masters. It is not possible to estimate the actual number of blacks who came from Saint Domingue, but there can be little doubt about their presence, indeed their prominence, in New York: they appear to have been involved in most of the black unrest in the city in the following decade.[11] For instance, French-speaking blacks made up a surprisingly high proportion of the runaway slaves advertised in New York newspapers in the 1790s.[12] In 1792 Zamor, a native of Guinea just arrived from Port-au-Prince, ran away from his master and was "supposed to be lurking about this city among the French negroes."[13] In 1796 a wave of arson was widely attributed to the French blacks. Even more disturbing for the white population, French blacks, as we saw in the previous chapter, instigated a major riot in 1801. That year Thomas Eddy pointed out in his account of the state prison that one-third of the black prisoners were immigrants from "European colonies, in the West Indies and Africa."[14] There can be little doubt that most of these blacks came from Saint Domingue.[15]

In the first decade of the nineteenth century the total population of New York City continued to increase rapidly, and by 1810 there were over ninety thousand people living there. The black population also grew quickly, though at a lower rate than the total population. In 1810 the percentage of blacks in the population had fallen

TABLE 22
Free Black Population in New York City, 1790–1810

Year	Free Black Households	Free Blacks in Free Black Households	Free Black Population	Free Blacks in White Households	% of Free Blacks in White Households
1790	157	678	1,036	349	33.7
1800	676	2,115	3,332	1,152	34.6
1810	1,228	4,815	7,470	2,495	33.4

Sources: U.S. Bureau of the Census, *Heads of Families at the First Census of the United States Taken in the Year 1790: New York* (Washington, D.C., 1909); U.S. Bureau of the Census, Second Census of the United States, 1800, M32, Record Group 29, National Archives, Washington, D.C.; U.S. Bureau of the Census, Third Census of the United States, 1810, M252, Record Group 29, National Archives.

Note: The figures for free blacks in white households and those in free black households do not add up to those for total free black population because they do not include free blacks in prison, in the almshouse, in the hospital, and in debtor's prison. This category included 9 in 1790, 65 in 1800, and 160 in 1810.

to 9.7. The sources of the free black population increase gradually changed in the first decade of the nineteenth century. Migration from the surrounding countryside continued to play an important role, but as the situation in Saint Domingue stabilized, immigration from the Caribbean dwindled.[16] By 1810, however, the Gradual Manumission Act was beginning to have an effect, and for the first time freed city slaves had an appreciable impact on the size of the free population. The number of slaves declined both absolutely and relatively, until by 1810 only 16.2 percent of New York's black population were still slaves.

WHAT DID FREE BLACKS in New York do? About one in three lived in white households (see table 22). Some, who were genuinely free, did so by choice or because of the nature of their work, usually domestic service. But as we saw in chapter 2, many who were classified as free by the census taker were actually restricted by some form of indenture. This sort of arrangement, whereby the master freed the slaves but retained control of their labor, was institutionalized in the Gradual Manumission Act of 1799. Under the terms of the act, the children born of slaves after July 4, 1799, were freed, but had to serve the owners of their mothers until they were twenty-five (females) or twenty-eight (males).

TABLE 23
Occupations of Heads of White Households Containing
Free Blacks in New York City in 1800

Occupation	Heads of Households N	%	Free Blacks in White Households N	%
Merchant	256	40.0	398	41.6
Professional	56	8.7	82	8.5
Retail	53	8.3	63	6.6
Official	21	3.3	39	4.1
Service	42	6.5	62	6.5
Maritime	18	2.8	19	2.0
Artisan	93	14.5	132	13.8
No occupation and/or widow	83	13.3	140	14.6
Miscellaneous	17	2.6	22	2.3
	639	100.0	957	100.0

Sources: U.S. Bureau of the Census, Second Census of the United States, 1800, M32, Record Group 29, National Archives, Washington, D.C.; *Longworth's American Almanack, New-York Register, and City Directory, for the Twenty-Fourth Year of American Independence* (New York, 1799); *Longworth's American Almanack, New-York Register, and City Directory, for the Twenty-Fifth Year of American Independence* (New York, 1800); *Longworth's American Almanack, New-York Register, and City Directory, for the Twenty-Sixth Year of American Independence* (New York, 1801).

Note: The 1800 census listed 778 white households containing 1,152 free blacks—139 (17.9 percent) of the households, containing 195 (16.9 percent) of the free blacks, were not matched with the directories.

The occupations of the heads of white households containing free blacks strongly suggest that most free blacks were employed as domestic servants (see table 23). Sixty percent of the households in which free blacks lived were headed by merchants, retailers, officials, and professionals (mostly lawyers and doctors). Free blacks in these residences typically lived in the attic rooms and cellars and performed similar duties to those of slaves. In both 1790 and 1800 one in three of the white households containing free blacks also owned slaves, and it is difficult to believe that the treatment of the two groups varied to any significant extent.

Little is known of the occupational structure of the blacks living in free black households in the late eighteenth and early nineteenth

TABLE 24
*Occupations of Male Free Black Heads of Households
in New York City*

Occupation	1800			1810	
	N	%	Mulattoes	N	%
Laborer (e.g., mariner)	43	38.7	8	114	43.5
Service	6	5.4	2	20	7.6
Food (e.g., oysterman)	14	12.6	3	22	8.4
Artisan	42	37.8	15	75	28.6
Retail	2	1.8	1	18	6.9
Professional	0		0	5	1.9
Miscellaneous	4	3.6	2	8	3.1
	111	100.0	31	262	100.0

Sources: U.S. Bureau of the Census, Second Census of the United States, 1800, M32, Record Group 29, National Archives, Washington, D.C.; *Longworth's American Almanack, New-York Register, and City Directory, for the Twenty-Fourth Year of American Independence* (New York, 1799); *Longworth's American Almanack, New-York Register, and City Directory, for the Twenty-Fifth Year of American Independence* (New York, 1800); *Longworth's American Almanack, New-York Register, and City Directory, for the Twenty-Sixth Year of American Independence* (New York, 1801); U.S. Bureau of the Census, Third Census of the United States, 1810, M252, Record Group 29, National Archives; *Longworth's American Almanack, New-York Register, and City Directory; For the Thirty-Fifth Year of American Independence* (New York, 1810); *Elliot and Crissy's New-York Directory, For the Year 1811, and 36th of the Independence of the United States of America* (New York, 1811).

centuries. Historians have generally relied on a few sporadic comments from travelers' accounts to cover the period before the 1850 federal census, in which for the first time occupations were included.[17] However, by linking the early federal censuses with the city directories, it is possible to extract a surprising amount of information about the heads of free black households.[18] Table 24 identifies the occupations of 111, or about one in five, of the males heading households in the 1800 census and 262, or about one in four, of the males heading households in the 1810 census. Obviously there are problems in using statistics that represent only a minority of the total black male work force: free black heads of households were more likely to be skilled than dependent members of households, and the bias of the directories toward the skilled further skews the figures. On the other hand, these are probably the best figures we are ever going to have. Though they must be interpreted with caution, the statistics in table 24 used in conjunction with other material allow access to an important part of the black past that has previously remained obscure.

What, then, do these statistics show? First, that about four out of every ten of the male blacks matched with the directories were either laborers or mariners. These figures undoubtedly underestimate the number of blacks involved in such work. Mariners and laborers are notoriously underrepresented in sources like the directories; in fact, it is surprising that so many were included. In the quarter-century after the Revolution over a third of the trade of the United States went through New York, which provided work for many blacks in the merchants' warehouses, on the docks loading cargoes, and on the ships themselves. William Strickland, one of the more observant of the travelers who visited New York in that period, noted that most of the "inferior" labor about town was done by blacks.[19] Ira Dye's analysis of the protection certificate applications suggests that about one-fifth of Philadelphia's maritime work force in this period was made up of blacks, and although a similar study cannot be attempted for New York, there seems little reason to assume any substantial difference between the two cities.[20]

Many newly freed blacks pieced together an existence as day laborers. Since they were often accused of petty crimes, court records occasionally allow us a glimpse of their lives. John, a free black man accused of theft in September 1801, "kept house" up at the collect, the freshwater pond in the North Ward. He was married, but his wife had been forced to leave New York to find work. For the previous three months she had been employed by a Mrs. Lawrence in Newark. A little over a year before John had gone as a sailor on a voyage to Cadiz, Spain. More recently he had been hired by Icard and Stafford's, where he had "wrought" as a laborer. He quit Icard and Stafford's, probably after being accused of theft, worked for half a day for a Mrs. Hio, then traveled to Newark to visit his wife for a week or so. On his return he was arrested on a charge of grand larceny but was later acquitted.[21] This combination of laboring and working as a sailor seems to have been quite common. But such an existence was always marginal, and these blacks were extremely vulnerable each winter and whenever there was a downturn in the economy. The coroner's report on John Richards, a black

man found dead in New York in January 1804, succinctly noted that
he had languished and died "from the Want of Bedding, Cloathing,
and the Common Necessaries of Life and the too frequent use of
Spirituous Liquors." [22]

Probably the most surprising finding shown in table 24, however,
is the number of free black males who did other work. In 1800 more
than one in three were classified as artisans, and by 1810, after the
hard years of the Embargo, nearly three in ten blacks were still in
this category.[23] Even allowing for the caveats about the bias of such
statistics toward skilled blacks, the figures are high. It is clear from
the directories that blacks possessed a wide variety of skills. They
worked, for example, as carpenters, coopers, cabinetmakers, uphol-
sterers, sailmakers, butchers, and bakers. Many skilled blacks probably worked for whites, but at least a few set up their own businesses.
Timothy Weeks of 4 Reed Street "followed shoemaking" in some
sort of partnership with William Johnson, another black, who lived
on Prince Street in the Fifth Ward.[24] Black artisans often appeared
in white business records.[25] Alexander Anderson, who supported his
medical studies by working as an engraver, noted a number of times
in his diary that he had cut tobacco stamps for many of the black
tobacconists in the city.[26] Some black artisans became quite well
known. Years later John Francis, a New York antiquarian, remembered that Peter Williams, sexton at the Methodist church on John
Street, was "striving to sustain a rival opposition in the tobacco line,
with the famous house of the Lorillards." [27] Peter Williams, a free
black, was listed as a tobacconist in both 1800 and 1810.

The figures in table 24 provide an instructive contrast with the
only comparable material from any other city in this period. Gary
Nash has analyzed the special listings of free blacks in the Philadelphia directories of 1795 and 1816.[28] Nash's material suffers from
the same shortcomings and distortions as do the figures in table
24. His definition of "artisan" is narrower than mine, excluding, for
example, sawyers, whom I have included. But even if the narrower
definition is used New York blacks were more than twice as likely to
possess a skill than were Philadelphia blacks.[29] A number of factors
explain this large discrepancy. Unlike their Philadelphia counterparts, who had used mainly white indentured servants, New York
artisans had relied heavily on slave labor throughout the eighteenth
century. As late as 1790, as we saw earlier, artisans were actually the

largest slaveholding group in New York, outnumbering both merchants and retailers. Undoubtedly, therefore, more blacks in New York were trained in these skills under slavery than was the case in Philadelphia. It should also be remembered that slavery still existed in New York: free blacks were not necessarily representative of the whole black population. Blacks who managed to buy their freedom or were manumitted for some other reason, or who came from Saint Domingue, were probably an exceptional group possessing unusually high levels of skill.

Support for the contention that the black artisans were an exceptional group can be found in the high number of skilled blacks who were mulattoes. For some unknown reason, the census taker for New York City in 1800 added in brackets after the name of the black head of household the term "mulatto" or the term "black."[30] As far as I know, this is the earliest extensive listing of the racial origins of blacks in America, and it is interesting to note that this unusual concern with color occurred in the midst of the substantial migration from Saint Domingue, where racial distinctions were always much finer than in America. Nearly half of the mulattoes identified in the directories had a trade (see table 24). More than one in three of the artisans were mulattoes, and if the less-skilled sawyers, all of whom were "black," are taken out this figure rises to nearly one in two.

Free blacks and slaves were heavily involved in the selling of goods in the streets and markets, many traveling from Long Island and New Jersey to sell their produce.[31] Free blacks living in New York were also prominent in the markets, although the directories again underestimate their importance. The blacks' presence was most noticeable in the oyster trade, which they dominated. The 1810 directory listed twenty-seven oystermen, of whom at least sixteen, or about 60 percent, were free blacks. Most of these black oystermen probably hawked their wares in the streets, but two of the blacks in the 1810 directory had both home and work addresses, which among whites was a sign of relative well-being. The figures in table 24 are not really good enough to allow an extensive analysis of the differences between 1800 and 1810. Nevertheless, the material does support the tentative conclusion that between 1800 and 1810 blacks began to move into some of the lesser professions and also to become small proprietors. The black shift into the oyster houses was the logical extension of their dominance of the trade. The 1810 directory included only two oyster houses, one of which was owned by a black. In the 1811 directory another black-owned oyster house appeared. The oyster house was to become a fashionable haunt of nineteenth-century New Yorkers, and these blacks were the forerunners of Thomas Downing, who ran a famous and luxurious establishment in the 1830s.[32] Free blacks also became involved in small establishments such as taverns, which were mostly concerned with the provision of food and drink.[33] By 1810 there were also two black teachers and, for the first time, a black clerk.

Although analysis of directory and census material yields much new and valuable information on the occupational structure of the free blacks, it provides only snapshots of that structure at ten-year intervals. What is missing is any element of dynamism or mobility. Yet it is impossible to work for any length of time with this material without being impressed by the shifting nature of the population. Free blacks appear in the directory one year but are omitted in the next. Only a handful of blacks listed in the census of 1800 can be identified with any degree of certainty in that of 1810.[34]

Occasionally information that allows a more detailed reconstruction of black lives has survived. The case of Alexander Whistelo is an example. Whistelo, a free black, was involved in a notorious trial in 1807 after the commissioner of the almshouse sued him over his failure to support his alleged bastard child. The published account of the case not only provides fascinating insights into the racial ideas of prominent New York doctors, who tried to establish whether the father of the child was black or white, but it also reveals interesting details of Whistelo's employment patterns. At the time he was supposed to have fathered the child Whistelo was a mariner. From the testimony of Lucy Williams, the mother, it appears that between August 1805 and January 1807 Whistelo made four voyages, the longest from May 1 to August 4, 1806, and the shortest lasting eight days in January 1807 at about the time the child was born. His employment as a sailor was sporadic. Presumably in the slack time he either lived off his earnings or followed the pattern discussed earlier and found employment as a laborer. When brought to trial in mid-1807, he was working as a coachman for Dr. David Hosack.[35] Whistelo won his case and faded back into obscurity, but he appears in the 1810 census and is listed in the directory as the

TABLE 25

Female-Headed Free Black Households in New York City, 1790–1810

Year	Total Free Black Households	Female-Headed Free Black Households		Total Blacks in Free Black Households	Free Blacks in Female-Headed Free Black Households	
		N	%		N	%
1790	157	27	17.2	678	84	12.4
1800	676	127	18.8	2,115	325	15.4
1810	1,228	214	17.4	4,815	711	14.8

Sources: U.S. Bureau of the Census, *Heads of Families at the First Census of the United States Taken in the Year 1790: New York* (Washington, D.C., 1909); U.S. Bureau of the Census, Second Census of the United States, 1800, M32, Record Group 29, National Archives, Washington, D.C.; U.S. Bureau of the Census, Third Census of the United States, 1810, M252, Record Group 29, National Archives.

owner of a small grocery shop. A similar occupational mobility was probably experienced by many free blacks, although the generally upward nature of Whistelo's movement was perhaps unusual.

Though little is known about black female occupations, many of the black women living in male-headed households were also active in the work force, supplementing the household income. Most of these women were employed in domestic work, usually as servants. In addition, a large number of women were themselves heads of households. Women headed somewhere between one in five and one in six of the black households in the three censuses (see table 25). This figure may exaggerate the number of female-headed households, as at any one time a number of husbands were probably away at sea. For example, Diana Lawrence, who lived on Fayette Street and worked as a servant for a Mrs. Hazelton, was married, but in December 1803 her husband, Samuel Lawrence, was at sea.[36] However, many of these women did act for long periods of time as the virtual heads of their households. Some coped with this status rather too well. William Thomas arrived back from a voyage to the East Indies to discover that his wife, Mary, "had not been as true to his bed as she ought to have." He accused her of committing adultery, "which She admitted to be true and in some Measure boasted in what She had been guilty."[37] Among the migrants from the surrounding countryside were single women attracted by the prospect of work and life in the city. Sally Gale, born and brought up in Huntington on Long Island, moved to New York in 1797. A week after she had arrived she obtained a job at New York Hospital, where she worked as a nurse for about seven months.[38] The city was one of the few environments where such unattached women could earn a living.

Unfortunately the directories are of little use in determining the occupations of free black women. In 1800 twelve, or nearly one in ten, of the females heading black households were listed in the directories. In 1810 the figure rose marginally to twenty-six, or about one in eight. The occupations of all of these women were domestic. Some were seamstresses, one was a "pye-baker," and others were mantua-makers. By far the most important occupation, however, was "washer," with seven out of the twenty-six women matched in 1810 in this category. All of these figures vastly underestimate the number of working women in the free black population. Only one woman was identified as a market woman, yet black women played a very prominent role as sellers of produce in New York markets and streets.

Information on black women and their occupations is scarce. Thomas F. De Voe recorded an account of a remarkable woman, supposedly a slave freed by George Washington, who near the turn of the century lived on the corner of John and Cliff streets. She opened a store in the basement of the house and sold milk, butter, eggs, and "cookies, pies and sweetmeats of her own manufacture; and she also took in washing for several bachelor gentlemen in the neighborhood." On Washington's birthday she baked her "Washington cake" and fed "some of the first men, old and young." During the yellow fever epidemics the butchers gave her sacks of sheep heads, enabling her to feed the scores of abandoned cats with the brains.[39]

Many free black women lived a precarious existence, and inevitably some turned to petty crime. Nancy, formerly the slave of Francis Van Dyke, a chocolate maker, stole a striped cotton apron from a line and "Carried it off to a Cook Shop in East George and there pledged it for something to eat as she was hungry."[40] The slightest misfortune could invite disaster. The child of Betsey Miller, who lived near the New Furnace on Greenwich Street, caught measles. Having "no money to help herself with and not being able to go out to work on account of her sick child," Miller stole from an unattended money drawer, but was quickly apprehended.[41]

From necessity or choice others turned to another occupation that did not appear in the directories—prostitution. Moreau de St. Méry, who paid more attention to these matters than most travelers, noted that "women of every color can be found in the streets, particularly after ten o'clock at night, soliciting men and proudly flaunting their licentiousness in the most shameless manner."[42] Alexander Anderson, the engraver, encountered an example of such "shameless" behavior on his way home one night when he stopped to relieve himself. "As I was busy against the wall, a mulatto wench came up to me in a very familiar manner, but finding I was not too disposed to make free with her begg'd my pardon, pretending she mistook me for some other person."[43] There were many brothels in New York, and black women ran quite a few of them. Neighbors protested about the presence of such establishments, as court records show, but the unchecked flow of complaints strongly suggests that brothels were an accepted part of city life. Asked in court where he resided, the free black Anthony Delacroix bluntly replied: "in a whore house near the New Market."[44] In 1802 Amos Curtis, a city marshal, finally decided to do something about the brothel in the cellar kitchen in his own residence at 83 Chambers Street. On entering the premises he had "found in one part of the said Nancy Cobus' House a White Man in the very fact of Committing adultery with a Black Woman and in another Room in the said Nancy's House he found one White Man undressed and in bed with two Black Women."[45]

Women were much more restricted in their choice of occupations than men. The skilled jobs that a proportion of free black men could obtain paid more and were less tedious than the domestic tasks to which women were largely consigned. Nevertheless, the availability of work, whether it was washing or prostitution, made the city a viable, if precarious, place in which women who headed households could live.

The material from the city directories suggests that the free black occupational structure, particularly for males, was more open than historians have assumed. Not surprisingly, a large proportion of the newly freed blacks performed laboring jobs in and around New

York. At the bottom of the social structure in the port city was a
constantly changing and shifting pool of blacks who eked out an
existence, often by combining short-term laboring jobs with work
as sailors. But by comparison with contemporary Philadelphia or,
more poignantly, with New York later in the century, New York
in the immediate postslavery period afforded a black male a much
greater chance to work at a skilled trade. Of course there were limits
to this mobility—there were no black merchants or lawyers. However, around the turn of the century New York offered recently
freed blacks considerably more opportunities than did other American cities to make a reasonable living and even, in a few instances,
to establish their own businesses. Analysis of the directories suggests that the industrialization that impacted so strongly on New
York City in the first half of the nineteenth century diminished
rather than increased the occupational opportunities available to
free blacks.

FREEDOM ALLOWED BLACKS the chance to begin to put the Afro-
American family on a surer footing, and as we saw with the example of John Moranda, some blacks eagerly seized this opportunity. Moranda's case, though suggestive of the strength of family
bonds and of black determination to overcome the institution's
splintering impact on the slave family, is perhaps even more elo-
quent about the difficulties free blacks still faced. Once John Moranda had secured his own liberty it took him another three years,
and we can only imagine the parsimonious and arduous existence
he endured during this period, to accumulate the money necessary
to buy the freedom of the rest of his family. The fact that slavery
ended gradually in this region decisively influenced the contours
of the free black family in the late eighteenth and early nineteenth
centuries. Unlike slaves in the South, those in New York and New
Jersey were liberated only slowly, over a number of years. Thus the
members of most slave families, typically owned by at least two
masters, were not freed at the same time, and many black families
were still separated by the hated institution.

Even when the whole of a family had managed to free itself there
was still considerable pressure on the family unit. Although, as we
have seen, New York City offered free blacks more of a chance to

secure decent employment than did any other American city at this time, it is important to keep that fact in perspective. Employment as a domestic often meant that blacks lived under the employer's roof and thus were separated from the rest of the family—even in 1810 one in three blacks labeled as "free" by the census taker were residing in a white household. Furthermore, many blacks existed on the margins by picking up day-laboring jobs here and there, and for such persons winter and downturns in the economy could have a devastating impact. In 1801, for example, John's wife, being unable to find employment in the city, had to leave their house near the collect to take a position as a domestic in Newark, New Jersey.[46]

The movement of free blacks to the city introduced further pressures on the black family. Free blacks migrating to New York have left only the faintest imprint on the historical record, but it appears likely that it was often individual blacks who first moved to the city. Uncertainty about prospects in the metropolis and lack of money probably prevented many families moving as a unit. A rare glimpse of the trauma that this situation could involve is contained in the diary of Elihu Smith, a young Connecticut-born physician who lived in New York in the 1790s. In 1795 Smith, as a favor to a friend in his hometown of Litchfield, sought out a free black named Cash Africa in New York. Africa had left his wife and children in Litchfield and traveled alone to the city, presumably with the intention of either bringing his family there or of making some money and returning to Litchfield. Smith wrote back to his friend that after some trouble he had found Cash Africa: "I made a proper representation to him, of the condition in which his wife & her children were; & made use of your name, as you desired me. The fellow *promises well*. That, you know, he always does. I have, however, found out with whom he lives; &, if he does not fulfill his engagements, I shall apply to his master." A short while later Smith noted in his diary that he had delivered a letter to Cash Africa from his wife and that Cash Africa had sent seven yards of baize to his wife and children for clothes. It seems, however, that Smith was later forced to carry out his threat, for he delivered five dollars from Cash Africa's employer to the family in Litchfield.[47] This incident illustrates some of the problems and tensions associated with the migration of free blacks to the city. It also provides a good example of the kind of white paternal interference, always more likely in rural areas, that

many freed blacks were no longer prepared to tolerate and that undoubtedly spurred on many to move from the area where they had
been enslaved.

Unfortunately the bare details in the early censuses preclude an
extensive statistical analysis of the free black family in these for-
mative years. The census taker listed only the name of the head of
household and the number of members in it. This number, which
varied from one to eighteen, was not broken down by age or sex, and
consequently we have little idea of what constituted a household.
(As Gary Nash has noted, some of these larger units were probably
large extended or augmented household units, where a family put
up boarders or relatives and friends freshly arrived from the country.) [48] The census material from 1800, however, the year the census
taker included the racial designation of the black head of household, does provide some fascinating and tantalizing insights into
the nature of sexual relations between the races. Casual sexual contact between white and black occurred all the time, but occasionally
there are brief references in print to more long-lived relationships.
In 1803, for example, the *New York Evening Post* included in a list of
those who had died in the yellow fever epidemic Mary Carmer of 56
E. Rutgers Street, a "very light complexioned mulatto" who had a
"white sailor husband." The newspaper thought this case worthy of
a brief comment not because of the racially mixed marriage, which
was mentioned incidentally, but because of the public way Carmer
died (she had a fit near the tea water pump and had to be taken to
the almshouse, "where she expired in the yard"). [49] The 1800 census
also contains evidence of more permanent relationships. Typically,
miscegenation is thought to have taken place between white men
and black women, but it is impossible to determine whether the free
black living in a white household was a female, let alone whether
the free black was more than a servant. [50] Mary Carmer, for instance,
would have appeared in the census as one free black of unknown sex
in a white household headed by a white man: there would have been
no indication that she was the wife of the head of the household.
Nevertheless, we do know that in 1800 there were eleven households
headed by a black male that contained white women. For instance,
John Francis, a hairdresser, headed a household that consisted of
one other black apart from himself and a white female between the
ages of twenty-seven and forty-six. John Williams lived in a house-

hold that included five other blacks and two white females between seventeen and twenty-six years of age. Five out of the eleven house-holds were headed by blacks like John Williams, whom the census taker categorized as "mulatto." In 1800 the remarkably high figure of one out of every fifty black households headed by a male con-tained one or more white females. That such living arrangements occurred openly, whether or not there was a sexual relationship, starkly contrasts with the situation in New York in the 1830s, where rumors that blacks were about to "mullatoize" and take over white neighborhoods were a factor in the antiabolition riots.[51]

If the censuses are of only limited value, other sources do allow the piecing together of an impressionistic picture of some aspects of free black family life. For the most part, however, court records and brief snippets in the newspapers reveal the failures and messy end-ings rather than the long-lived and stable relationships. They show the havoc that poverty and enforced separations continued to wreak on the black family. In 1802, for example, Sarah Thomas, a washer-woman, and David Smith, a sailor, who had been living together in Thomas Street, had a falling out. Thomas had Smith charged and convicted of the theft of two gold rings and some clothes.[52] What is intriguing about this and many other cases in the court records is that free blacks often turned to white authorities for help in sort-ing out their problems. The results were not always so happy for the women. In April 1805, Henry Laurence, a mulatto, jealous of the attention he believed other men gave his wife and doubting her faithfulness to him, cruelly beat her. She complained to the magis-trate but apparently received little help. Further enraged, Laurence purchased some ratsbane, spread it on several slices of bread, and fed it to his wife, who after several days of agony died. Laurence was executed on October 4, 1805.[53]

In the case of John Vallier more than supposition was involved; there was no doubt that his wife had committed adultery. Return-ing home early one day in 1805 Vallier discovered his wife in bed with Isorn Harris, who quickly debunked in classic style through the window. Vallier's wife then left him for Harris, and when Vallier confronted both of them she refused to return. Later Vallier came across Harris alone in the street and asked him if he was ashamed of himself for ruining both Vallier and his family, to which Har-ris replied that "he was a single man and would ketch any woman

he could either married or single." It was not long after this that
Vallier shot and killed Harris.[54] Mention has already been made of
the case of William Thomas, a sailor who returned from the East
Indies to discover that his wife "had not been as true to his bed as
she ought to have." A "much agitated" Thomas determined to kill
himself, but the pistol misfired. He then found his wife, killed her,
and again tried to end his own life. This time, however, "by Chance
unaccountable to him he missed himself." Thomas was found guilty
of assault and battery but not murder.[55]

For blacks at the bottom of the social structure, struggling to
make ends meet, an unwanted pregnancy could mean disaster. In
1801 a black woman far advanced in pregnancy and living in the
almshouse died after a slave named Peter "wantonly" drove a carriage over her.[56] Pregnancy was particularly disastrous for single
women. In a number of cases newly born children were abandoned
in places where they would easily be found: in 1803, for instance, a
man driving a hearse to the almshouse discovered a bundle near the
gate. The bundle turned out to be a mulatto child who was about
a week old and "abundantly supplied with cloathing."[57] In another
case a black woman was quickly apprehended after she abandoned
her newborn mulatto child on Barley Street. When questioned by
the police she related that, with labor approaching and "having no
home or any place whatsoever," she went to the poorhouse but
was turned away. She had given birth in an open yard and left her
child. The woman was committed to jail for trial on the charge of
abandoning her infant.[58]

But black women were not mere victims of their circumstances
and in particular of male violence. Even in the court records one
sees signs of a female culture and of significant female networks
of acquaintances and friends. Probably this pattern is most obvious in cases involving black prostitutes, but occasional hints occur
in other contexts. In 1801, for example, Sally Abels, while "sitting
down peaceably by the fireside in her own house in Hague Street,"
was assaulted by her husband, Jupiter Abels, who stabbed her in the
breast with a fork. Details of the case are sparse, but we know that
it was two free black women neighbors who first ministered to the
wound and later came forward to testify on Sally Abels's behalf.[59]
Admittedly such evidence is often allusive and possibly open to
other interpretations, but it seems likely that in this and other cases

such relationships played an important role in helping to sustain black women in what were often difficult circumstances.

As slavery slowly wound down in the early years of the nine-teenth century many black families in and around New York City were reunited and were able, often for the first time, to live under one roof. But there was a fragility to black life and particularly the black family in these years. The press of economic circumstances continued to render the existence of these families precarious. The sort of work that many black men and women were compelled to accept—as seamen and in domestic service—did not pay very well and often entailed lengthy absences from home. Court records, in particular, paint a dismal picture of the impact of such an uncer-tain and hard existence on the lives of many free blacks, particu-larly women.

LITTLE IS KNOWN about free black residential patterns in New York City in the late eighteenth and early nineteenth centuries. His-torians, relying mainly on the occasional comments of travelers, have glossed over the subject, attempting only a few generalizations about the concentration of black housing in what are seen as em-bryonic ghettos.[60] A much more detailed picture comes into focus, however, if one analyzes the data contained in the city's censuses of 1790, 1800, and 1810 (see maps 5, 6, and 7).

The most striking point, particularly for readers familiar with the ghettos of twentieth-century America, is that black households were well distributed throughout the city. Figures from the index of dissimilarity, which measures the amount of segregation in the city, are very low by later nineteenth- and twentieth-century stan-dards.[61] The colonial city was a "walking city" of mixed neigh-borhoods and relatively little spatial segregation of classes, and the distribution of free black households reflected these characteristics. As one goes through the census it becomes clear that black house-holds were usually clustered in groups of between two and five, but what is more noticeable is that these clusters were often in very close proximity to the houses of prominent members of the New York elite.[62] In the years after the Revolution, however, and just as free blacks emerged as an important and statistically significant ele-ment in the population, the spatial organization of the city began to

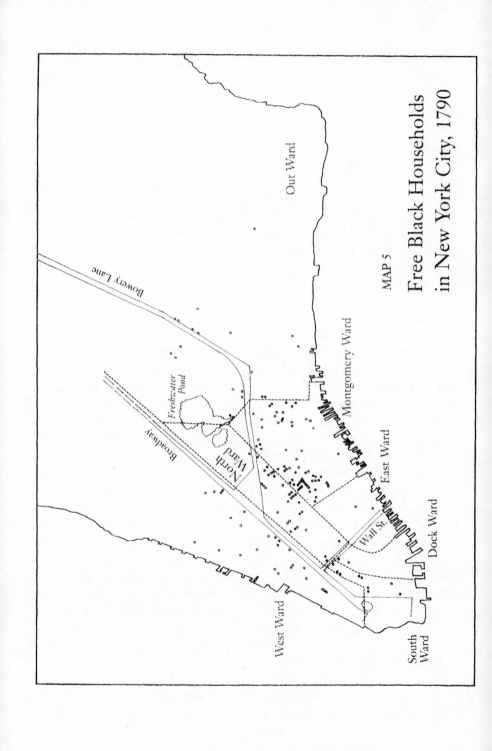

MAP 5

Free Black Households
in New York City, 1790

change. That change was related to economic developments. As the production of goods and services in this rapidly expanding urban center was divorced from the household and wage labor was introduced, the laboring classes were forced into rented accommodation. It became less common for employees to live and work under their masters' roofs. The old mixed neighborhoods began to give way to the more rigid class segregation of the "industrial city."[63] The industrial city would not emerge fully for some time, but its antecedents can be discerned early in the nineteenth century in New York's black residential patterns.

Like freed rural slaves, free urban blacks apparently chose not to live in areas where slavery was still entrenched. In 1790 there were only four black households in the Dock and East wards. These two wards were by far the heaviest slaveholding wards in the city; in 1790, 41 percent of the white households in the East Ward and 37 percent in the Dock Ward contained slaves. Farther north in John Street, on the other hand, a significant grouping of black households clustered around the John Street Methodist Episcopal Church. The link between that important institution in black community life and the black households was clear to at least one slaveholder, who advertised that his runaway was probably being sheltered "in some negro house near the Methodist meeting house in John Street."[64]

The majority of free blacks who, over the next two decades, attempted to find housing in the city appear to have moved into the area north of John Street. By 1810 most free blacks were settled in a broad band from the Hudson River in the Fifth Ward, through the collect (or freshwater pond) in the Sixth Ward, and down to the East River. What was increasingly happening, then, was that free blacks were becoming concentrated in the emerging working-class wards. Much of the land in this area was at best marginal—it was marshy, ill-drained, and particularly in the Fourth and Sixth wards, was used for such semi-industrial activities as tanning, a trade notorious for its bad odors. Black settlement in the area was centered around that pillar of black community life—the church. In 1796 black members of the Methodist Church in New York had obtained permission from the Reverend Francis Asbury, bishop of the American Methodist Episcopal church, to set up a separate church in a house on Cross Street, between Mulberry and Orange streets (just southeast of the freshwater pond on the maps). Subsequently

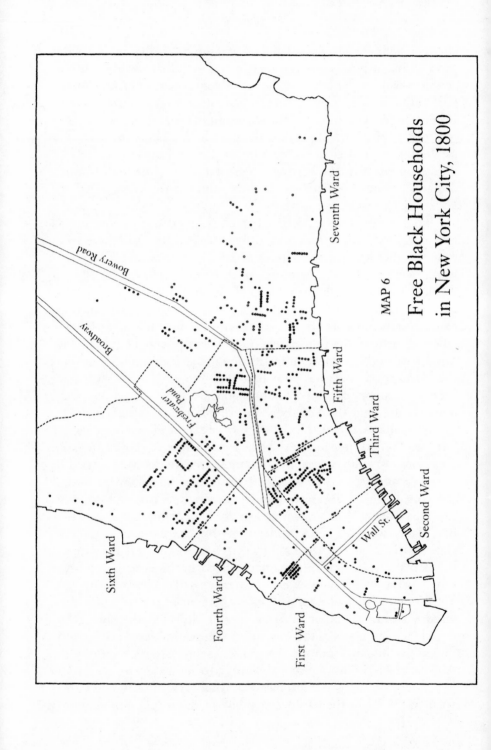

MAP 6

Free Black Households
in New York City, 1800

this area attracted a large number of black households, and in the 1830s it attained worldwide notoriety as the Five Points Slum. In 1800 members of the new congregation built the Zion Methodist Episcopal Church on the corner of Leonard and Church streets in the Fifth Ward. That area had been owned by the Anglican Church and opened up for settlement relatively late; but by 1810 many blacks had established residences there near their place of worship.[65] The census data suggest this was a common pattern; churches were built and the establishment of black households would follow. In this particular area black institutions, notably the church, appear to have fostered the development of a strong sense of community among blacks who consequently were probably better off in some ways than their white neighbors.[66]

When free blacks first entered the housing market the city was expanding rapidly in population and physical size. Slaves had nearly always lived in their masters' houses, usually in the attic rooms or cellars, but newly freed and immigrant blacks had to find their own accommodation, and at a time when housing was in short supply. Blacks fresh from the countryside often stayed with friends or relatives. Robert Havens came to the city from Cow Harbor on Long Island and spent a short time "with his Aunt Peggy Banks in a Cellar three Doors from Frankfort Street in William Street."[67] Others lived in households as lodgers. Silvia, a slave from Brunswick, New Jersey, who came to New York for a few days, boarded with Jane White in Rector Street.[68] In 1801 Jacob Spellman, a sailor who had arrived from New Bern, North Carolina, the previous winter, lodged in a house in Orange Street.[69] Many of the single transient blacks at the bottom of the social hierarchy lived in places that were little more than flophouses. Details brought out in a court case in 1799 suggest the nature of their life-styles. At least five black males lived in one room in a house on Mulberry Street. Figaro, a French black, was probably a longtime resident. Peter Mathew had been in the room two days, John Jersey and Jacob Claire for about three weeks, and John Caesar for two months.[70] Similar sorts of establishments appear to have existed for women. Nancy Cooke testified at the trial of Alexander Whistelo that Lucy Williams, mother of Whistelo's alleged child, had lived with her for six weeks in a room that contained not much more than two beds. Evidently the two women had little to do with one another. Cooke did not feel quali-

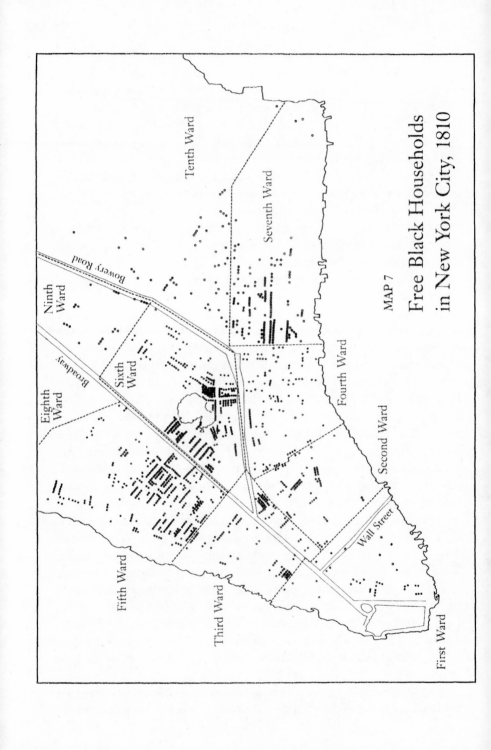

MAP 7

Free Black Households
in New York City, 1810

First Ward

Second Ward

Third Ward

Fourth Ward

Fifth Ward

Sixth Ward

Seventh Ward

Eighth Ward

Ninth Ward

Tenth Ward

Broadway

Bowery Road

Wall Street

fied to comment on Williams's character, although she was able to remember that a very "light" man had stayed one night.[71]

Even as early as the 1790s a few blacks owned the houses in which they lived. In 1796 William Platt, a black sawyer, willed his house at 49 Cedar Street to his wife.[72] But as with an increasing number of white New Yorkers, the vast majority of free blacks lived in rented accommodation. Information contained in the directories and censuses shows that black households typically occupied only a portion of a house. Some blacks lived in the outbuildings at the rear (Ruth Dusenbury, a free black woman, lived in a "backhouse" on Cliff Street, near John Street) and others rented apartments, but the part of the house most closely associated with free blacks was the cellar.[73] The prevailing architectural style in New York featured high-ceilinged cellars under the raised front stoop. These cellars, which were half-underground, were easily separated from the rest of the house to allow multiple occupancy.[74]

Occasionally the testimony given in court cases furnishes particulars of the lives of these black cellar occupants. When Thomas Cooney was charged with grand larceny in 1804, he and his wife, Margaret, were operating a grocery store at 22 Harman Street in the Seventh Ward. The cellar kitchen in this house was rented to Ruth Smith, a "yellow woman," for five shillings a week. She in turn had taken in a boarder, John Young, a black man. In the course of his testimony Young mentioned an equally complicated arrangement that existed just down the street, where James Anderson, a black, had lived "at Clarry Brown's who lives under a grocery store in Harman Street beyond George Street."[75]

Such details deepen our understanding of the black residential pattern shown on the maps. Although the concentration of black households became more marked over the twenty-year period, we should remember that these blacks lived among white households. In 1800 the largest consecutive listing of black households, that on Ann Street, contained only eight. Though by 1810 there were three streets in the Fifth Ward with nine or ten black households in a row, only two areas of any size were almost exclusively black. By the early years of the nineteenth century, Theatre Alley (near Broadway at the top of the Third Ward on map 7) was recognized as a black neighborhood. In 1802 the manager of the theater complained bitterly about the "noisy mob of Negroes and vulgar boys" who hung around the door begging for checks from patrons, which they then "promptly sell again at half price, or for what they can get." [76] By my calculations, the 1810 census listed nineteen black and two white households in the alley. The other substantially black neighborhood was in the area later called the Five Points. In 1810 there were twenty-four black and two white households (totaling eighty-nine blacks and seven whites) near the corner of Little Water and Cross streets, eleven black households in a row farther down Cross Street near Orange Street, and ten black households in a row on the adjoining Mulberry Street.

Generally, however, free blacks were not segregated in black enclaves. The type of segregation that did occur was of a curious vertical kind, foreshadowing the experience of Ralph Ellison's Invisible Man, whose basement residence was not in Harlem but in a border area. A medical report regarding the Bancker Street area in the Fourth Ward graphically illustrates one of the consequences of this segregation.

> Out of the 48 blacks, living in 10 cellars, 33 were sick, of whom 14 died; while, out of 120 whites, living *immediately over their heads* in the *apartments of the same houses, not one* even had the fever. [77]

Conditions in the cellars were often appalling. Medical reports on the numerous epidemics that ravaged New York in these years speak of the cellars accumulating water and every type of refuse in rainy weather and of the threat they posed to health. One of the first victims in the 1805 epidemic was a black woman who lived in a "very filthy cellar" on Greenwich Street. [78]

But there is a more obvious point: far from being separated, black and white lived in one another's pockets. This pattern is further established by numerous complaints found in the court records. In 1800, for example, Susan Brasher, a free black woman who lived at the corner of Ferry and Cliff streets, complained about John Stoddart. Stoddart, a laborer who had accommodation in the upper part of the same house, was perpetually drunk and cruelly beat and abused his pregnant wife. [79] In 1804 several whites protested about the behavior of York, a resident of Gold Street. York apparently spent most of his time drunk and was given to cursing, swearing, and quarreling, so that "the whole neighborhood is continually disturbed by the disorderly behaviour of the said York." [80]

Blacks may have lived in cellars, but as Ellison's invisible protagonist reminds us, there are "warm holes" as well as "cold holes."
In spite of the squalor in which they often had to exist, New York's
blacks were able to create a vibrant underground culture. Cellars
and cellar kitchens allowed easy and, for the slaves, unsupervised
access to the streets and fostered the development of complex networks of relationships. Occasionally we get a clearer view of this
urban black culture, which flourished in the area around Bancker
Street. In 1799 an advertisement for Peter, a mulatto runaway slave,
described him as a "great dancer and a very quarrelsome fellow, and
is noted as such in the negro dancing cellars in the city." Peter was
evidently captured and sold, but within a few months he absconded
again. A second advertisement informed readers that Peter was well
known in the vicinity of Lumber Street and "in the negro dancing
cellars on Bancker Street by the appellation of Hazard's Peet."[81] In
1802 Henry Thompson, a black, was convicted of keeping a disorderly house on Oliver Street near the intersection with Bancker
Street. Day or night, the complainant alleged, up to fourteen men
could be found playing dice, cards, and "Divers other games" in
Thompson's establishment.[82] Women, too, were drawn to the area.
One night in 1805, Caty Thomas, Phoebe Brown, and Grace Kelley
went uptown to a tavern and dance house on East George Street
run by Gilbert Williams, a black. Here they encountered Benjamin
Dunbar and Harry, a black who was a regular participant in the
Sunday evening service at the African Church but who also had
a reputation as a young man about town, and danced until about
half past ten. Moving on to another tavern on Cheapside Street,
also run by a black, they continued dancing until two o'clock in
the morning.[83] These blacks, some slave, some free, came to the
Bancker Street area from all over town. Here they could gamble,
drink, listen to music, meet members of the opposite sex, and most
important, for it appears to have been an especially valued medium
of self-expression, dance.

IT WAS ON THE STREETS, in the markets, and in the numerous dives
and gin joints of New York that much of black life took place. Our
access to this world is now restricted to snatched glimpses, distorted by disapproving white eyes and gleaned from such sources
as the court records, but one can still discern the shadowy out-

lines of a network of petty criminal activity that, almost inevitably, was associated with this underground culture in the cosmopolitan port city.

In the next chapter we shall see that there was a thriving market in used clothing on the city streets, where an indigent black could readily raise some cash by selling such items as shoes, coats, trousers, and the like. But clothing was only one of many types of goods bought and sold by blacks. Although much of this trade was doubtless legitimate, there was also considerable potential for stolen items to be quickly resold. Some blacks were driven to theft by their circumstances. It takes little imagination, for example, to understand why in December in New York City an impoverished Samuel Tonkin should have stolen a few sticks of firewood.[84] But with others theft was less an act of desperation and more a way of life. The black criminal infrastructure of New York City appears to have been quite sophisticated. In 1802, for example, Sannon, a slave, stole a watch and some cigars, which he sold to another black who in turn sold them to another. Eventually the goods ended up in New Haven.[85] At times whites were involved as well: in 1804 a black woman stole a watch and sold it to James Clark, a pedlar, who augmented the income he received from plying his trade by acting as a fence for stolen property.[86]

The techniques blacks used to steal varied from the breaking into and entering of premises at night to more subtle activities. Two blacks went into a store, tried on a few pairs of shoes, and pocketed those that fit the best in their cavernous greatcoats; a black woman secreted a pair of shoes under her dress.[87] In another case a group of blacks used a classic stratagem: one occupied the storekeeper while another quickly passed goods to his two companions outside.[88] Others took advantage of the gullibility of some whites. In 1799 an outraged New Yorker inserted a notice in the *Daily Advertiser* detailing the activities of a "Black Swindler." A sixteen-year-old black female had knocked on the door and used "the name of a Lady" to borrow an expensive dress, allegedly to have a copy made. The "Lady" must have been well known for the "request was immediately complied with," but neither dress nor girl had since been sighted.[89] Some were even more brazen. When John Hunter decided, in 1798, to steal a pile of timber belonging to a coachmaker on Broad Street, he hired a white cartman to turn up at the site very early in the morning. Hunter helped the cartman load the cart with twenty-three planks and three boards and then directed him to deliver the timber to a dock, where Hunter sold it to the captain of a schooner. From the testimony of the captain it appears that Hunter had a thriving trade in lumber and had made it known along the waterfront that he could quickly fill any orders.[90]

Much of this trade, licit and illicit, took place in the numerous bars and taverns of the bustling city. In 1786 the *Daily Advertiser* claimed that there were eight hundred taverns in New York, a number that must have increased substantially in the 1790s and early 1800s as the population of the city trebled.[91] Quite a few were either black establishments or were patronized largely by blacks. Complaints of rowdy behavior were commonplace: in 1800, for example, exasperated neighbors registered their objections to the "drinking, and Rioting and Quarrelling and fighting at late hours of the night" that regularly occurred at 26 Cedar Street.[92] The character of another tavern situated across town near the tea water pump house was revealed in an 1802 case. A brawl involving more than a dozen blacks started after a black stubbed out a "segar" in someone else's drink. After the fight John Moore, a black who had attracted a goodly proportion of the blows, belligerently announced that "if any Negro in New York should give him three saucy words he would be the means of his death." That this was no idle threat was demonstrated soon after when the body of another black, Thomas Jackson, was fished out of the East River.[93]

Alcohol was an important part of black life. A few drinks in a tavern slaked the thirst after a hard day's labor and offered a brief respite from the constraints of white society; several more drinks offered an oblivion from which whites could be excluded. New York slaveowners constantly inveighed against their slaves' "abuse" of alcohol. Pro's owner somewhat facetiously described him as "a great talker and smoker and no hater of spirituous liquor."[94] Others were very concerned at the way alcohol could transform slaves into a troublesome property. David Nichols's slave Roe, for example, was "much given to intoxication, at which time he is very quarrelsome." Similarly, Jacob, a twenty-year-old slave, was normally "very plausible" and well behaved, but was very "fond of spirituous liquors, and when a little intoxicated is very talkative, apt to be noisy and sometimes impudent."[95]

In a succession of cases in the 1790s and early 1800s free blacks in varying degrees of intoxication were brought before the white authorities. Tobias, detained in December 1798, was so drunk he was incapable of uttering a word.[96] In 1804 William Hayslop celebrated his release from prison by getting blind drunk. Accused of theft the next day, he could only lamely claim that he "was so much intoxicated with liquor that he does not know whether he took the said piece of Striped Cotton or not but if he did steal the said Piece of Cotton he is willing to pay for it."[97] The court was about as impressed with Hayslop's story as it was with that of William Rollins, who confessed to theft but pointed out that "he was in a Christmas Frolic when he did it and is willing to pay eight Dollars to make it up."[98] In April 1805 John Primrose, another free black just discharged from prison, was accused of the theft of some cloth from a shop on Maiden Lane. While Primrose could remember quite well events up to twelve o'clock on the morning of his release, things were a bit blurred after that. In fact the "Examinant was so much intoxicated last evening and Afternoon that he does not know whether he was in Maiden Lane at all or not."[99] Such cases are, of course, extreme. Not many blacks regularly drank themselves into a stupor, but material from the court cases and fragmentary references from other sources make it clear that alcohol was an important part of the lives of many New York blacks, both slave and free.

Court records also bring out well the differences and divisions among the black population. Historians, usually most interested in relations between black and white, have often found a unity of purpose among blacks that stretches the bounds of credulity. In particular, reliance on the slippery idea of a black "community," a concept that derives much of its analytical force from the encircling white oppression, has masked the extent to which blacks argued, fought, and struggled among themselves. Blacks stole goods and money from each other as well as from whites. In 1804, for example, Solomon Lane made off with the takings of a black oysterman.[100] Gangs of black youths preyed on other blacks. In 1801 Tom Peters pilfered a fifty-dollar note from his master and changed it at a house on William Street. Word probably spread that Peters had come into some money, for a few nights later when he went to Ricketts Circus Peter Clark and Lewis Francis maneuvered him into a corner and relieved him of half the money left in his pocket book.[101] In 1804,

a young black, Richard Smock, was engaged by a sailor to carry a
trunk from the Fly Market to another part of town. On the way
he was cornered by three youths, two black and one white, who
smashed open the trunk, took out the money they found inside, and
threw the trunk into the East River.[102]

As we have already seen, blacks instigated legal action against
other blacks in order to curb noisy neighbors or to help sort out
messy domestic separations. These were not isolated cases but
formed part of a broader pattern.[103] A few incidents clearly demonstrate that blacks were familiar enough with white institutions not
just to use but (in ways reminiscent of the southern slaves' Br'er
Rabbit stories) to exploit them in order to achieve their aims. In the
fall of 1803, for example, Cesar Jackson played dice with a French
Negro and lost twenty-five dollars. Jackson, not happy at his "luck"
and probably keen to exploit his opponent's unfamiliarity with the
language and customs of New York, claimed that the French Negro
was using false dice and demanded his money back, but this "being
refused him he sent his Wife for the Watch men." Jackson's ruse
failed, however, as both the money and the dice were pocketed by
the watch.[104] When Exodus Thompson was accused of stealing a
turkey from a stall in the market, another black, Joseph Freeman,
came forward and testified that he had taken "particular notice of
the said Exodus and saw him go off with the said Turkey in a Clan-
destine Manner." Although Thompson claimed complete ignorance
of any turkey he easily supplied a motive for Freeman's damaging
testimony: "not long since [Exodus Thompson] gave the above
named Joseph Freeman a good Sound Beating for which he has no
Doubt he now comes forward to swear against Examt."[105] Similar
tactics could, on occasion, be tried against whites. One morning in
1803 the mistress of a free black, Diana Lawrence, discovered not
only that her servant was drunk but also that she had stolen a lamp
and secreted it in the "necessary tub." On being accused of theft
Diana Lawrence threatened her employer that "if she dared to say
that she . . . had stolen her Lamp . . . she would prosecute her."[106]

The spare details and dry language of court records tend to flat-
ten out black behavior, making it appear little different from that
of whites who broke the same laws. Alcohol was an important part
of white life; whites thieved and bought and sold stolen goods; and
whites, too, had a remarkably strong belief in the efficacy of the

legal system as a means of solving their problems. What was different was the context of this black behavior: the black population of New York was of such a size that an (often literally) underground black life flourished and blacks dealt with one another face-to-face. The meaning for blacks of much of this behavior remains obscure (in large part because of the limited details in the sources), but there can be little doubt that it confirmed every prejudice and stereotype the authorities, and whites generally, ever held about blacks.[107] In the next chapter I shall examine other facets of this New York black life — in particular the ways in which blacks talked, dressed, and used their bodies — in relation to which it is possible to pinpoint subtle differences between white and black behavior, differences that I will argue constitute a distinctive "style" marking blacks off from their white contemporaries.

7

A Question of Style

As ELIHU SMITH, a young physician, and William Dunlap, his dramatist friend, strolled through the streets of New York on an October day in 1795, their attention was attracted to the appearance of a black passerby. The man, Smith recorded that evening in his diary, had been "very flippantly drest . . . with legs like two semi-circles." The fellow was, Dunlap had quipped, "a very great beau *(bow)—about the legs*."[1] Smith's description and Dunlap's pun suggest that the black's appearance was alien and comic. Something— not just the shape of the man's legs, but his clothes, their colors, or the two in combination—was not right. Neither of the two friends would have considered venturing abroad in such attire.

The sense of cultural distance conveyed by this incident is rather more subtle than that usually considered in studies of blacks in America. Over the last twenty years historians have revolutionized our understanding of black culture, but they have generally concentrated on the rural areas of the South. There blacks, when they were not a majority of the total population, were at least a sizable minority. Most were slaves, living and working on plantations and separated from the whites by a physical and cultural gulf. Such factors have been emphasized by historians who have examined aspects of black culture that were strongly influenced by an African past. Black cultural distinctiveness has been seen largely as a function of demography, the high black to white ratios in the plantation South allowing sufficient social space for African patterns to be important in shaping the day-to-day life of blacks. Under these circumstances the cultural gap between the races was wide and the process of acculturation a matter not of years but of generations.[2]

As we have seen, the situation in and around New York City was different. Although in 1800 New York's black population of 5,865 was second in size only to Charleston's, the more significant point is that free blacks and slaves made up only about 10 percent of the city's inhabitants. New York's black population was being further distinguished from that of the South at this time by changes in the balance between its free and slave components. In the colonial period virtually all of the blacks in the city had been slaves, but in the quarter-century after the Revolution the migration into the city of free blacks from the countryside and the West Indies, and the passage of the gradual abolition measure in 1799, reversed this situation. By 1810 only 16.2 percent of a much larger black population of 8,918 were still enslaved, and New York had become the largest center of free blacks in America.

Economic changes were, too, helping to bring the races together. The gradual demise of slavery was part of a larger shift from bound labor to wage labor that was transforming the city and, in the process, incorporating blacks into the emerging working class. By 1810 quite a few of New York's free blacks were artisans, some were in domestic service, and others pieced together a livelihood by alternating between laboring around the docks or the city and working as sailors. But neither in employment nor in residence were these blacks and the dwindling number of slaves segregated. They often labored alongside working-class whites and occupied similar types of housing in the same areas of the city. On the face of it, the vast majority of New York blacks seem to have been incorporated successfully into the dominant culture.

Yet, as is suggested by the reaction of Elihu Smith and William Dunlap to the "flippantly" dressed black, the relationship between whites and blacks in New York was not so simple. In part because of an African influence often conveyed by African-born West Indian migrants, the process of acculturation did not create an exact replica of the dominant culture. Smith and Dunlap were certainly well aware that more than skin color distinguished the two races. Even when blacks wore the same clothes and spoke the same language as other inhabitants of the city, they did so in ways that were distinctive. A sense of the difference that I have in mind is best conveyed through the concept of "style," particularly as it has been developed in England in studies focusing on youth subcultures such as those

of the teddy boys, mods, and punks. Here style means the process
by which objects, such as the Edwardian suit of the teddy boy or
the safety pin of the punk, are taken from the dominant culture
and given a new meaning in the context of the subculture.[3] In this
chapter I intend to examine the way New York blacks used style—
through the language they spoke, through the clothes they wore,
and through gesture and bodily movements—to create their own
subculture.

Runaway advertisements provide the major body of evidence that
I will use in this attempt to reconstruct, if only in a limited fashion, the world New York blacks fashioned for themselves. There are
of course problems in relying on such material. Runaways were by
definition a select group, and consequently certain segments of the
black population—in particular males, mulattoes, the young, and
the African and West Indian born—are, as we saw earlier, overrepresented. Possibly as a result of these biases the runaway sample
will tend to magnify and to exaggerate the cultural traits that I intend to argue are the constituent elements of the New York black
style. But as we are unlikely to come up with sources that are any
more revealing, historians must either attempt, however tentatively,
to piece such fragmentary and difficult material together or write
these blacks even farther out of American history.[4] At the very least,
a close analysis of the runaway advertisements, buttressed by insights from other sources, should reveal one end of the spectrum
of black stylistic behavior in and around New York City at the end
of the eighteenth century and help us to understand that New York
blacks did not enter their freedom in a vacuum but as people with
a cultural life-style that made them distinct.

INCREASINGLY, historians of the black experience have recognized
the vital role that language played in culture, but their attention has
been directed mainly at the South. Gerald Mullin used the ability
of Virginian runaway slaves to speak English as an indicator of
their degree of acculturation. Peter Wood, in his pioneering study
of colonial South Carolina, concluded that it would be difficult to
overestimate the importance of Gullah in the formation of black
culture on the tidewater plantations.[5] Charles Joyner has gone a step
further and placed language at the center of his analysis of black

culture on Waccamaw Neck, South Carolina, in the 1850s. Joyner argues that the process of creolization—a linguistic term meaning the convergence of two or more languages into an essentially new native tongue—can be used as a paradigm for understanding Afro-American culture. The English contribution to this language was principally lexical, the African contribution mostly grammatical. Anything but static, this creole language continued to be influenced by English and various African languages. Applied to culture, the concept of creolization enabled Joyner to focus on the unconscious grammatical principles that underpinned black behavior.[6]

The study of the speech of blacks outside the South Carolina tidewater has been left largely to linguists. Though primarily concerned with problems of teaching and communication in the ghettos in the 1960s, William Stewart and J. L. Dillard have sketched the broad outlines of the history of black English in America.[7] It appears that many blacks in New York, as elsewhere on the mainland from Georgia to Nova Scotia, spoke a version of English that Dillard has called, rather inaccurately, a plantation creole. Varieties of black English, Dillard points out, in a warning equally relevant to the study of the black subculture in New York, did not deviate from standard English in an exotic fashion. But although the individual differences might often appear to be of little consequence, cumulatively they were of great importance in revealing the operation of a syntax at variance with that of the whites. Language, like culture, has to be analyzed as a whole, rather than one word at a time.[8] Though Dillard mainly relied on a few literary texts for his evidence, there are numerous other examples of black speech—in the newspapers and almanacs of the 1790s and early 1800s for example.[9] What is clear from these sources is that the use of black speech became a convention that, in the manner of the later minstrel show, allowed whites to satirize various aspects of contemporary life, from political events to the wearing of corsets. Widespread acceptance of this convention strongly suggests that the language of most blacks was perceived to be different from that of white New Yorkers.

Runaway advertisements provide much specific evidence about the language of individual blacks. One in four of the descriptions of runaways in the sample (316 out of 1,232) mentioned the ability of the slaves to speak English. Slaveowners, anxious to identify and reclaim their runaways, tried to categorize them succinctly by references to their "good English" or "broken English," terms that became accepted codes signifying the level of acculturation of the slaves. Of these 316 slaves, 229 or nearly three in four spoke English well or fluently. In 1804, for example, Silas Condit's slave Sharp spoke "good English," and a few years earlier, in 1788, Lewis Mulford's runaway Jacob could, rather unusually for a slave, both "read and speak English remarkably well."[10] Though such statements were almost certainly qualified by an implicit rider that the English being described was good for a black, the language of these slaves was probably close to standard English. Occasionally blacks even incorporated some of the regional dialects into their language: Grotis, who had been brought up on Long Island, was, according to his owner, John Brazier, "yankeyfied in his speech, and likewise slow in his motion."[11] On the other hand more than one in four of the blacks (87 out of 316) were described as using "bad" or "broken" English, or even as being incapable of uttering a single word in the language of their owner. The wording of some of the more detailed advertisements suggests that more was involved than an inability to master the language. Telemaque, for example, spoke "broken English with fluency,"[12] and other runaways were characterized as using a "negro English." It is likely that these blacks spoke a creole language.

Runaway advertisements are particularly effective in drawing attention to the unusually complex linguistic and cultural interaction that occurred in New York. On the mainland, African- and American-born blacks generally came in contact only with a relatively homogeneous English-speaking population. The state of New York, however, was noted for its ethnic diversity and particularly for the large Dutch component in its population. The Dutch in New York City had long been anglicized, but there was a large Dutch-speaking population in the surrounding area, on the western end of Long Island and in New Jersey, who made a living supplying the metropolis with food. These farmers were heavily involved in slavery: in some areas of Kings County on Long Island more than 60 percent of households owned slaves, a rate that would not have been out of place in the South. Slaves from these areas were influenced by Dutch culture, and many were brought up speaking a version of this language. At the very least 75 of the 1,232 runaways were fluent in Dutch.[13]

Not surprisingly, the presence of a Dutch-derived language in
the New York area sometimes made communication between blacks
difficult. In 1744 Alexander Hamilton, a Maryland doctor traveling
for his health, made one of the earliest known attempts to record
a conversation between two blacks. As Hamilton approached New
York, Dromo, his slave, went on ahead to ask the way. Hamilton
rode up and

> found him discoursing a negroe girl, who spoke Dutch to him.
> "Dis de way to York?" says Dromo. "Yaw, dat is Yarikee," said
> the wench, pointing to the steeples. "What devil you say?" re-
> plies Dromo. "Yaw, mynheer," said the wench. "Damne you,
> what you say?" said Dromo again. "Yaw, yaw," said the girl.
> "You a damn black bitch," said Dromo, and so rid on.[14]

Fifty years later similar problems existed. Although the evidence is
not conclusive, it seems that the three-way cultural interaction that
occurred in New York created a situation analogous to twentieth-
century Louisiana. Throughout the eighteenth century the Dutch
influence probably played a similar role to that of French Creole
in Louisiana, complicating and reinforcing the patterns of "negro
English" and delaying the decreolization process.[15] In 1792 John De
Wint's runaway Maria spoke "very broken English and good Negro
Dutch," and there were many other blacks like Maria who were
more fluent in Dutch than in English.[16] Cuff, who ran away from
his owner, Abraham Allen of Hackensack, in 1789, spoke "broken
English as he was brought up in a Dutch family," while thirteen
years later a black named Will, the slave of David Banks of Newark,
spoke "Low Dutch and middling good English, although he frequently gives his words the Dutch accent."[17] This Dutch influence
was particularly important in New York City in the quarter-century
after the Revolution. There had always been a movement of blacks
between the rural and urban areas, with slaves often traveling to the
city to sell their owners' produce; runaway advertisements provide
abundant evidence that many such slaves expected to find refuge
there. In the 1790s and early 1800s, however, freed rural blacks from
the countryside where Dutch culture continued to be significant
moved permanently into the city in large numbers and became an
important part of the rapidly growing urban free black population.
    This pattern was further reinforced by an influx of blacks from

the Caribbean, particularly from Saint Domingue, that occurred at the same time. Many of these blacks, brought in as slaves by émigrés fleeing the great rebellion in the French colony, had only recently been enslaved. In 1802 Nassau, a sixteen-year-old slave belonging to D. C. Dinnies, was described as speaking very broken English as he was "but 18 months from the coast of Africa." The language of such blacks was more African, and possibly some spoke what the linguists have called West African Pidgin English.[18] In 1800 a runaway named Beliour was said to speak a "little in African dialect," and in the same year Henry Spingler advertised that his slave Phillis, who was forty-five years old, African born, and scarred by country marks, spoke with a "mixture of her natural dialect."[19] Quite a few of these blacks, however, had spent enough time in the West Indies to have picked up a European language, usually French. Over the whole period from 1771 to 1805 fifty-six of the runaways were described as speaking French; forty-seven of these slaves, however, absconded between 1791 and 1805. It is therefore not surprising that the surviving records from the New York District Court in the 1790s and early 1800s show that at times an interpreter was needed to translate the testimony of blacks.[20] Some blacks had a smattering of both languages. A Guinea-born black who ran away in 1794 spoke "a little English and a little French."[21] These languages were rather different from the ones spoken by Europeans, as John Lavallier acknowledged in 1805 when he described Joseph, who had originally come from Louisiana, as able to speak both "negro English and negro French."[22] Many other miscreants were bilingual and some were even trilingual. In 1789 Lindor, who called himself a native of the West Indies, was able to speak "pretty good English, French and creole."[23]

The evidence that we possess concerning the language of New York blacks is far from perfect: not only are we forced to rely on runaway advertisements, but also the majority of slaveowners were regrettably silent on the abilities of their runaways to speak English. Nevertheless the evidence can still support the conclusion that there was a variety of black language styles in and around New York City, ranging along a continuum from those who spoke a language close to that of standard English, through creole-speaking blacks, to, at the other end, a few speakers of African languages. The majority of New York blacks were probably clustered near the former, or more acculturated, end of the spectrum, a conclusion that is supported by the evidence from one special use of language, the naming of free blacks and slaves.

Under slavery, New York blacks were often named by their masters and frequently, though not always, were given only one name. Some masters indulged themselves, displaying their classical knowledge in names such as Cato or Caesar, or their sense of humor in names such as Romeo or Pleasant Queen Anne.[24] Black reaction to such thoughtless or calculated humiliation surfaces in the runaway advertisements, which make it clear that many masters expected their slaves to use alternative names when they absconded. Charles Arding, for example, anticipated that his runaway would quickly abandon the appellation Flummary.[25] Such name changing was more than just a matter of disguise, as quite often the master could specify the name likely to be assumed by the slave. Some advertisements even imply that there was tacit acceptance by slaveowners of a dual system of nomenclature, with one name used by the master and the other by the blacks. One runaway, for example, was a "man named Cato but calls himself Curtis Johnson"; another, "named York, calls himself Jacob."[26] The formulaic wording of these notices, with the passive "named" followed by the active "calls himself," underlines the fact that the name bestowed by the master was not necessarily the one used by the blacks.[27]

The preferred names of the runaways provide an interesting guide to the values of the slaves. Generally, the classical and the shortened given names associated with slavery were shunned.[28] Joseph Blackwell's slave Caesar chose "William" and not the diminutive "Will" or "Billy."[29] Similarly, a few advertisements indicate that the desire to assume a surname was a source of tension between slave and master. Theo. Fowler knew his slave as Scip, but "[a]mongst the black people he goes by the name Scipeo Bailey."[30] Surnames were a sign of freedom. Not only did they give slaves a sense of dignity inappropriate to their servile status, but in America's patrilineal culture, surnames also flowed from paternity and so from exclusive marriage (both formally denied to slaves).

It was in this period near the turn of the century that many of the former slaves swelling New York's free black population first acquired a surname, a process that can be studied systematically by using the census records.[31] In the first census in 1790 only the given names of most free blacks were included, with fewer than 15 percent of the small number of the listed free black heads of households having a surname. But by the time of the 1800 census the position had changed. Although there were more than four times as many free black heads of households 94 percent were recorded as having a surname.[32]

What sort of surnames did these blacks choose? A few took the family names of former slaveowners, but the vast majority followed the more normal pattern of the runaways and eliminated all possible connection with slavery. The Dutch were heavily involved in slaveholding in east New Jersey and New York, yet Dutch surnames were rare, a Mingo Roosevelt being a conspicuous exception. A few blacks — New Year Evans, Royal Cromwell, and Hudson Rivers are examples — celebrated their freedom with what Gary Nash has aptly called an "etymological flourish." Some, like the rather more threatening Thomas Paine, took the names of the famous. Overwhelmingly, however, the blacks chose very common and neutral surnames. In 1800 the three most common surnames — Johnson, Williams, and Thomas — accounted for 8.1 percent of the names of all free blacks. In 1810 the top three — Johnson, Williams, and Smith — accounted for nearly 11 percent of all the black names listed in the census. In fact, in 1810 4.5 percent, or about one in twenty-two, of all the heads of free black households had the surname Johnson. Such names were also common among the white population, but to nowhere near the same extent.[33] The use of such surnames probably reflected, in part, the desire for anonymity prevalent among many former slaves, a desire that had helped draw rural blacks to the metropolis. In their choice of names most New York blacks indicated quite realistically that their hopes and aspirations, and particularly their desire to be free, were conceived within the framework of a white world.

Much of the evidence about the language and naming patterns of New York blacks, then, points toward an overall process of acculturation and anglicization. But there is also enough material to suggest that in New York at the end of the eighteenth century the African past of these blacks was still of importance. Even the evidence from the nomenclature of the blacks is not totally one-sided: there were some African given names among the free blacks — the 1800 census included a few blacks, not mulattoes, such as Quaquo

Minnisee and Cuffee McClair, with African day names—and there
are more in the runaway advertisements.[34] Similarly, a significant
minority of New York blacks spoke a language that was nearer the
African end of the linguistic spectrum. In 1799 Augustus Griffin
of Oysterponds, Long Island, commenting on the language of two
elderly Africans, noted that John Tatoo "talked much plainer english than Jack, whose pronounciation was much broken."[35] What
is significant in this case is that Jack had been brought over from
Africa fifty-five years previously. In part because of the influx of
African and West Indian blacks in the 1790s, but also because of the
complicating influence of the Dutch culture in the city's hinterland,
New York continued to provide an environment where blacks such
as Jack could use a variety of language styles.

LINGUISTIC DIVERSITY was only one aspect of black cultural distinctiveness. In 1794 William Strickland noted that one of the few
features that distinguished New York City from England was the
number of blacks in the streets, blacks "who may be seen of all
shades till the stain is entirely worne out."[36] Strickland's striking
metaphor raises the important issue of the blacks' appearance. Historians who have touched on this subject have, like Strickland, generally confined themselves to the matter of color, over which blacks
had no control. Yet in other areas blacks quite consciously shaped
the visual impact of their bodies. They did so to a significant extent
through the clothes they wore, a matter that historians have usually
examined in a different context—as an example of paternalism or as
a measure of the physical well-being of slaves.[37] Here, I would like
to try to examine the cultural meaning of the appearance of New
York blacks.[38]

   For the most part free blacks and slaves wore garments similar
to those of the rest of the working population of New York. The
clothing free blacks were able to afford, and that given to slaves by
their masters, was usually made of cheap homespun material. Typically, males wore either overalls or a pair of trousers, a shirt, often a
waistcoat, and a jacket. Females usually wore a petticoat and a dress
or gown.[39] Yet in spite of the limitations imposed by their position at
the bottom of society many blacks took a great deal of care of, and
pride in, their attire. Some slaveowners made precisely this point

in their runaway notices. A twenty-four-year-old runaway named Cuff, for example, "took with him a great variety of good cloaths is fond of dress and always appears very clean and smart." Other advertisements, such as that for Isaac Varian's slave Molly, who was "very fond of dress," help to suggest the important role clothing played in the lives of some blacks.[40]

Clothing helped to distinguish the hours of work from the hours of leisure and, in the case of those still enslaved, the master's time from the slave's. Many New York blacks, such as the West Indian runaway Lindor, who was "very fond of dressing well on some occasions," took the utmost pains with their appearance before going out, often to the dancing cellars uptown in and around Bancker Street.[41] In 1802 Isabella Thomas, a free black woman living on James Street, asked her servant girl friend Elizabeth Mumford "to lend her a handkerchief to wear to a dance."[42] Similarly, important occasions like funerals and weddings required a certain standard of dress. When Frank Pero, the slave of David Dixon, was about to be married, he borrowed some thirty dollars from his friend John Jackson, who was also a slave. Having paid the minister a dollar for the marriage ceremony, he spent the rest of the money on a blue coat, a pair of blue pantaloons, a waistcoat, a pair of shoes, and a hat from a shop at the corner of Ann Street and Broadway.[43]

Evidence concerning New York blacks is scarce and hard to come by, but quite strikingly, surviving fragments are commonly centered around clothing, further suggesting the importance of apparel to the blacks. Extra money that slaves occasionally received from their masters, earned by doing odd jobs in their free time, or stole was often spent on clothes. In 1798, when Samuel Robertson was convicted of stealing twelve dollars from Elizabeth Graham, his mistress, he confessed that he had used the money to buy a jacket, a hat, and a pair of shoes from a black woman who lived on Cliff Street.[44] Although most of our knowledge of this facet of black life stems, as in this case, from court records, such behavior illustrates a broader pattern.

As the last example shows, blacks did not have to spend their money in white-owned stores. A thriving market in secondhand clothes operated in New York. In 1804, for instance, a free black named John Young bought a pair of corduroy pantaloons from James Anderson, a black seaman, for two dollars.[45] Not surprisingly, the original source of some of the merchandise could not bear too close a scrutiny; judging from the surviving court records, the crime of which both free blacks and slaves most commonly were accused was the theft of either clothing or material. In another incident in 1804, a free black named John Thomas stole a blue coat from the door of John Sickle's tailor shop on the corner of Nassau Street and Maiden Lane.[46] Many cases brought before the courts involved servants, either free or slave, taking advantage of their position to steal goods from their masters. Sally Smith, a young indentured black girl, confessed to taking numerous items of clothing from John O'Brien while she was living in his house as a servant.[47] Sometimes blacks stole the garments for their own use, but generally items of clothing were quickly resold, being only marginally less negotiable than currency. In 1804 Nancy, a recently freed black, took a striped cotton apron from a clothesline on Bedlow Street and exchanged it for some food in a cook shop on East George Street.[48]

Even though many New York blacks wore the same items of clothing as whites, the overall effect was often distinctive. Just as with the creole language, the vocabulary, or individual piece of clothing, may have been similar, but the grammar was different. Of course, such nuances are extremely hard to pick up nearly two hundred years later, but reactions such as those of Dunlap and Smith to the "flippantly" dressed black have occasionally survived. In 1796 when Ned Cornell, an indentured black of about sixteen, absconded from the almshouse, the advertisement placed in the *Argus* included the comment that he "also took with him a long fine coat and a pair of boots which he usually wears together and makes a fairly grotesque appearance."[49] In this case, as in the Dunlap and Smith episode, the combination of clothes obviously offended white sensibilities.

West Indian blacks, who were either African born or had lived in a culture heavily influenced by African patterns, were often noted for their distinctive appearance. Peggy, a thirty-seven-year-old runaway who was born on Saint Eustatius, was described as dressing "in the style of the West Indian wenches."[50] This West Indian "style" may well have incorporated combinations of clothes and colors considered unusual within Euro-American culture, but the feature that attracted particular comment was the use of a handkerchief as a head covering. To extend the analogy with language, this was a case where blacks broadened the vocabulary of clothing. Charles Joyner, in his study of South Carolina, concludes that the white bandanna handkerchiefs commonly worn by women reflected continuity with African tradition and demonstrated a high degree of personal pride.[51] Undoubtedly they fulfilled a similar function in New York. There, however, colors other than white were used: Suke generally wore a black handkerchief; Isabella wore a striped one on her head and another on her neck.[52] Handkerchiefs were often part of male attire also. Lindor "commonly wears an handkerchief on his head, according to the West India fashion."[53] Another characteristic associated with black Caribbean males was the use of one or two earrings. Wanno, a twenty-two-year-old runaway, had a ring in one of his ears and, according to his owner John Taylor, "looks and talks like a West India negro."[54]

The most important factor contributing to the distinctive appearance of the blacks was their hair. In descriptions of runaways slaveowners often emphasized the physical difference between white and black by using terms like "wool" or "negro hair." Orlando Patterson has argued in *Slavery and Social Death* that, contrary to the common view, it was not so much color but hair type that became critical as a mark of servility in the Americas.[55] If this was the case in New York, it makes the distinctive way in which blacks styled their hair all the more significant. Mingo, who ran away in 1801, wore his hair either "tied or friz'd below his hat."[56] A runaway named Jim had "a very bushy woolly head, and often plats and ties his hair."[57] Henry Rogers's opinion that Abraham, his twenty-eight-year-old slave, was a "surly looking fellow" was probably due at least in part to the way the runaway wore his hair "much bushed out."[58]

Blacks living in and around New York styled their hair in a variety of ways. Some wore it tied in a queue. Abraham Polhemus's runaway, a mulatto named Jack, gathered his hair behind, and Daniel, who absconded from a ship in 1804, wore "his hair tied in a short tight queue."[59] A few had almost all of their hair in plaits. An eighteen-year-old runaway named Morris wore "his hair about 4 inches long, which is usually plaited and turned up."[60] Others, like Calvin Woodruff's Jack, wore their earlocks braided.[61] According to Thomas De Voe, there was a pattern to these different styles. In his description of the breakdown contests on Catharine Slip, De Voe states that the New Jersey blacks, mostly from Tappan, wore their forelocks plaited with tea leads, while the Long Island blacks had their hair in a queue tied with a dried eelskin.[62] The evidence from the runaway advertisements is, however, rather more confused and does not support such a neat geographic division.

In the case of black females, it is clear that these hairstyles reflected continuity with an African past. Styles like that of Mary, who wore her hair "braided in several parts of her head," or Caty, who had short hair but wore "a braid of long hair tied to her head," were common in West Africa.[63] The situation with black males is more complex. According to Melville Herskovits, black males in West Africa and the New World cut their hair close and wore it unparted. The sole exception that Herskovits noted was what he termed the "local elaboration" in Dutch Guiana, where males also braided their hair.[64] It may be little more than coincidence, but it is interesting to note that such styles in New York were generally associated not with the Africans and West Indians, but with American-born blacks, particularly those brought up in the Dutch areas.

There are indications that the cultural meaning of some black male hairstyles was ambiguous, paradoxically hinting on the one hand at both difference from whites and an African past, and on the other, at similarity and acculturation. Again, it is the language used to describe hair arrangement that provides the clue. The hair of some blacks, often derogatorily termed "wool" to emphasize its difference from that of whites, appears to have been styled to resemble the appearance of the fashionable wigs worn by the New York elite. Jim, a twenty-five-year-old runaway who lived near the Hoboken ferry opposite New York and could speak both Dutch and English fluently, tied "his hair in a cue, with an eel skin, but sometimes combs it about his head and shoulders in the form of a whig."[65] Even the word *queue*, which was frequently used to describe the plaited hair of blacks, was closely associated with wigs. De Voe used the same language to describe the hair of the Long Islanders when he noted that they sometimes "combed it about their head and shoulders, in the form of a wig, then all the fashion."[66] Of course there was one crucial difference — the color of the blacks' hair was the opposite of the light-colored wigs. That being so, the effect must at times have been dangerously close to parody. Consider for example the appearance of Jack Jackson, who ran away in 1794. Like many other blacks, Jackson was fond of clothes and often dressed in a "rather beauish" fashion, wearing his "wool turn'd up and a comb behind." According to a postscript to the runaway advertisement, he had been seen on the Kingsbridge Road resplendent in a "dark blue coat, with a velvet collar and his *wool powdered.*"[67]

New York blacks functioned as bricoleurs, to borrow Claude Lévi-Strauss's term, drawing from both their African past and the dominant Euro-American culture to create an appearance that, considered as a whole, was new.[68] If, as in the case of hairstyles, individual components of this style revealed an ambiguity of meaning, the effect was magnified in the overall visual impact of the blacks. In part this originated from the juxtaposition and contrast between a coiffured head of hair or a bandanna handkerchief and clothes worn by whites. But it also derived from context. Blacks who wore expensive clothing or fashioned their hair to resemble a wig gave a fresh meaning to these items. This was particularly so when they dared to take on the trappings of the elite. The effect cannot have been too dissimilar from that of the mods in the 1960s, whose smart dress, according to one commentator, was all the more disturbing because of the impression they gave of "actors who are not quite in their places,"[69] a perception that, in the case of New York blacks, was heightened by their color. In spite of, or because of, the talk of manumission and the eventual passage of the gradual abolition act, well dressed and in particular expensively dressed blacks caused considerable unease in the white population.

In part such unease resulted from white suspicions of the means blacks had employed to obtain the clothes. In the wake of the widespread yellow fever epidemics in the 1790s many whites believed that blacks had taken advantage of their supposed immunity to the disease to pillage the partly evacuated cities. John Bernard, an actor, recorded that it was commonly remarked in Philadelphia that "you might know where the fever had been raging by the Sunday dress of the black women."[70] Undoubtedly, similar comments circulated in New York. The assumed link between crime and smartly dressed blacks has been a constant theme in Afro-American history, and in this period, as we have seen, there was at least some justification for these views. But more was involved. Consider for example the language used to describe the free wife of one runaway slave: she had "lately been detected thieving—is noted for gay and fanatical dressing—and is particularly fond of wearing feathers in her hat."[71]

Similar behavior in a white woman could hardly have drawn such a reaction. Free blacks, such as this woman, or slaves, such as the runaway described as "genteely dressed,"[72] represented an inversion of the natural order, with all the attendant dire consequences. Even in pre-Freudian times, the black apprehended on Long Island after assaulting a white woman can hardly have allayed such fears by claiming that his name was Handsome Dick.[73]

In 1941 Melville Herskovits pointed out that such routine activities as walking, sitting, talking, laughing, singing, and dancing presented a very promising field for the study of African retentions in the New World. Referring to a film he had made of an Ashanti ceremony in the village of Asokore, Herskovits noted that the dance he recorded was virtually identical to the Charleston.[74] Long before Herskovits made his suggestion some slaveowners were well aware of the nature of the distinctive motor behavior of blacks. Nowhere is this more obvious than in descriptions in runaway advertisements of the way blacks walked. In 1785, for example, Sam, according to his owner James Hepburn of New Windsor, Middlesex County, New Jersey, had "a very wide remarkable walk."[75] Will, another Jersey runaway, "throws out his feet and toes in a singular manner walking very wide."[76] At times it is possible to see white New Yorkers grappling with the language as they try to capture the alien movement of their slaves: Tom "spraddled"; another black named Tom walked "loggy leaning forward"; and Nat had a "remarkable waddle in his walk, which makes him appear as if he was wounded in the hips."[77] Other phrases such as "a kind of rocking in his walk" or a "peculiar swing in his gait" suggest the rhythmic harmony that Kenneth Johnson would later characterize as one of the most important elements in the walk of blacks in the ghettos.[78] However, descriptions such as "an awkward swaggering walk" or "walks with a strut" probably resonate most strongly with twentieth-century readers.[79]

Other body movements and mannerisms are also described in the advertisements, often in terms that reflect quite acute observation of the ways in which blacks conducted themselves in conversation. This was the context with which slaveowners were most familiar and within which readers of their advertisements would most likely come across the runaways. For some slaves, obviously adept at managing encounters with whites, descriptions took the form of a warning. Cudjo was "a fellow of great cunning and may forge a very plausible story on the road, as he is much addicted to lying."[80] A few blacks were noted for their aggressive demeanor. Hannah had a "loud voice and saucy tongue."[81] Scip, whose attitude toward his master was obviously disdainful, spoke "with a great deal of boldness and impertinence and walks with a strut."[82]

Other blacks had similar attitudes but exhibited them in a more subtle fashion. Movements of the body, in particular the eyes, gave slaves and free blacks an opportunity to release their hostility non-verbally, and thus to avoid retribution. By their very nature such strategies only rarely enter what, for the eighteenth century anyway, is predominantly a white historical record. But with the aid of some studies of black behavior in twentieth-century ghettos it is possible to detect an occasional example of nonverbal hostility. Such studies make clear that one of the better-known ways of expressing impudence and disapproval of an authority figure is "rolling the eyes." This movement is usually preceded by a stare, but not one in which there is eye contact. After the stare the eyes are moved from one side of the socket to the other, the eyelids being lowered, and the movement being always away from the other person. Sometimes the eye movement is accompanied by a slight lifting of the head or a twitching of the nose.[83] Consider, then, the case of Bill, who ran away in 1804. He "casts his eyes to the ground and raises them when spoken to, at which time he has a habit of inclining his head rather one side."[84] Although these descriptions are not identical there is at least the possibility that Bill may have been engaged in something rather akin to "rolling the eyes." This movement may or may not have had its origins in West Africa, but it is generally recognized as being distinctively black. Kenneth Johnson has pointed out that nonblacks often fail to recognize it and see its significance.[85]

If some blacks on occasion were able to handle whites with ease, others had difficulty. Cuff, who spoke both Dutch and broken English, was likely if "cross examined" to stutter considerably, and Han had a "remarkable impediment in her speech so as to be scarcely understood when answering questions."[86] The most common mannerism attributed to the runaways in their confrontations with whites was a "down look." Pompy used "plain English but when spoken to has a down look," and Aaron was "a remarkable man having a down look scarce to be equalled, and always appears as if his eyes were half shut."[87] The "down look" of these blacks contrasts markedly with the behavior of white convicts as described in runaway advertisements. Roger Ekirch in his discussion of convict runaways in the Chesapeake cites examples that all emphasize eye contact: "bold staring"; "hard looking man"; "very remarkable way of staring anyone in the face."[88] Although this is hardly conclusive it does tend to suggest that the black "down look" has cultural origins and is not just an example of lower-class behavior. This refusal, or inability, of many slaves to look their masters or other whites in the eye during verbal encounters reinforced prejudices about the unreliability and shiftiness of the blacks, an attitude conveyed in one owner's observation that his slave Charles had a "down sultry look."[89]

But slaveowners may well have been misinterpreting the behavior of their slaves. For blacks in both West Africa and twentieth-century America, avoiding eye contact with people is a nonverbal way of acknowledging their power and authority. Herskovits pointed out that averting the eyes, and even the face, when speaking to elders or other respected persons was an element of African etiquette.[90] Historians are by now very familiar with the important role African-derived traditions played in resistance to slavery, but it is just as likely that patterns of accommodation were influenced by similar factors. Slaves like Nero, who was "very obliging, stammers a little when he speaks, [and] has rather a down look"[91] in the presence of his owner, may well have been drawing on an African-derived gestural vocabulary to acknowledge their subordinate position.[92]

The relationship between white and black in New York was never one of complete subservience. The above-mentioned Nero may well have been acquiescent, as his owner suggested, in his day-to-day dealings with whites, but the master's opinion survives only through the agency of, ironically, a runaway advertisement. Nor, it should be added, was the relationship one of constant antagonism. Black behavior was far too complex to be neatly bundled into categories labeled "accommodation" or "resistance." The style constructed, both consciously and subconsciously, by New York blacks fully demonstrates these complexities.

THE AMBIGUITIES of this black style are well illustrated in the following example. Among the Forman Papers in the New-York Historical Society is a small notebook kept by an unknown white woman living near Mount Pleasant in Westchester County.[93] The notebook is part diary and part letter and appears to have been designed to inform a friend of the details of local life. From November 1798 to August 1799 there are regular, but very brief, entries, mostly about the weather. Occasionally there are more detailed references to local elections or a funeral. But in 1799 there is a change: "As there is nothing extroriadary throug [the] present month September," the author writes, "I shall omit & fill up [the] remainder with a short History of Sambo's manuvers through [the] Winter." What follows is a ten-page attempt by a white to understand the behavior of her slave named, ironically enough, Sambo.[94]

Until New Year's Eve Sambo had been a "fine boy" who stayed close at home and was "very Submissive." This behavior induced his owners to allow him, like other blacks in the country, to have a little liberty. Just before the holidays they had "new sized him from stem to stern (as the Old man said he did by Harriet when he left her in Ireland)." Fitting out Sambo with new clothes reinforced the slaveowners' paternalistic self-image. The treatment of the occasion by the author, particularly the bracketed reference to the family's history, was designed both to show that Sambo was treated like a member of the family and to allow the narrator to organize, and try to comprehend, Sambo's later actions within the framework of the parable of the prodigal son. Sambo was given permission to go out in his new clothes but was "beged & requested" to behave himself and return "according to orders." But Sambo did not come home until daylight the next morning. Further, his owners later found out that he had not only stolen two geese but also tried to incriminate Old Cato, a free black living in the vicinity, by leaving the severed heads on his doorstep. The miscreant was taken to court and received a hundred lashes the same day.

Sambo had been earning some extra money by going every morning and evening to a Mr. OBrion's, where he cut firewood and foddered the cattle. One Sunday he "mounted his new Cloathes" and collected the twelve shillings OBrion owed him for four weeks work, which combined with two dollars he had won at a "husslin frollick" gave him more than enough money for a "bout." Sambo was not sighted until the next evening, when the "Doctor," who appears to have been the writer's husband, was "lucky enough to nab him" in Mount Pleasant and took him home.

> The Doctr. then reversed [the] Parable in Scripture & Strip'd him of his new Apperral put on his rags & shaved his head which he had for some time before taken much pains in plaiting & tying his wool in which he had a considerable cue.

Although some of the document appears to be missing at this point, it seems that Sambo had also stolen something on this latest expedition. He was taken to court again and sentenced to seventy lashes "well laid on." Soon afterward he was caught breaking into Josiah West's mill in search of cider. The court was "collected" by a little after sunrise, and "Sixty lashes was his Doom." Sambo then ran away for a time but eventually returned. He remained at home for a few weeks but was "unsetled & good for little." This period of relative quiet ended when Sambo was caught breaking into Conover's store looking for liquor. He was sent to the courthouse and put in the dungeon for a month. On each of the following three Saturdays Sambo was given a hundred lashes. After the last of these whippings he was taken home where, according to the writer: "Sambo with his sore back was that evening as happy as a lord, has ever since been contented at home & more faithfull than he ever was before. has played no tricks since so far we flatter ourselves a reformation has taken place at length. God grant it may continue for I am sure we have beene well worne out with trouble with him."

What is striking about this case is the extent to which the writer, in an attempt to understand the slave's behavior, centers the narrative around Sambo's appearance and in particular his clothes. In fact, the struggle for control of Sambo took place quite literally over his body. To Sambo's owners the clothes represented their benevolence and paternalism. It is clear, though we are viewing the incident through the eyes not of Sambo but of his owner, that his garments meant something different to Sambo. The slave's new clothes and carefully styled hair had become closely associated in his mind with good times, drinking, and gambling. It is significant that, in an effort to control his recalcitrant behavior, Sambo's body was scarred by the whip. When that failed the doctor not only took back the clothes, but went to the extraordinary length of shaving Sambo's head, a symbolic castration that also had biblical antecedents.[95]

Finally, after receiving a fearful number of lashes, Sambo returned like the prodigal son to the fold, "more faithful" than before. But his return was as abrupt and unexplained as his departure. In the last sentence in the notebook the writer attributes Sambo's deleterious behavior to his thirst for rum and surmises that "if he should drink too deep he dont care what he does & may play his old pranks over again." However, as the opaque penultimate sentence — "It is true when the Holy Days come on the White Folks are right down mad as the Negro song says" — and, indeed, the perceived need to record the episode on paper, suggest, the writer found Sambo's love of drink an unsatisfactory, or at least incomplete, explanation. Though removed by two hundred years from "Sambo's manuvers" and compelled to view them through the eyes of an anonymous white woman, we may at least speculate that the symbolic importance of clothing and appearance was something that, if whites and blacks did not fully articulate, they nevertheless understood.

THE MATERIAL collected and analyzed in this chapter clearly demonstrates the existence of a style among *some* New York blacks. But the often fragmentary and difficult nature of such material requires that more general conclusions must be cautiously and tentatively worded. On any particular facet of black behavior — language, clothing, hairstyles, or bodily movements, for example — most owners of runaways made no comment at all. Only a minority, for example, described the way in which their runaways walked. But silence concerning the walking styles of other blacks does not mean that those styles were identical to those of whites. Undoubtedly there existed a range of walking styles among the blacks, with some being merely less extravagant or exaggerated than others. They are not to be ignored on that account. The hallmarks of any style are variation and change, and it is hardly surprising that uniformity in walking, or in any other facet of black behavior, did not exist.

What, then, was the importance of the black style detected here? Unlike most blacks in the South, New York blacks were not sheltered from the full impact of white culture by the existence of a plantation community.[96] By the early years of the nineteenth century they were being drawn inexorably into the emerging working class of the city. As evidenced by the increasingly violent tenor of race relations and particularly the riots of the 1830s, whites were scarcely enamored of this prospect. Although their reaction was less aggressive, New York blacks, through the way they spoke, the manner in which they dressed, and their bodily movements and gestures, made it clear that they viewed this process, if not with hostility, then at least with ambivalence. Not only did the style of New York blacks reinforce, albeit in a less dramatic form than in the South, continuities with their African past and differentiate black from white in the rapidly changing metropolis, but as we have seen it was also of considerable importance in the day-to-day lives of black New Yorkers attempting to live in a white world. The piecing together of fragmentary and often neglected evidence and the patient teasing out of its significance reveal that the story of New York blacks was not simply one of rapid and wholesale assimilation, but more one of creative adaptation to an often hostile world.

Epilogue

WE ARE NOW in a better position to understand that there were grounds for the "Citizen of Color" to claim, in 1814, that blacks were advancing under the protection of New York's liberal laws and that "we dwell in safety and pursue our honest callings, none daring to molest us, whatever his complexion or circumstances." At the end of the Revolution the vast majority of New York City blacks were slaves: three decades later the black population of the metropolis had nearly trebled and most of its members were now free. The blacks themselves had played a large role in this transformation and, aided by an infusion of Africans and West Indians, were creating their own distinctively black way of life in the metropolis. Not only was slavery gradually ending, but also free blacks were flourishing in the urban environment. Blacks attended the African Free School and the African Church, and as recently as 1813 it was said that a city election had been decided by black votes.[1] Blacks were being given, too, a chance to pursue their "honest callings" and, to an extent not seen in any other northern urban center, were finding their way into the ranks of the artisans and petty proprietors. The satisfaction that came from knowing they were playing an important role in the life of the city, the air of celebration that marked the black response to the Committee of Defense's call for help, seemed justified despite the clear danger presented by the English.

Yet with the benefit of hindsight it is clear that the position of blacks was precarious and that the undoubted gains of those decades were based on fragile ground. Several small, but nevertheless disturbing, incidents boded ill for the future. One evening in September 1801, Louis Cooney, a black man who ran a small shop adjoining

the museum on Greenwich Street, was accosted by three men of
the watch. Roughly, they ordered him home. Cooney retorted that
he was home and showed them his door. The watch began shov-
ing him against the window of the house. Determined to stand up
for his rights, Cooney insisted that it was not ten o'clock; he was a
free man and would go inside when he pleased. Eventually William
Waldron, the keeper of the museum, went to Cooney's rescue, but
by that time he had been badly bashed, particularly about the kid-
neys. That night he lost a lot of blood through his penis.[2] A similar
incident occurred in June 1803. Louis Hart, a black hairdresser who
lived on Water Street, was standing outside his house when Lewis
Humphrey, a mariner, began beating the black woman who lived in
Hart's cellar. The woman pushed the sailor away and ran into the
cellar, and when Humphrey then attempted to open the door with
a knife Louis Hart protested. Humphrey then asked Hart "if the
House was his to which he replied that it was whereupon he immediately struck the deponent who not being willing to fight with
him went into the House." Humphrey left but returned half an hour
later with six shipmates. They broke into the cellar and assaulted
the black woman. They then moved upstairs into Hart's house, beat
him with sticks, smashed some of his property, and stole a quantity of silver teaspoons.[3] The reactions of the black men involved in
these assaults may have been different, but the significance of the
violence was the same: poor whites from the neighborhood had attacked those free blacks who, as evidenced by their ownership of
property, were managing to get ahead.[4]

The critical days of August 1814 were one of the last occasions
on which the optimism of the "Citizen of Color" was plausible.
New York blacks had become free just as the social organization of
the city was undergoing a fundamental transformation. The movements of blacks from their masters' houses to the cellars and from
slave to wage labor are telling examples of the dislocations that accompanied this transformation. Initially some blacks prospered in
the uncertain transition between the gradual ending of slavery and
the onset of what Sean Wilentz has labeled "metropolitan industrialization." But over the ensuing decades the opportunities available
to this first generation of free blacks, opportunities that they had
eagerly exploited, would disappear under a relentless barrage of
discrimination and prejudice, a dismal story that has been treated

comprehensively elsewhere.[5] Increasingly blacks became part of the emerging working class, and the heightened competition for jobs between blacks and whites would have its inevitable result. The violence directed at Hart and Cooney was unusual at the turn of the century. By the 1820s and 1830s it had become common.

Notes

Introduction

1. August Meier and Elliot Rudwick, *Black History and the Historical Profession, 1915–1980* (Urbana, Ill., 1986). For an excellent critical account of the recent writing on blacks and slavery, see Peter Novick, *That Noble Dream: The "Objectivity Question" and the American Historical Profession* (New York, 1988), 472–91.

2. Papers presented at the conference at Purdue University in October 1983 have been published in Darlene Clark Hine, ed., *The State of Afro-American History: Past, Present, and Future* (Baton Rouge, La., 1986).

3. Meier and Rudwick, *Black History and the Historical Profession*, 144.

4. On the impact of the WPA interviews, see, for example, Norman R. Yetman, "Ex-Slave Interviews and the Historiography of Slavery," *American Quarterly* 36 (1984): 181–210.

5. Henry S. Cooley, *A Study of Slavery in New Jersey* (Baltimore, 1896); A. Judd Northrup, "Slavery in New York: A Historical Sketch," *State Library Bulletin* 4 (1900): 243–313. See also the studies of other northern colonies: William Johnston, *Slavery in Rhode Island, 1755–1776* (Providence, 1894); George H. Moore, *Notes on the History of Slavery in Massachusetts* (New York, 1866); Bernard C. Steiner, *History of Slavery in Connecticut* (Baltimore, 1893); Edmund Raymond Turner, *The Negro in Pennsylvania: Slavery—Servitude—Freedom, 1639–1861* (Washington, D.C., 1911).

6. See Simeon F. Moss, "The Persistence of Slavery and Involuntary Servitude in a Free State (1685–1866)," *Journal of Negro History* 35 (1950): 289–314; Edwin Olson, "Social Aspects of Slave Life in New York," *Journal of Negro History* 26 (1941): 66–77; Leo H. Kirsch, Jr., "The Negro and New York, 1783–1865," *Journal of Negro History* 16 (1931): 382–473; Edgar J. McManus, *A History of Negro Slavery in New York* (Syracuse, N.Y., 1966); Edgar J. McManus, *Black Bondage in the North* (Syracuse, N.Y., 1973).

7. McManus, *Black Bondage in the North*, x.

8. There have been a few local studies of slavery. For a solid study of Long Island, see Richard Shannon Moss, "Slavery on Long Island: Its Rise and Decline During the Seventeenth Through Nineteenth Centuries" (Ph.D. diss., Saint John's University, 1985). See also Ralph Ireland, "Slavery on Long Island: A Study in Economic Motivation," *Journal of Long Island History* 6 (1966): 1–12; Thomas J. Davis, "Three Dark Centuries Around Albany: A Survey of Black Life in New York's Capital City Area Before World War I," *Afro-Americans in New York Life and History* 7 (1983): 7–23; Thomas J. Davis, "New York's Long Black Line: A Note on the Growing Slave Population, 1626–1790," ibid., 2 (1978): 41–59; Francis D. Pingeon, "Slavery in New Jersey on the Eve of Revolution," in *New Jersey in the American Revolution*, Papers Presented at the First Annual New Jersey History Symposium 1969 (Trenton, N.J., 1970): 41–53. For New York City, see Thomas J. Davis, "Slavery in Colonial New York City" (Ph.D. diss., Columbia University, 1974); Thomas J. Davis, "'These Enemies of Their Own Household': A Note on the Troublesome Slave Population in Eighteenth-Century New York City," *Journal of the Afro-American Historical and Geneaological Society* 5 (1984): 133–47.

9. See Kenneth Scott, "The Slave Insurrection in New York in 1712," *New-York Historical Society Quarterly* 45 (1961): 43–74. The most detailed and useful account of 1741 is Thomas J. Davis, *Rumor of Revolt: The "Great Negro Plot" in Colonial New York* (New York, 1985). See also Ferenc M. Szasz, "The New York Slave Revolt of 1741: A Re-examination," *New York History* 48 (1967): 215–30; Leopold S. Launtiz-Schurer, Jr., "Slave Resistance in Colonial New York: An Interpretation of Daniel Horsmanden's New York Conspiracy," *Phylon* 41 (1980): 137–52. One other incident in Albany has received attention: Don R. Gerlach, "Black Arson in Albany, November 1793," *Journal of Black Studies* 7 (1977): 301–12.

10. For some useful comments on the distortions resulting from concentrating on rebellions and revolutions rather than on the more prosaic forms of everyday resistance, see James C. Scott, *Weapons of the Weak: Everyday Forms of Peasant Resistance* (New Haven, Conn., 1985), xv–xvi and passim.

11. McManus, *Black Bondage in the North*, x.

12. David Brion Davis, *The Problem of Slavery in the Age of Revolution, 1770–1823* (Ithaca, N.Y., 1975); Winthrop D. Jordan, *White over Black: American Attitudes Toward the Negro, 1550–1812* (Chapel Hill, N.C., 1968).

13. In addition to the relevant chapters in the work cited earlier, see Edgar J. McManus, "Antislavery Legislation in New York," *Journal of Negro History* 46 (1961): 207–16. More generally see Leon F. Litwack, *North of Slavery: The Negro in the Free States, 1790–1860* (Chicago, 1961), 3–29; Arthur Zilversmit, *The First Emancipation: The Abolition of Slavery in the*

North (Chicago, 1970); A. Leon Higginbotham, *In the Matter of Color: Race and the American Legal Process—The Colonial Period* (New York, 1978).

14. As well as the work previously cited, see Edwin Olson, "The Slave Code in Colonial New York," *Journal of Negro History* 39 (1944): 147–65; Carl Nordstrom, "The New York Slave Code," *Afro-Americans in New York Life and History* 4 (1980): 7–25; William M. Wiecek, "The Statutory Law of Slavery and Race in the Thirteen Mainland Colonies of British America," *William and Mary Quarterly*, 3d ser., 34 (1977), 258–80.

15. Vivienne Kruger's dissertation gives a comprehensive account of the black family and is a valuable contribution. See Vivienne L. Kruger, "Born to Run: The Slave Family in Early New York, 1626–1827" (Ph.D. diss., Columbia University, 1985). Ira Berlin has also provided a brief overview of the outlines of black culture in all of the northern colonies. Although, as the reader will discover, I disagree on a few points, I must also confess to considerable admiration for the way Berlin, well aware of the sorts of issues being canvassed by historians of the South, has fashioned a synthesis out of a rather unhelpful historiography. See Ira Berlin, "Time, Space, and the Evolution of Afro-American Society on British Mainland North America," *American Historical Review* 85 (1980): 44–78.

16. Jessica Kross, *The Evolution of an American Town: Newtown, New York, 1642–1775* (Philadelphia, 1983). This book is only the most glaring example. Similar criticisms could be made of the work of many other historians.

17. Thomas J. Davis, ed., *The New York Conspiracy by Daniel Horsmanden* (Boston, 1971).

18. Gary B. Nash, "Slaves and Slaveowners in Colonial Philadelphia," *William and Mary Quarterly*, 3d ser., 30 (1973): 223–56; Gary B. Nash, " 'To Arise Out of the Dust': Absalom Jones and the African Church of Philadelphia, 1785–95," in Gary B. Nash, *Race, Class, and Politics: Essays on American Colonial and Revolutionary Society* (Urbana, Ill., 1986), 323–55; Gary B. Nash, *Forging Freedom: The Formation of Philadelphia's Black Community, 1720–1840* (Cambridge, Mass., 1988). Nash has also published two more-general articles, although they are based on his extensive knowledge of Philadelphia. See Gary B. Nash, "Forging Freedom: The Emancipation Experience in the Northern Seaports, 1775–1820," in Ira Berlin and Ronald Hoffman, eds., *Slavery and Freedom in the Era of the American Revolution* (Charlottesville, Va., 1982), 3–48; Gary B. Nash, "The Social Evolution of Preindustrial Cities, 1700–1820: Reflections and New Directions," *Journal of Urban History* 13 (1987): 115–45. See also Jean R. Soderlund, *Quakers and Slavery: A Divided Spirit* (Princeton, N.J., 1985), a much broader study than its title might suggest; Jean R. Soderlund, "Black Women in Colonial Pennsylvania," *Pennsylvania Magazine of History and Biography* 107

(1983): 49–68. For the later period, see Julie Winch, *Philadelphia's Black Elite: Activism, Accommodation, and the Struggle for Autonomy, 1787–1848* (Philadelphia, 1988).

19. At this point I should warn the reader that, as mentioned in the Preface, the New York City in this book is "loosely defined": wherever the material has allowed me to do so I have also drawn evidence from the city's immediate hinterland. My primary concern is with the city itself, but the life of the city was inextricably tied to the surrounding country-side. This observation becomes particularly important when one looks at slavery. New York City was situated in the middle of the heaviest slave-owning region north of the Mason-Dixon line: blacks from the surround-ing countryside came to the city to sell their masters' or their own produce in the markets, to seek out the company of friends and relatives, and to avoid their masters when they ran away. It therefore makes little sense to take New York City out of its context — its hinterland on the rest of Manhattan Island, the western end of Long Island, Staten Island, and the neighboring counties of New Jersey that came within the orbit of the metropolis.

20. See William D. Piersen, *Black Yankees: The Development of an Afro-American Subculture in Eighteenth-Century New England* (Amherst, Mass., 1988). There is also a lot of work on blacks and slavery in the northern colonies and states in progress at the moment.

21. Armstead L. Robinson, "The Difference Freedom Made: The Emancipation of Afro-Americans," in Hine, ed., *State of Afro-American History*, 51–74, especially 51.

22. See, for example, Eric Foner's exemplary *Nothing But Freedom: Emancipation and Its Legacy* (Baton Rouge, La., 1983).

23. The quantity and quality of recent work about New York City are remarkable. See Hendrik Hartog, *Public Property and Private Power: The Corporation of the City of New York in American Law, 1730–1870* (Chapel Hill, N.C., 1983); Sean Wilentz, *Chants Democratic: New York City and the Rise of the American Working Class, 1788–1850* (New York, 1984); Peter George Buckley, "To the Opera House: Culture and Society in New York City, 1820–1860" (Ph.D. diss., State University of New York at Stony Brook, 1984); Graham Russell Hodges, *New York City Cartmen, 1667–1850* (New York, 1986); Christine Stansell, *City of Women: Sex and Class in New York, 1789–1860* (New York, 1986); Thomas Bender, *New York Intellect: A His-tory of Intellectual Life in New York City, from 1750 to the Beginnings of Our Own Time* (New York, 1987); Paul A. Gilje, *The Road to Mobocracy: Popular Disorder in New York City, 1763–1834* (Chapel Hill, N.C., 1987).

A Note to the Reader

1. For a much more detailed account of the problems of using this tax list, see Herbert S. Klein and Edmund P. Willis, "The Distribution of Wealth in Late Eighteenth-Century New York," *Histoire Sociale—Social History* 18 (1985): 259–83.

2. See Sharon V. Salinger and Charles Wetherell, "Wealth and Renting in Prerevolutionary Philadelphia," *Journal of American History* 71 (1985): 826–40.

3. Bruce Martin Wilkenfield, *The Social and Economic Structure of the City of New York, 1695–1796* (New York, 1978), 158–62.

Chapter One

1. William Strickland, *Journal of a Tour in the United States of America, 1794–1795*, ed. J. E. Strickland (New York, 1971), 43–44, 63–64, 228–30.

2. The totals from the 1771 census are collected in Edgar J. McManus, *A History of Negro Slavery in New York* (Syracuse, N.Y., 1966), 199. Carl Bridenbaugh, ed., "Patrick M'Robert's Tour Through Parts of the North Provinces of America," *Pennsylvania Magazine of History and Biography* 59 (1935): 142.

3. Ira Rosenwaike, *Population History of New York City* (Syracuse, N.Y., 1972), 15.

4. All the figures from the 1790, 1800, and 1810 censuses come from my own count. For a more detailed account of the origin of these figures, see A Note to the Reader.

5. The 1789 tax list excluded the propertyless poor. See Herbert S. Klein and Edmund P. Willis, "The Distribution of Wealth in Late Eighteenth-Century New York," *Histoire Sociale—Social History* 18 (1985): 259–83.

6. Gary B. Nash, "Slaves and Slaveowners in Colonial Philadelphia," *William and Mary Quarterly*, 3d ser., 30 (1973): 247–48; James A. Henretta, "Economic Development and Social Structure in Colonial Boston," ibid., 22 (1965): 85.

7. The estimates of the total numbers in these categories come from the 1790 directory. By my count there were 248 merchants, 605 retailers, 163 professionals, and 1,620 artisans.

8. Historians have made a much better job of analyzing the position of eighteenth-century white women in Philadelphia than in New York, and I have drawn on their work. See Carole Shammas, "The Female Social Structure of Philadelphia in 1775," *Pennsylvania Magazine of History and Biography* 107 (1983): 69–83; Claudia Goldin, "The Economic Status of Women in the Early Republic: Quantitative Evidence," *Journal of Interdis-*

ciplinary History 16 (1986): 375–404. More generally, see Mary Beth Norton, "The Evolution of White Women's Experience in Early America," *American Historical Review* 89 (1984): 593–619 and the work cited in her footnotes.

9. See Betsy Blackmar, "Re-walking the 'Walking City': Housing and Property Relations in New York City, 1780–1840," *Radical History Review* 21 (1979): 131–48.

10. David J. Jeremy, ed., *Henry Wansey and His American Journal, 1794* (Philadelphia, 1970), 137; Strickland, *Journal of a Tour*, 64.

11. *American Minerva*, March 15, 1797; *New York Evening Post*, April 2, 1805.

12. On the role of blacks in the maritime work force, see Ira Dye, "Early American Merchant Seafarers," *Proceedings of the American Philosophical Society* 120 (1976): 349; Gary B. Nash, "Forging Freedom: The Emancipation Experience in the Northern Seaports, 1775–1820," in Ira Berlin and Ronald Hoffman, eds., *Slavery and Freedom in the Era of the American Revolution* (Charlottesville, Va., 1982), 8–10.

13. *Daily Advertiser*, September 7, 1801, November 13, 1794; *Argus*, September 24, 1795; *Minerva*, May 26, 1796.

14. See Alfred Young, "The Mechanics and the Jeffersonians: New York, 1789–1801," *Labor History* 5 (1964): 247–76; Alfred F. Young, *The Democratic Republicans of New York: The Origins, 1763–1797* (Chapel Hill, N.C., 1967); Howard B. Rock, *Artisans of the New Republic: The Tradesmen of New York City in the Age of Jefferson* (New York, 1979); Sean Wilentz, *Chants Democratic: New York City and the Rise of the American Working Class, 1788–1850* (New York, 1984); Graham Russell Hodges, *New York City Cartmen, 1667–1850* (New York, 1986).

15. Wilentz, *Chants Democratic*, 36.

16. For a brief account of opposition from tradesmen to the use of slaves in skilled trades in the first half of the century, see Richard B. Morris, *Government and Labor in Early America* (New York, 1965 [orig. pub. 1946]), 182–83.

17. The comparison with Philadelphia is most instructive. Jean Soderlund dates the entry of Philadelphia artisans into slaveholding to the period from 1730 to 1750. In the years just prior to the Revolution, as Gary Nash has shown, nearly half of the city's slaves were owned by artisans or men associated with maritime enterprises. In an excellent article Sharon Salinger outlines the decline in usage of all forms of bound labor by artisans from approximately the middle of the eighteenth century. I would suggest that in New York City, with its long tradition of using slaves rather than indentured servants, artisan use of slave labor probably peaked after midcentury and then began to decline along the lines argued by Salinger

for Philadelphia. Jean R. Soderlund, *Quakers and Slavery: A Divided Spirit* (Princeton, N.J., 1985), 63–64; Nash, "Slaves and Slaveowners in Colonial Philadelphia," 249–50; Sharon V. Salinger, "Artisans, Journeymen, and the Transformation of Labor in Late Eighteenth-Century Philadelphia," *William and Mary Quarterly*, 3d ser., 40 (1983): 62–84; see also Sharon V. Salinger, *"To Serve Well and Faithfully": Labor and Indentured Servants in Pennsylvania, 1682–1800* (New York, 1987).

18. Wilentz, *Chants Democratic*, 38–40. See also Rock, *Artisans of the New Republic*, 129–32.

19. The list of members at the incorporation of the General Society is in Thomas Earle and Charles T. Congdon, eds., *Annals of the General Society of Mechanics and Tradesmen of the City of New York, from 1785 to 1880* (New York, 1882), 22–23. I compared these members with my lists of the 1790 and 1800 slaveholders and their occupations, drawn from the manuscript censuses and the city directories, in order to obtain the figures in the text.

20. *American Minerva*, August 3, 1796; *Daily Advertiser*, November 29, 1798, September 9, 1800; *Argus*, February 1, 1797; *Daily Advertiser*, February 1, 1797.

21. In 1786 males composed 42.6 percent of the total black population, or 896 of 2,103 (free blacks were not differentiated from slaves in this census). In early 1806, figures from the city council revealed that 864, or 44.0 percent, of 1,960 free blacks and 818, or 39.9 percent, of the 2,048 slaves were male. Both counts were taken after particularly disruptive events — in 1786 the city was still recovering from the British occupation during the Revolution, and the 1806 census was designed to assess the impact of the yellow fever epidemic and the consequent mass departures on New York City's population. Nevertheless, it seems clear that females outnumbered males in both the slave and free populations in this period, conforming to the patterns found in other American cities in the nineteenth century. (McManus, *History of Negro Slavery in New York*, 200; Enumeration of the Inhabitants of the City of New York, Census File 1806, Records of the Common Council, Municipal Archives, New York City). For other nineteenth-century cities, see Leonard P. Curry, *The Free Black in Urban America, 1800–1850: The Shadow of the Dream* (Chicago, 1981), 8–12.

22. For an account of the role of black women in a plantation society, see Carole Shammas, "Black Women's Work and the Evolution of Plantation Society in Virginia," *Labor History* 26 (1985): 5–28. Also see the excellent Elizabeth Fox-Genovese, *Within the Plantation Household: Black and White Women of the Old South* (Chapel Hill, N.C., 1988).

23. *Daily Advertiser*, December 10, 1790.

24. Again the comparison with Philadelphia is instructive. Jean Soder-

lund has argued that in colonial Philadelphia some occupational groups such as innkeepers and widows were more likely than others such as craftsmen and merchants to own female slaves. Sharon Salinger argues that later in the eighteenth century the changing sexual composition of Philadelphia's indentured servants provides evidence of changing work roles. Toward the end of the century artisans owned fewer servants (down from 46.6 percent of servant owners in 1767 to 13.3 percent in 1791) and merchants owned more (up from 33.3 percent in 1767 to 60.7 percent in 1791). In the same period females increasingly constituted a larger percentage of all indentured servants. Similarly, in Baltimore at the end of the eighteenth and beginning of the nineteenth century, as Charles Steffen has shown, the shipbuilders, the heaviest users of slave labor, usually owned male slaves. In the case of New York, I would suggest that there was a sexual division of black labor and that artisans or ship captains, for example, would have owned a higher percentage of black males than merchants or professionals. Jean R. Soderlund, "Black Women in Colonial Pennsylvania," *Pennsylvania Magazine of History and Biography* 107 (1983): 60; Soderlund, *Quakers and Slavery*, 63; Salinger, "Artisans, Journeymen, and the Transformation of Labor in Late Eighteenth-Century Philadelphia," 66–68; Charles G. Steffen, *The Mechanics of Baltimore: Workers and Politics in the Age of Revolution, 1763–1812* (Urbana, Ill., 1984), 39.

25. For an account of the importance of renting and a caution about some of the shortcomings of measuring wealth rather than income, see Sharon V. Salinger and Charles Wetherell, "Wealth and Renting in Prerevolutionary Philadelphia," *Journal of American History* 71 (1985): 826–40.

26. *Abstracts of Wills on File in the Surrogate's Office, New York City, 1665–1800*, 17 vols. (New York, 1892–1909), 14:294, 308.

27. *Recollections of Samuel Breck* (Philadelphia, 1877), 90.

28. François Alexandre Frédéric, duc de La Rochefoucauld-Liancourt, *Travels Through the United States of North America, the Country of the Iroquois, and Upper Canada in the Years 1795, 1796, 1797*, 2 vols. (London, 1799), 2:457–58.

29. On the mixed neighborhoods of the colonial city, see Carl Abbott, "The Neighborhoods of New York City, 1760–1775," *New York History* 55 (1976): 35–53. On the spatial transformations of the city, see Blackmar, "Re-walking the 'Walking City' "; Elizabeth Strother Blackmar, "Housing and Property Relations in New York City, 1780–1850" (Ph.D. diss., Harvard University, 1980); Allan R. Pred, *The Spatial Dynamics of U.S. Urban-Industrial Growth, 1800–1914: Interpretive and Theoretical Essays* (Cambridge, Mass., 1966).

30. Timothy Dwight, *Travels in New York and New England*, ed. Barbara M. Solomon, 4 vols. (Cambridge, Mass., 1969), 3:200, 226. On Long

Island more generally, see Ralph H. Gabriel, *The Evolution of Long Island* (Port Washington, N.Y., 1960 [orig. pub. 1921]).

31. "Memoirs of an Emigrant: The Journal of Alexander Coventry M.D." (Typescript prepared by the Albany Institute of History and Art and the New York State Museum, 1978), 69, 145.

32. On New Jersey, see Peter O. Wacker, "Patterns and Problems in the Historical Geography of the Afro-American Population of New Jersey, 1726–1860," in Ralph E. Ehrenberg, ed., *Pattern and Process: Research in Historical Geography* (Washington, D.C., 1975), 25–71 and especially the maps on 44–47; Peter O. Wacker, *Land and People: A Cultural Geography of Preindustrial New Jersey: Origins and Settlement Patterns* (New Brunswick, N.J., 1975). The appendix in this last book (at 416–17) conveniently collects the totals from the 1790, 1800, and 1810 New Jersey censuses.

33. U.S. Bureau of the Census, *A Century of Population Growth: From the First Census of the United States to the Twelfth, 1790–1900* (Washington, D.C., 1909), 281–91. Unfortunately, there is no figure for Virginia because the census schedules have been lost. The overall figure for New York State was 14.2 percent.

34. Strickland, *Journal of a Tour*, 41.

35. U.S. Bureau of the Census, *Century of Population Growth*, 116–24, especially table 51 on 123, 274–75. Of late there has been some controversy over the exact way to use surnames to estimate the numerical importance of ethnic groups in the population. Most of this has been centered on the alleged influence of the Celts in the South. A seemingly interminable series of articles between Forrest McDonald and Grady McWhiney on the one hand and Rowland Berthoff on the other has argued the point. The latest entrant in the lists includes a full bibliography. See Rowland Berthoff, "Celtic Mist over the South," *Journal of Southern History* 52 (1986): 523–46 and the inevitable rejoinder on 547–50. There has also been some reworking of the Dutch figures, particularly by Thomas L. Purvis. See Thomas L. Purvis, "The European Origins of New Jersey's Eighteenth-Century Population," *New Jersey History* 100 (1982), 15–31; Thomas L. Purvis, "The European Ancestry of the United States Population," *William and Mary Quarterly*, 3d ser., 41 (1984): 85–101; Thomas L. Purvis, "The National Origins of New Yorkers in 1790," *New York History* 67 (1986): 133–53. Even if all agree eventually and the figures change, I do not think that will alter the basic point: in 1790 inhabitants of Dutch origin were more likely to own slaves than those from any other important ethnic group. On the Dutch in New York more generally, see Alice P. Kenney, *Stubborn for Liberty: The Dutch in New York* (Syracuse, N.Y., 1975); Eric Nooter and Patricia U. Bonomi, eds., *Colonial Dutch Studies: An Interdisciplinary Approach* (New York, 1988).

36. Strickland, *Journal of a Tour*, 74.

37. La Rochefoucauld-Liancourt, *Travels Through the United States*, 2:233.

38. John Ezell, ed., *The New Democracy in America: Travels of Francisco de Miranda in the United States* (Norman, Okla., 1963), 99.

39. La Rochefoucauld-Liancourt, *Travels Through the United States*, 2:216, 1:369.

40. Strickland, *Journal of a Tour*, 163.

41. Kenneth Roberts and Anna M. Roberts, trans. and eds., *Moreau de St. Méry's American Journey, 1793–1798* (Garden City, N.Y., 1947), 272.

42. J. P. Brissot de Warville, *New Travels in the United States*, ed. Durand Echeverria (Cambridge, Mass., 1964), 227–28.

43. Edward Countryman, *A People in Revolution: The American Revolution and Political Society in New York, 1760–1790* (Baltimore, 1981), 248–49. Arthur Zilversmit has demonstrated that Dixon Ryan Fox's contention that the passage of the 1799 act was due to a vote along party lines is incorrect. Zilversmit concludes that abolition was not identified with either party but, in fact, split the parties. See Arthur Zilversmit, *The First Emancipation: The Abolition of Slavery in the North* (Chicago, 1970), 182–83.

44. Quoted in Zilversmit, *First Emancipation*, 160. On a number of occasions in the 1790s the opposition of the Dutch to attempts to end slavery had wider political ramifications. In 1792, when John Jay, former president of the Manumission Society, was running for governor, John Wynkoop expected that the "*Dutch Inhabitants*" of Ulster County, "a great majority" of whom "possess *many slaves*," would "probably vote against him for that reason alone." Similarly, in 1799, a few days after the passage of the Gradual Manumission Act, a minor dispute arose over one Van Vechten's comment that "the Yankees had already obtained too much influence in our Government and that it was high time the Dutch people should rally against them." John Wynkoop to Peter Van Schaack, February 23, 1792, Van Schaack Papers, Library of Congress; Van Vechten to John Sanders, April 9, 1799, Letterbook for 1799, Sanders Family Papers, New-York Historical Society.

45. Quoted in Kenney, *Stubborn for Liberty*, 215.

46. Isaac Weld, *Travels Through the States of North America and the Provinces of Upper and Lower Canada During the Years 1795, 1796, and 1797*, 2 vols. (London, 1800), 2:372.

47. Diary of Dr. Samuel Thompson of Setauket, Long Island, New York Public Library.

48. Claude G. Bowers, *The Diary of Elbridge Gerry, Jr.* (New York, 1927), 50.

49. *New York Journal*, January 8, 1789; *Greenleaf's New York Journal*,

April 26, 1794, July 29, 1796; *New Jersey Journal*, April 4, 1792; *Centinel of Freedom*, April 24, 1807.

50. Nash, "Slaves and Slaveowners in Colonial Philadelphia," 244–46. See also Alan Tully, "Patterns of Slaveholding in Colonial Pennsylvania: Chester and Lancaster Counties, 1729–1756," *Journal of Social History* 6 (1973), 284–305.

51. La Rochefoucauld-Liancourt, *Travels Through the United States*, 2:450.

Chapter Two ·

1. Thomas M. Doerflinger, *A Vigorous Spirit of Enterprise: Merchants and Economic Development in Revolutionary Philadelphia* (Chapel Hill, N.C., 1986), 335–44; Hendrik Hartog, *Public Property and Private Power: The Corporation of the City of New York in American Law, 1730–1870* (Chapel Hill, N.C., 1983), 82–100. See also Jacob M. Price, "Economic Function and the Growth of American Port Towns in the Eighteenth Century," *Perspectives in American History* 7 (1974): 123–86; Michael Kammen, "'The Promised Sunshine of the Future': Reflections on Economic Growth and Social Change in Post-Revolutionary New York," in Manfred Jonas and Robert V. Wells, eds., *New Opportunities in a New Nation: The Development of New York After the Revolution* (Schenectady, N.Y., 1982), 109–43.

2. Thomas C. Cochran, "The Business Revolution," *American Historical Review* 89 (1974), 1449–66; Thomas C. Cochran, *Frontiers of Change: Early Industrialism in America* (New York, 1981); Allan R. Pred, *Urban Growth and the Circulation of Information: The United States System of Cities, 1790–1840* (Cambridge, Mass., 1973).

3. Sean Wilentz, *Chants Democratic: New York City and the Rise of the American Working Class, 1788–1850* (New York, 1984), 12–13 and passim. See also Sean Wilentz, "Artisan Republican Festivals and the Rise of Class Conflict in New York City, 1788–1837," in Michael Frisch and Daniel J. Walkowitz, eds., *Working Class America: Essays on Labor, Community, and American Society* (Urbana, Ill., 1983), 37–77.

4. On street numbering, see William Strickland, *Journal of a Tour in the United States of America, 1794–1795*, ed. J. E. Strickland (New York, 1971), 62–63.

5. On the poor, see Raymond A. Mohl, "Poverty in Early America, A Reappraisal: The Case of Eighteenth-Century New York City," *New York History* 50 (1969): 5–27; Raymond A. Mohl, *Poverty in New York, 1783–1825* (New York, 1971); Robert E. Cray, "White Welfare and Black Strategies: The Dynamics of Race and Poor Relief in Early New York, 1700–1825," *Slavery and Abolition* 7 (1986): 273–89.

6. Hartog, *Public Property and Private Power,* 156 and passim.

7. Wilentz, *Chants Democratic.*

8. Strickland, *Journal of a Tour,* 63, 229.

9. Thomas J. Davis, "Slavery in Colonial New York City" (Ph.D. diss., Columbia University, 1974), 191, 212. Edgar J. McManus asserts that slavery in New York after the Revolution was "an obsolete and expensive system of labor." See Edgar J. McManus, "Antislavery Legislation in New York," *Journal of Negro History* 46 (1961): 214. Similarly, Simeon Moss, writing of New Jersey, claims that the "spirit of independence" played no small part in the "decline" of slavery in that state and that it was "gratifying" to see a "more uniform decline" in the slave population in the fifty years after 1790, conveniently glossing over the fact that, as is apparent from his own tables, the slave population did not reach its peak until 1800. See Simeon F. Moss, "The Persistence of Slavery and Involuntary Servitude in a Free State (1685–1866)," *Journal of Negro History* 35 (1950): 298, 302–3.

10. Sidney I. Pomerantz, *New York, an American City, 1783–1803: A Study of Urban Life* (New York, 1965), 221.

11. See, however, Vivienne L. Kruger, "Born to Run: The Slave Family in Early New York, 1626–1827" (Ph.D. diss., Columbia University, 1985), 724–84. Kruger argues that the New York Manumission Society played a vital role in manumissions. She has located a "sample" of 2,045 recorded manumissions for the six southern counties of New York. However, as best as I can make out, she has not found any sources for New York City other than those used here (see 1010–16 for her account of her sources). Even using her figures for all six counties, a minimum of 83 percent of manumissions occurred after the passage of the 1799 act, and, in fact, the majority occurred after 1810. The gross statistics of New York City's slave population—an increase from 2,057 in 1790 to 2,534 in 1800—offer little support for an argument that the New York Manumission Society had much impact, at least before 1800.

12. Harry B. Yoshpe, "Record of Slave Manumissions in New York During the Colonial and Early National Periods," *Journal of Negro History* 26 (1941): 78–104, especially 86.

13. *Abstracts of Wills on File in the Surrogate's Office, New York City, 1665–1800,* 17 vols. (New York, 1892–1909), 15:78, 128.

14. Ibid., 96.

15. Ibid., 14:300.

16. Ibid., 137.

17. For an illuminating discussion of the application of "personalism" to slavery in the South, see Suzanne Lebsock, *The Free Women of Petersburg: Status and Culture in a Southern Town, 1784–1860* (New York, 1984), 112–45,

especially 137–41. In many ways, though, men in New York who manumitted slaves exhibited the characteristics that Lebsock views as part of "personalism" — particularly in the way they chose to free personal favorites and kept others in bondage (which resembles the way white Petersburg women discriminated between their heirs).

18. *Abstracts of Wills*, 15:110–12.

19. Gary Nash noted a similarly high rate of turnover among urban slaveowners in the tax lists of 1767 and 1769 in Philadelphia. Perhaps slaves were a more flexible form of property in an urban environment than many historians have realized. Gary B. Nash, "Slaves and Slaveowners in Colonial Philadelphia," *William and Mary Quarterly*, 3d ser., 30 (1973): 243.

20. Rosenwaike cites an estimate that as many as four thousand may have come to New York. Ira Rosenwaike, *Population History of New York City* (Syracuse, N.Y., 1972), 22. Also see John Baur, "International Repercussions of the Haitian Revolution," *Americas* 26 (1970), 394–418.

21. *Argus*, June 9, 1795.

22. For an excellent account of the origins and workings of the Philadelphia merchant community, which probably did not differ that much from New York, see Doerflinger, *Vigorous Spirit of Enterprise*.

23. Of the 121 merchants in 1800 who could be traced back to 1790, 50 were retailers and 10 of that 50 had no slaves in 1790.

24. The list of stockholders is from Henry W. Domett, *A History of the Bank of New York, 1784–1884, Compiled from Official Records and Other Sources at the Request of the Directors* (New York, 1884), 136–39. Females and institutions were left out for the purposes of comparing the list with the 1790 and 1800 censuses.

25. The list of subscribers to the New York Manufacturing Society was published in the *Daily Advertiser*, March 17, 1789. These subscribers were then matched with the 1790 and 1800 censuses. See also Thomas E. V. Smith, *The City of New York in the Year of Washington's Inauguration: 1789* (Riverside, Conn., 1972 [orig. pub. 1889]), 108–9.

26. Doerflinger, *Vigorous Spirit of Enterprise*, 283–334.

27. See Sharon V. Salinger, "Colonial Labor in Transition: The Decline of Indentured Servitude in Late Eighteenth-Century Philadelphia," *Labor History* 22 (1981): 165–91; Sharon V. Salinger, "Artisans, Journeymen, and the Transformation of Labor in Late Eighteenth-Century Philadelphia," *William and Mary Quarterly*, 3d ser., 40 (1983): 62–84; Sharon V. Salinger, *"To Serve Well and Faithfully": Labor and Indentured Servants in Pennsylvania, 1682–1800* (New York, 1987).

28. See Wilentz, *Chants Democratic*; Betsy Blackmar, "Re-walking the 'Walking City': Housing and Property Relations in New York City, 1780–1840," *Radical History Review* 21 (1979): 131–48.

29. On bakers, see Allan R. Pred, *The Spatial Dynamics of U.S. Urban-Industrial Growth, 1800–1914: Interpretive and Theoretical Essays* (Cambridge, Mass., 1966), 205–7; Howard B. Rock, "The Perils of Laissez-Faire: The Aftermath of the New York Bakers' Strike of 1801," *Labor History* 17 (1976): 372–87; Howard B. Rock, *Artisans of the New Republic: The Tradesmen of New York City in the Age of Jefferson* (New York, 1979), 183–201; Wilentz, *Chants Democratic*, 139–40.

30. Rock, *Artisans of the New Republic*, 205–7, 210–11; Wilentz, *Chants Democratic*, 137–39.

31. Lebsock, *Free Women of Petersburg*, 26–27.

32. Claudia Goldin concludes that in Philadelphia in the 1790s there was a high degree of probability that the widow would assume the deceased husband's business or trade. See Claudia Goldin, "The Economic Status of Women in the Early Republic: Quantitative Evidence," *Journal of Interdisciplinary History* 16 (1986): 398. See also Lisa Wilson Waciega, " 'A Man of Business': The Widow of Means in Southeastern Pennsylvania, 1750–1850," *William and Mary Quarterly*, 3d ser., 44 (1987): 40–64.

33. It is difficult to work out the extent to which New York blacks were kidnapped or sold illegally to the South. The Reports of the Standing Committee of the New York Manumission Society (the surviving papers are in the New-York Historical Society) contain many instances where they took action to prevent either of these occurrences. Every now and again warnings were published in the newspapers suggesting that blacks should be wary. On March 23, 1786, for example, "Justica" warned in the *Daily Advertiser* that Captain Tinker and the sloop *Maria* were back in the North River. Previously Tinker had allegedly offered a black two crowns to carry a jug of vinegar to the ship in the hope of kidnapping him. Similarly, in 1801 there was a major riot when a Madame Volunbrun tried to sell twenty blacks to the South (this will be dealt with more fully later). Undoubtedly many whites were successful in such activities—but it is impossible even to guess how many blacks were affected.

34. By far the best account of the impact of the economy on the merchants is contained in Doerflinger, *Vigorous Spirit of Enterprise*.

35. *Daily Advertiser*, January 10, 1791.

36. The best accounts of this process are Blackmar, "Re-walking the 'Walking City' "; Elizabeth Strother Blackmar, "Housing and Property Relations in New York City, 1780–1850" (Ph.D. diss., Harvard University, 1980).

37. Timothy Dwight, *Travels in New York and New England*, ed. Barbara M. Solomon, 4 vols. (Cambridge, Mass., 1969), 3:431.

38. François Alexandre Frédéric, duc de La Rochefoucauld-Liancourt, *Travels Through the United States of North America, the Country of the Iro-*

quois, and Upper Canada in the Years 1795, 1796, 1797, 2 vols. (London, 1799),
2:457–58.

39. On the separation of work from residence, see Pred, *Spatial Dynamics of U.S. Urban-Industrial Growth,* 207–9.

40. Pred used the 1800 city directory and counted 115 persons with a
place of residence different from the workplace. My figure of 94 slaveowners with separate houses comes from the 1799, 1800, and 1801 directories, and not just the 1800 directory. Further, individuals who either
owned or rented buildings next to one another—for example, 35 and 37
Broad Street—were included, as this would still enable a clear distinction
to be made between work and residence.

41. Blackmar, "Re-walking the 'Walking City,'" 143.

42. Charles H. Haswell, *Reminiscences of an Octogenarian of the City of
New York (1816–1860)* (New York, 1897), 69. Unfortunately, historians of
domestic service have little to say on the early part of the nineteenth
century and are much more informative for later periods. See Daniel E.
Sutherland, *Americans and Their Servants: Domestic Service in the United
States from 1800 to 1920* (Baton Rouge, La., 1981).

43. Edmund Phillip Willis, "Social Origins of Political Leadership in
New York City from the Revolution to 1815" (Ph.D. diss., University
of California, Berkeley, 1967), 59–61. The link between slaveowning and
shipbuilding certainly existed in New York, but it was nowhere near as
important as in Baltimore. On Baltimore, see Charles G. Steffen, *The Mechanics of Baltimore: Workers and Politics in the Age of Revolution, 1763–1812*
(Urbana, Ill., 1984), 39–41.

44. Willis, "Social Origins of Political Leadership in New York City,"
59–61.

45. Probably the best account of the legislation ending slavery in New
York and New Jersey is contained in Arthur Zilversmit, *The First Emancipation: The Abolition of Slavery in the North* (Chicago, 1970), 139–200.

46. As we shall see later, many of these blacks actually negotiated an
early release from their owners. Regardless of this, the legislature had
given the owners the option of retaining the services of these blacks until
they reached their twenties.

47. *Daily Advertiser,* August 5, 16, September 1, 1788.

48. Yoshpe, "Record of Slave Manumissions in New York," 83.

49. Ibid., 98.

50. There is, of course, a vast literature on the end of slavery in the
South, and much of it is excellent. See, for example, Barbara Jeanne Fields,
*Slavery and Freedom on the Middle Ground: Maryland During the Nineteenth
Century* (New Haven, Conn., 1985); Eric Foner, *Nothing but Freedom:
Emancipation and Its Legacy* (Baton Rouge, La., 1983); Eric Foner, *Recon-*

struction: America's Unfinished Revolution, 1863–1877 (New York, 1988). See also the works cited in Foner's very useful historiographical article, "Reconstruction Revisited," *Reviews in American History* 10 (1982): 82–100.

51. For a very detailed account of the workings of the act and the way in which the provisions about abandoning infant children were exploited by slaveowners, see Kruger, "Born to Run," 818–86.

52. For a number of excellent essays on the impact of industrialization on the countryside, see Steven Hahn and Jonathan Prude, eds., *The Countryside in the Age of Capitalist Transformation: Essays in the Social History of Rural America* (Chapel Hill, N.C., 1985). See also Allan Kulikoff, "The Transition to Capitalism in Rural America," *William and Mary Quarterly*, 3d ser., 46 (1989): 120–44. For an interesting account of Long Island and the impact of New York City in the first half of the nineteenth century, see Elizabeth Johns, "The Farmer in the Works of William Sidney Mount," *Journal of Interdisciplinary History* 17 (1986): 257–81.

53. Rosenwaike, *Population History of New York City*, 28–32.

54. Kenneth Roberts and Anna M. Roberts, trans. and eds., *Moreau de St. Méry's American Journey, 1793–1798* (Garden City, N.Y., 1947), 172.

55. Peter O. Wacker, "Patterns and Problems in the Historical Geography of the Afro-American Population of New Jersey, 1726–1860," in Ralph E. Ehrenberg, ed., *Pattern and Process: Research in Historical Geography* (Washington, D.C., 1975), 25–71 and especially 44–47.

56. On Queens, see Joseph S. Tiedemann, "Queens County, New York, Quakers in the American Revolution: Loyalists or Neutrals?" *Historical Magazine of the Protestant Episcopal Church* 52 (1983): 215–27; Joseph S. Tiedemann, "Communities in the Midst of the American Revolution: Queens County, New York, 1774–1775," *Journal of Social History* 18 (1984), 57–58; Joseph S. Tiedemann, "A Revolution Foiled: Queens County, New York, 1775–1776," *Journal of American History* 75 (1988): 417–44; Jessica Kross, *The Evolution of an American Town: Newtown, New York, 1642–1775* (Philadelphia, 1983).

57. Rosenwaike, *Population History of New York*, 31.

Chapter Three

1. John Jay to Egbert Benson, September 18, 1780, in Richard B. Morris, ed., *John Jay: The Making of a Revolutionary, Unpublished Papers, 1745–1780* (New York, 1975), 823.

2. Winthrop D. Jordan, *White over Black: American Attitudes Toward the Negro, 1550–1812* (Chapel Hill, N.C., 1968), 335, 485.

3. See, for example, Jordan, *White over Black*; David Brion Davis, *The*

Problem of Slavery in the Age of Revolution, 1770–1823 (Ithaca, N.Y., 1975);
Duncan J. MacLeod, *Slavery, Race, and the American Revolution* (Cambridge, 1974).

4. Jordan, *White over Black*, 429–81.

5. This chapter is based on my reading of an extensive range of material
from Pennsylvania, New York, and New Jersey. I read the extant issues of
all magazines published between 1770 and 1800: *American Magazine* (1787–
1788); *American Monthly Review* (1795); *American Moral and Sentimental
Magazine* (1797–1798); *American Museum* (1787–1792); *American Universal
Magazine* (1797–1798); *Arminian Magazine* (1789–1790); *Christian Scholar's
and Farmer's Magazine* (1789–1791); *Columbian Museum* (1793); *Dessert to the
True American* (1798–1799); *Experienced Christian's Magazine* (1796–1797);
Lady's Magazine (1792–1793); *Lady and Gentleman's Pocket Magazine of Literary and Polite Amusement* (1796); *Literary Miscellany* (1795); *Literary Museum*
(1797); *Medical Repository* (1797–1800); *Methodist Magazine* (1797–1798);
Monthly Magazine and American Review (1799–1800); *Monthly Military Repository* (1796–1797); *New Jersey Magazine* (1786–1787); *New York Magazine*
(1790–1797); *New York Weekly Magazine* (1796–1797); *Philadelphia Magazine
and Monthly Review* (1799); *Philadelphia Minerva* (1795–1798); *Philadelphia
Monthly Magazine* (1798); *Porcupine's Political Censor* (1796–1797); *Rural
Casket* (1798); *Rural Magazine* (1798–1799); *Theological Magazine* (1796–
1799); *Time Piece* (1797–1798); *United States Christian Magazine* (1796);
United States Magazine (1794); *Universal Asylum and Columbian Magazine*
(1786–1792); *Weekly Magazine of Original Essays* (1798–1799). The number of newspapers published in these states was vast; I was able to read
only a selection: *Albany Centinel* (incomplete issues, 1800–1806); *Albany
Register* (1793–1794); *American Minerva* (1793–1796); *Argus* (1795–1797);
Centinel of Freedom (1796–1810); *Daily Advertiser* (1785–1805); *Federalist;
New Jersey Gazette* (1798–1800); *Greenleaf's New York Journal* (1794–1800);
Hudson Weekly Gazette (1787); *Jersey Chronicle* (incomplete issues, 1795–
1796); *Long Island Courier* (1799–1803); *Minerva* (1796–1797); *New Jersey
Gazette* (1777–1786); *New Jersey Journal* (1789–1793); *New York Evening Post*
(1801–1805); *New York Gazette and Weekly Mercury* (1771–1783); *New York
Journal* (1786–1794); *Rivington's New York Gazette* (varying titles, 1773–
1783). I read all the almanacs published in these states between 1770 and
1800 listed in Charles Evans, comp., *American Bibliography*, and reproduced
in the microprint series *Early American Imprints*. For the years 1801–1810
I looked at all the almanacs for these states in the Rare Book Room of the
New York Public Library. In addition I made my way, painfully, through
all the novels published in America before 1810 listed in Lyle H. Wright's
American Fiction and reproduced in the microfilm series *American Fiction,*

1774–1905. Finally, I read or skimmed every item published in New Jersey, New York, and Pennsylvania between 1770 and 1800 reproduced in the microcard edition of Evans not already listed above.

6. For an analysis of the *Columbian Magazine*, see Lawrence J. Friedman, *Inventors of the Promised Land* (New York, 1975), 3–43. For an analysis of the *New York Magazine*, see David Paul Nord, "A Republican Literature: A Study of Magazine Reading and Readers in Late Eighteenth-Century New York," *American Quarterly* 40 (1988): 42–64.

7. Frank Luther Mott, *A History of American Magazines, 1741–1850* (Cambridge, 1957), 39.

8. Mott, *History of American Magazines,* 100–3; Nord, "Republican Literature," 47.

9. "Observations on the Gradation in the Scale of Being Between the Human and Brute Creation. Including Some Curious Particulars Respecting Negroes," *Columbian Magazine,* January and February 1788. Virtually every piece in a magazine, newspaper, or almanac referred to in the rest of this chapter was reprinted in at least one other publication; however, to save space only one citation is given. For a more detailed consideration of these racial ideas, see Jordan, *White over Black,* 438–542; John C. Greene, "The Debate on the Negro's Place in Nature, 1780–1815," *Journal of the History of Ideas* 5 (1962): 384–96.

10. "A Comparative View of the Faculties of Memory, Reason, and Imagination of Negroes (from Jefferson's *Notes on the State of Virginia*)," *Columbian Magazine,* March 1788.

11. Benjamin Rush's paper was read to the American Philosophical Society on July 14, 1792, but not published for several years. "Observations Intended to Favour a Supposition that the Black Colour (as it is called) of the Negro Is Derived from Leprosy," American Philosophical Society, *Transactions* (Philadelphia, 1799). It was also reprinted as "Reasons for Ascribing the Colour of Negroes to Leprosy," *American Magazine and Monthly Review,* April 1800.

12. "A Letter from James McHenry," *New York Magazine,* October 1791.

13. "Account of a Wonderful Talent for Arithmetical Calculation in an African Living in Virginia," *American Museum,* January 1789. William Piersen argues that New England slaves engaging in feats of memory were drawing on skills common to the griot castes of Africa. See William D. Piersen, *Black Yankees: The Development of an Afro-American Subculture in Eighteenth-Century New England* (Amherst, Mass., 1988), 100.

14. Rush to Belknap, August 19, 1788, in L. H. Butterfield, ed., *Letters of Benjamin Rush,* 2 vols. (Princeton, N.J., 1951), 1:482.

15. "The African's Complaint," *Philadelphia Minerva,* April 29, 1797.

16. "On the Different Species of Mania," *Columbian Magazine*, December 1786; "African Magnanimity," *American Museum*, March 1790; "The Slave—A Tale Too True," *New York Weekly Magazine*, January 6, 1796.

17. Mukhtar Ali Isani, "'Far From Gambia's Golden Shore': The Black in Late Eighteenth-Century Imaginative Literature," *William and Mary Quarterly*, 3d ser., 36 (1979): 353–72.

18. "Diary of a Surinam Planter," *Time Piece*, August 14, 1797.

19. "Refined Cruelty," *Rural Magazine*, July 7, 1798; "An Account of Some of the Cruelties Exercised on the Negro Slaves in Surinam," *Philadelphia Magazine and Monthly Review*, September 1798.

20. Robin Winks uses the term "pious pornography" to describe the slave narratives in the nineteenth century with their "horrific tales of whipping, sexual assaults and explicit brutality." Robin Winks, ed., *Four Fugitive Slave Narratives* (Reading, Mass., 1969), vi. See also Frances Smith Foster, *Witnessing Slavery: The Development of Ante-Bellum Slave Narratives* (Westport, Conn., 1979), 20–21.

21. "For the New York Magazine," *New York Magazine*, June 1791.

22. When the blacks did speak in the sentimental pieces it was usually in rather stilted English. Occasionally the black view, or more correctly, a black view, was printed in the magazines. In 1789, for example, the *Museum* published a forceful and cogent letter from a black about slavery. Ironically the letter was reprinted from England. "Letter on Slavery. By a Negro," *American Museum*, July 1789.

23. "The Slave—A Tale Too True," *New York Weekly Magazine*, January 6, 1796.

24. "The Slave—A Fragment," *New York Magazine*, February 1797.

25. This power relationship was illustrated in a similar fashion in the accounts of conversion of blacks by whites. See "Conversion of An African Woman," *Theological Magazine*, November and December 1796; "Authentic Memoirs of the Conversion of a Negro," *United States Christian Magazine*, vol. 1, no. 2, 1796.

26. "The Paradise of Negro Slaves. A Dream," *Columbian Magazine*, January 1787. For an interesting interpretation of this piece as Rush's "guilt-drenched vision," see Gary B. Nash, *Forging Freedom: The Formation of Philadelphia's Black Community, 1720–1840* (Cambridge, Mass., 1988), 104–5.

27. *Philadelphia Minerva*, April 23, 1796. For a similar story, see "The Generous Slave," *Philadelphia Minerva*, January 6, 1798.

28. Frank Luther Mott, *American Journalism: A History, 1690–1960* (New York, 1960), 59.

29. *American Minerva*, December 9, 1793. For a content analysis of one important colonial paper, see Charles E. Clark and Charles Wetherell,

"The Measure of Maturity: The *Pennsylvania Gazette*, 1728–1765," *William and Mary Quarterly*, 3d ser., 46 (1989): 279–303.

30. Isani similarly notes the lack of material in the newspapers (Isani, "'Far From Gambia's Golden Shore',￼" 353). "Extraordinary Friendship of Two Negroes," *Philadelphia Minerva*, December 16, 1797; *American Minerva*, February 16, 1796.

31. "Rights of Black Men," *American Museum*, November 1792.

32. *Centinel of Freedom*, December 21, 1796; *American Minerva*, December 15, 1796; *Minerva*, September 2, 1797. Many people in the Middle Atlantic states (not to mention those in the South) had misgivings about Saint Dominguan blacks. In 1798 when a ship with a number of French blacks on board arrived in Philadelphia, the ship was moved to a position under the guns protecting the port on account of a "disposition" among the blacks. See *Centinel of Freedom*, July 3, 1798.

33. Quoted in Jordan, *White over Black*, 521.

34. *American Minerva*, October 12, 1796. See also the issues for July 12 and October 10, and François Alexandre Frédéric, duc de La Rochefoucauld-Liancourt, *Travels Through the United States of North America, the Country of the Iroquois, and Upper Canada in the Years 1795, 1796, 1797*, 2 vols. (London, 1799), 2:133–34.

35. James D. Hart, *The Popular Book: A History of America's Literary Taste* (New York, 1950), 43.

36. Quoted in Hart, *Popular Book*, 42.

37. David Hall, in particular, has argued that there is no sharp disjuncture between the literate and preliterate worlds and that ideas from print had a large impact on the preliterate "world view." My argument here is that almanac makers geared the material they printed to the margins of the preliterate world; the material has links both with the preliterate world and with the highly literate world of the magazines. Almanacs can get us closer to a "popular mentalité" than any other printed source in eighteenth-century America. See David D. Hall, "The World of Print and Collective Mentality in Seventeenth-Century New England," in John Higham and Paul K. Conkin, eds., *New Directions in American Intellectual History* (Baltimore, 1980), 166–80; David D. Hall, "The Uses of Literacy in New England, 1600–1850," in William Joyce, David D. Hall, Richard D. Brown, and John B. Hench, eds., *Printing and Society in Early America* (Worcester, Mass., 1983), 1–47. See also David D. Hall, *Worlds of Wonder, Days of Judgment: Popular Religious Belief in Early New England* (New York, 1989).

38. George Lyman Kittredge, *The Old Farmer and His Almanack* (Cambridge, Mass., 1920), vii.

39. The poems, particularly those of William Cowper, were the most

commonly reprinted pieces of antislavery literature in the almanacs. See, for example, *Burlington Almanac for . . . 1791* (Burlington, N.J., 1790); *The United States Almanac . . . 1794* (Elizabethtown, N.J., 1793). The few pieces of antislavery prose were invariably from the magazines.

40. *Poulson's Town and Country Almanac for . . . 1801* (Philadelphia, 1800).

41. Apart from a poem, "The Monkeys," in the *Balloon Almanac for . . . 1795* (Lancaster, Pa., 1794), the only other extensive reference to the black as ape that I found was in Charles Brockden Brown's novel *Arthur Mervyn*. On a coach trip his fellow passengers were a "sallow Frenchman from Saint Domingo," his ape, and two female blacks. As the hours passed the narrator "gazed at the faces of my *four* companions" and "took an exact account of the features, proportions, looks and gestures of the monkey, the Congolese and the creole Gaul. I compared them together, and examined them apart." Brockden Brown's protagonist came to no great conclusion, but there can be little doubt that the author was referring to the debates over the origins of race. Charles Brockden Brown, *Arthur Mervyn; or, Memoirs of the Year 1793* (Boston, 1827 [orig. pub. 1799–1800]), 138–39.

42. See, for example, *Hutchins Improved: Being an Almanac for . . . 1794* (New York, 1793), for rheumatism and *Franklin's Legacy: or the New York and Vermont Almanac for . . . 1799* (Troy, N.Y., 1798), for the stone.

43. *Centinel of Freedom*, August 23, 1803. The anecdotes, though mostly printed in the almanacs, were sometimes found in the newspapers. This New Jersey publication included a more diverse range of material than any other newspaper examined.

44. *The Merry Fellow's Companion* (Philadelphia, 1789), 26–27. This was one of two or three collections of anecdotes published at this time. It is assumed here that much the same audience had access to the almanacs and jest books.

45. *The Farmer's Calendar; or Fry and Southwick's Almanack for . . . 1798* (Albany, N.Y., 1797).

46. *Centinel of Freedom*, June 28, 1797.

47. *The United States Almanack for . . . 1801* (Elizabeth, N.J., 1800).

48. Lawrence W. Levine, *Black Culture and Black Consciousness: Afro-American Folk Thought from Slavery to Freedom* (New York, 1977), 298–368.

49. Little is known of black humor in the eighteenth century, but the traveler J. F. D. Smyth recorded the following example supplied by Richmond, his black servant. Richmond had been instructed to meet Smyth, but the black fell asleep in his canoe and his master was forced to walk a considerable distance through rough country. When the exhausted Smyth finally came across his servant he was told the following: "Kay mass (says he), you just leave me, me sit here, great fish jump up into de canoe; here he be, massa, fine fish, massa; me den very grad; den me sit very still,

until another great fish jump into de canoe; but me fall asleep, massa, and no wake till you come; now, massa, me know me deserve flogging, cause if great fish did jump into de canoe, he see me asleep, den he jump out again, and I no catch him; so, massa, me willing now take good flogging." An amused Smyth forgave his servant. This story is strikingly similar to the anecdotes from the almanacs presented in the text here. Quoted in Mechal Sobel, *The World They Made Together: Black and White Values in Eighteenth-Century Virginia* (Princeton, N.J., 1987), 33.

50. *Dickson's Balloon Almanac for . . . 1799* (Lancaster, Pa., 1798).

51. See Gerald W. Mullin, *Flight and Rebellion: Slave Resistance in Eighteenth-Century Virginia* (New York, 1972), 75–76. Similar advertisements can be found easily in the Middle Atlantic states: see, for example, *Argus*, August 5, 1796; *The Federalist*; *New Jersey Gazette*, June 30, 1800.

52. *Waterford Almanac for . . . 1807* (Waterford, N.Y., 1806).

53. *Centinel of Freedom*, November 30, 1796.

54. *The American Jest Book* (Philadelphia, 1789), 18–19.

55. *Hutchins Improved: Being an Almanac for . . . 1806* (New York, 1805).

56. *Centinel of Freedom*, October 23, 1806; *Encyclopedia* (Philadelphia, 1795), 12:794.

57. *Federal Almanac for . . . 1794* (New Brunswick, N.J., 1793).

58. *Father Abraham's Almanac for . . . 1796* (Philadelphia, 1795).

59. *Greenleaf's New York, Connecticut, and New Jersey Almanac for . . . 1792* (New York, 1791).

60. Gordon Wood, "Evangelical America and Early Mormonism," *New York History* 41 (1980): 359–86, especially 364.

61. It should be noted that I read virtually all extant almanacs in New York, New Jersey, and Pennsylvania for the period 1770–1800, but only a selection for the years from 1801 to 1810 (it was quite a large selection— all those in the Rare Book Room of the New York Public Library).

62. *Franklin's Legacy: or the New York and Vermont Almanack for . . . 1804* (Troy, 1803).

63. See, for example, *Courier and Long Island Advertiser*, October 2, 1804; *Centinel of Freedom*, August 24, 1810.

64. On the minstrel show, see Robert C. Toll, *Blacking Up: The Minstrel Show in Nineteenth-Century America* (New York, 1977); Sam Dennison, *Scandalize My Name: Black Images in American Popular Music* (New York, 1982); Richard Waterhouse, "The Internationalisation of American Popular Culture in the Nineteenth Century: The Case of the Minstrel Show," *Australasian Journal of American Studies* 4 (1985): 1–11.

65. Walter J. Ong, *The Presence of the Word: Some Prolegomena for Cultural and Religious History* (New Haven, Conn., 1967), 84.

66. Samuel Magaw, *A Discourse Delivered July 17, 1794 in the African Church* (Philadelphia, 1794), 9–10.

67. *Salmagundi*, March 7, 1807.
68. See, for example, McManus's claim that "whites in the North overwhelmingly supported the antislavery movement." Edgar J. McManus, *A History of Negro Slavery in New York* (Syracuse, N.Y., 1966), 182. For some similarly rash generalizations, see Edgar J. McManus, *Black Bondage in the North* (Syracuse, N.Y., 1973), 160–79.
69. Jordan, *White over Black*, 370–71.
70. There were 273 slaves in Philadelphia in 1790 and 55 in 1800. Gary B. Nash, "Forging Freedom: The Emancipation Experience in the Northern Seaports, 1775–1820," in Ira Berlin and Ronald Hoffman, eds., *Slavery and Freedom in the Era of the American Revolution* (Charlottesville, Va., 1982), 5.
71. See, for example, McManus's claim that the "lower classes" lacked the idealism found in the upper classes and had "neither sympathy for the Negro nor understanding of his problems." McManus, *History of Negro Slavery in New York*, 183.

Chapter Four

1. "Memoirs of an Emigrant: The Journal of Alexander Coventry M.D." (Typescript prepared by the Albany Institute of History and Art and the New York State Museum, 1978), 145.
2. *Our Revolutionary Forefathers: The Letters of François, Marquis de Barbé-Marbois During His Residence in the United States as Secretary of the French Legation, 1779–1785* (New York, 1929), 156.
3. François Alexandre Frédéric, duc de La Rochefoucauld-Liancourt, *Travels Through the United States of North America, the Country of the Iroquois, and Upper Canada in the Years 1795, 1796, 1797*, 2 vols. (London, 1799), 2:450.
4. Ira Berlin, "Time, Space, and the Evolution of Afro-American Society on British Mainland North America," *American Historical Review* 85 (1980): 44–78.
5. See Eugene D. Genovese, "The Treatment of Slaves in Different Countries: Problems in the Applications of the Comparative Method," in Laura Foner and Eugene D. Genovese, eds., *Slavery in the New World: A Reader in Comparative History* (Englewood Cliffs, N.J., 1969), 202–10.
6. Minutes of the New York Manumission Society for February 4, 1785, Papers of the New York Manumission Society, New-York Historical Society.
7. Report of the Committee of Resolutions Affecting Members of the Society Holding Slaves, February 1785, Papers of the New York Manumission Society.
8. The members of the New York Manumission Society were worked

out by going through the membership lists and minutes in the Papers of the New York Manumission Society. I then attempted to match these names with my lists of slaveholders taken from the 1790 and 1800 censuses.

9. Arthur J. Alexander, "Federal Officeholders in New York State as Slaveholders, 1789–1805," *Journal of Negro History* 28 (1943): 326–49, especially 330–31. Alexander also adduces two other pieces of "evidence" as to why we should not draw an erroneous conclusion. In 1782 Jay had asked a Mr. Benson to watch out for some old slaves on his father's property and gave him discretion to draw on £50 for that purpose. Second, Plato, one of Jay's father's slaves, was given the choice of which of Jay's children he would like to reside with: he chose John Jay.

10. George Pellew, *John Jay* (New York, 1980 [orig. pub. 1898]), 293–94.

11. Edgar J. McManus, *A History of Negro Slavery in New York* (Syracuse, N.Y., 1966), 168, 171, 182. This is a curious statement—I am unaware of any other agency of antislavery in New York State. Nevertheless, the tenor is not atypical of the usual assessments of the organization.

12. See, for example, McManus, *History of Negro Slavery in New York*, 161.

13. On the reapportionment, see Alfred F. Young, *The Democratic Republicans of New York: The Origins, 1763–1797* (Chapel Hill, N.C., 1967), 505–7; Mary-Jo Kline, "The 'New' New York: An Expanding State in the New Nation," in Manfred Jonas and Robert V. Wells, eds., *New Opportunities in a New Nation: The Development of New York After the Revolution* (Schenectady, N.Y., 1982), 24–26.

14. See David M. Ellis, "The Yankee Invasion of New York, 1783–1850," *New York History* 32 (1951): 3–17.

15. Probably because of language difficulties, historians have left the Dutch in the eighteenth century largely to one side. Hence what follows is largely speculation, but fragmentary references in the decades following the Revolution do suggest that there was a crisis over "Dutchness." The clearest indication of this comes from changes in the Dutch Reformed Church and, in particular, from conflicts over the language to be used in services, an important sign of ethnic consciousness. After the death of Domine Westerlo in 1790 the Albany Dutch Reformed Church never called another minister from the Netherlands. Farther down the Hudson in Kingston, according to Stuart Blumin, there was a generational struggle in 1808, which resulted in English replacing the Dutch language. Similarly, in a couple of letters in the Bancker Papers there are references to John B. Romayne, a young preacher, who could not accept the call to Paltz since he would be required to preach in Dutch for half the time "which would be too hard a task for him." Close examination of the voting patterns in the legislature and of the papers of politicians, a task that

was beyond the scope of both my limited resources and the subject of this book, would, I believe, turn up some evidence of the crumbling of the solid Dutch opposition to ending slavery. If there is any substance to them, such speculations raise fascinating possibilities, particularly when combined with Owen S. Ireland's analysis of the Germans in Pennsylvania and their attitude toward abolition. Charting the impact of the Revolution on these groups could broaden our understanding of race relations, slavery, and abolition in the Middle Atlantic states and even come up with a more satisfying interpretation of the end of slavery, emphasizing the ethnic diversity of the region, a factor that is acknowledged and then far too often ignored by historians. Alice P. Kenney, *Stubborn for Liberty: The Dutch in New York* (Syracuse, N.Y., 1975), 211–15; Stuart Blumin, *The Urban Threshold: Growth and Change in a Nineteenth Century American Community* (Chicago, 1976), 28–29; George W. Bancker to Abraham Bancker, June 30, November 11, 1798, Bancker Papers, New-York Historical Society; Owen S. Ireland, "Germans Against Abolition: A Minority's View of Slavery in Revolutionary Pennsylvania," *Journal of Interdisciplinary History* 3 (1973): 685–706.

16. Raymond A. Mohl, *Poverty in New York, 1783–1825* (New York, 1971), 20. See also M. J. Heale, "From City Fathers to Social Critics: Humanitarianism and Government in New York, 1790–1860," *Journal of American History* 63 (1976): 21–41.

17. For an excellent account of the development of a civic culture in New York in the eighteenth and early nineteenth centuries, see Thomas Bender, *New York Intellect: A History of Intellectual Life in New York City, from 1750 to the Beginnings of Our Own Time* (New York, 1987), 3–116. Many of the individuals in Bender's account were members of the New York Manumission Society.

18. This is based on my readings of the minutes of the New York Manumission Society through the 1790s. On the school generally, see Charles C. Andrews, *History of the New-York African Free-Schools* (New York, 1830).

19. Minutes of the Meeting of August 11, 1785, Papers of the New York Manumission Society. For an account of the society that, as the title would suggest, emphasizes social control, see John L. Rury, "Philanthropy, Self Help, and Social Control: The New York Manumission Society and Free Blacks, 1785–1810," *Phylon* 46 (1985): 231–41.

20. There was a large concern among such groups to regulate the behavior of the free black populations in the northern cities. On January 20, 1796, for example, the *American Minerva* printed a notice from the Convention of Deputies from the Abolition Societies (the notice was printed in many other papers as well). This group wished to see blacks act "worthy of the rank" of Freemen and "to justify the friends and advocates of your

colour in the eyes of the world." Then followed a list of nine suggestions for doing this, which included public worship, learning to read and write, simplicity in dress and frugality in family expenses, laying up earnings for children, and behaving toward all persons in a civil and respectful manner. In this way they could help remove "difficulties which have occurred in the general emancipation of such of your brethren as are yet in bondage."

21. The petition was published in the *Daily Advertiser*, March 14, 1786. (The emphasis in the quote is mine.)

22. This reticence about attacking slavery was evident in the 1790s as well. In 1793 a committee appointed to consider the feasibility of asking the legislature for a gradual abolition law concluded that such a request "would, in the *present situation of things*, be premature, and therefore *at this time*, it would not be advisable." Quoted in Arthur Zilversmit, *The First Emancipation: The Abolition of Slavery in the North* (Chicago, 1970), 176.

23. See *Daily Advertiser*, March 23, 1786, February 20, 1787.

24. Report of the Standing Committee for January 8, 1806, Papers of the New York Manumission Society. The reports of the standing committee detail numerous similar incidents.

25. The 132 signatories were listed in the *Daily Advertiser*, March 14, 1786. These names were then compared to my lists of slaveholders taken from the 1790 and 1800 censuses. In reality I compared only 129 of the signatories as three of the names in the newspaper were indecipherable.

26. *Daily Advertiser*, May 22, 1788.

27. *Western Constellation*, November 20, 1802.

28. *New Jersey Journal*, June 20, 1792.

29. Kenneth Roberts and Anna M. Roberts, trans. and eds., *Moreau de St. Méry's American Journey, 1793–1798* (Garden City, N.Y., 1947), 155–56.

30. Charles William Janson, *The Stranger in America, 1793–1806* (New York, 1971), 384–85. Another case reported here, that of a man cutting off the ear of a slave girl and fastening a padlock through a gash in the other ear, was also detailed in the *Daily Advertiser*, February 20, 1805. For details of more incidents of this type on Long Island, see Richard Shannon Moss, "Slavery on Long Island: Its Rise and Decline During the Seventeenth Through Nineteenth Centuries" (Ph.D. diss., Saint John's University, 1985), 161–66.

31. This is my impression from reading a lot of material. A more rigorous comparison would require examination of measurable items such as food, clothing, housing, length of working day, and general conditions of labor. See Genovese, "Treatment of Slaves in Different Countries," 203. If the sources that would enable such an examination exist, I unfortunately did not come across them.

32. Genovese, "Treatment of Slaves in Different Countries," 203.

33. See in particular Allan Kulikoff, *Tobacco and Slaves: The Development of Southern Cultures in the Chesapeake, 1680–1800* (Chapel Hill, N.C., 1986), 317–420. But see also Jean Butenhoff Lee, "The Problem of Slave Community in the Eighteenth-Century Chesapeake," *William and Mary Quarterly*, 3d ser., 43 (1986): 333–61.

34. *Daily Advertiser*, July 25, 1798. For an example of a buyer not wanting to purchase married slaves, see *Royal Gazette*, September 17, 1781.

35. *New York Gazette and Weekly Mercury*, February 14, 1774; *Royal Gazette*, February 26, 1780. For other examples of slaves being sold because of their children, see *New York Gazette and Weekly Mercury*, April 19, 1770, March 21, 1774, April 20, 1778.

36. *New York Gazette and Weekly Mercury*, April 8, 1776.

37. This observation is based on the systematic collection of all for sale notices published in the *New York Gazette and Weekly Mercury* (1771–1783), *Rivington's New York Gazette* (varying titles, 1773–1783), and the *New Jersey Gazette* (1777–1786). These notices detail somewhere in excess of seven hundred slaves. For the 1790s and early 1800s I read all the notices, but recorded only a few representative advertisements and any that were unusual. I also read and recorded the details of every will in New York State included in the published abstracts for the years 1770–1800 (totaling somewhere around fifteen hundred wills). Only very rarely were the family connections of slaves included (usually if the owner was manumitting them). However, the characteristic division of property between children and relatives usually resulted in a person's slaves being split up among several new owners. This inevitably must have impinged on at least some relationships not mentioned in the wills.

38. *New York Gazette and Weekly Mercury*, February 22, 1773.

39. Ibid., November 9, 1772; *New Jersey Gazette*, November 20, 1782.

40. *Centinel of Freedom*, September 23, 1806.

41. *New Jersey Gazette*, December 20, 1780.

42. *Rivington's New York Gazetteer*, June 2, 1774.

43. For a similarly grim view of the slave family in New York, see Vivienne Kruger's massive dissertation. Kruger's conclusions on the family at least are in accord with mine. New York blacks "ordinarily lived apart from both close family members and distant kin," and slaves were "randomly distributed rather than familially grouped into white households." Vivienne L. Kruger, "Born to Run: The Slave Family in Early New York, 1626–1827" (Ph.D. diss., Columbia University, 1985), 16, 21.

44. *The Diary of William Dunlap, 1766–1839*, 3 vols. (New York, 1929–1931), 1:118.

45. Such a view is at odds with the main thrust of slave historiography of late. However, I would suggest that the history of the slave family

badly needs reassessment. The standard reference remains Herbert Gutman's *The Black Family in Slavery and Freedom, 1750–1925* (New York, 1976). While Gutman was undoubtedly successful in his attempt to demolish the Moynihan Report, I would argue that he underestimated the impact of slavery on the slave family. In this regard the work of Manfra and Dykstra on the black stepfamily is very suggestive. Similarly Christie Farnham has recently raised a number of points that respectfully question Gutman's thesis. Whether Gutman was right or wrong about the South it should be remembered that his book, in spite of its title, is about that region. He considered the North in any depth only after slavery had ended, indeed after large numbers of southern blacks had migrated to the North in the decades following the Civil War. Jo Ann Manfra and Robert R. Dykstra, "Serial Marriage and the Origins of the Black Stepfamily: The Rowanty Evidence," *Journal of American History* 72 (1985): 18–44; Christie Farnham, "Sapphire? The Issue of Dominance in the Slave Family, 1830–1865," in Carol Groneman and Mary Beth Norton, eds., *"To Toil the Livelong Day": America's Women at Work, 1780–1980* (Ithaca, N.Y., 1987), 68–83.

46. See Thomas E. V. Smith, *The City of New York in the Year of Washington's Inauguration: 1789* (Riverside, Conn., 1972 [orig. pub. 1889]), 9.

47. On southern cities, see Richard C. Wade, *Slavery in the Cities: The South, 1820–1860* (New York, 1964), 55–79, especially 59; John P. Radford, "Race, Residence, and Ideology: Charleston, South Carolina in the Mid-Nineteenth Century," *Journal of Historical Geography* 2 (1976): 329–46.

48. Statement of Jake, *People v. Jake, a Slave of Cornelius Brinkerhoff,* filed December 4, 1804, box 19, District Attorney's Indictment Papers, Municipal Archives, New York City.

49. *New York Gazette and Weekly Mercury,* April 3, 1775, April 26, 1770.

50. *Minerva,* August 12, 1797.

51. Bound Volume, Forman Papers, New-York Historical Society.

52. *The Commissioners of the Alms House, vs Alexander Whistelo, A Black Man, Being a Remarkable Case of Bastardy, Tried and Adjudged by the Mayor, Recorder and Several Aldermen of the City of New York Under the Act Passed 6th. March 1801, For the Relief of Cities and Towns from the Maintenance of Bastard Children* (New York, 1808), 8. On the stereotype, see Joseph Boskin, *Sambo: The Rise and Demise of an American Jester* (New York, 1986), 133–34, 143, and passim.

53. *New York Journal,* March 10, 1792.

54. The diary is held in the New York Public Library, but the portions referred to here are more conveniently available in an appendix in Moss, "Slavery on Long Island," 322–28.

55. The best account of tobacco cultivation is Rhys Isaac's gloss on Landon Carter's diary in Rhys Isaac, *The Transformation of Virginia, 1740–1790*

(Chapel Hill, N.C., 1982), 22–30. See also T. H. Breen, *Tobacco Culture: The Mentality of the Great Tidewater Planters on the Eve of the Revolution* (Princeton, N.J., 1985), 46–55.

56. Statement of Andrew Powlis, *People v. Andrew Powlis*, filed August 8, 1805, box 24, District Attorney's Indictment Papers.

57. Thomas F. De Voe, *The Market Book: A History of the Public Markets of the City of New York* (New York, 1970 [orig. pub. 1862]), 322, 344–45. A breakdown, acrobatic dancing conducted within the confines of a raised plank, was the forebear of break dancing.

58. Diary of Dr. Samuel Thompson, July 20, 1800, New York Public Library. Material on black religion in the countryside is, as far as I can see, almost nonexistent. For a brief account of a Methodist meeting in Brooklyn, see Franklin Scott, trans. and ed., *Baron Klinkowström's America, 1818–1820* (Evanston, Ill., 1952), 108. See also Robert E. Cray, Jr., "Forging a Majority: The Methodist Experience on Eastern Long Island, 1789–1845," *New York History* 67 (1986): 285–303, although Cray pays scant attention to blacks, undoubtedly because of the paucity of sources.

59. Diary of Dr. Samuel Thompson, January 2, 1804; *Greenleaf's New York Journal*, February 2, 1796.

60. Diary of Dr. Samuel Thompson, June 15, 1803. "Coventry's Memoirs of an Emigrant" contains a lot of material on the activities of the local gentry in the lower Hudson Valley in the 1780s and 1790s.

61. Pierre Van Cortlandt to James Mandiville, January 5, 1799, in Jacob Judd, comp. and ed., *Correspondence of the Van Cortlandt Family of Cortlandt Manor, 1748–1800* (Tarrytown, N.Y., 1977), 595.

62. Dena J. Epstein, *Sinful Tunes and Spirituals: Black Folk Music to the Civil War* (Urbana, Ill., 1977), 66–67.

63. The most important of these and the one that surfaces in every account of Pinkster is James Eights, "Pinkster Festivities in Albany Sixty Years Ago," in Joel Munsell, ed., *Collections on the History of Albany, from Its Discovery to the Present Time*, 4 vols. (Albany, N.Y., 1865–71), 2:323–27.

64. The piece, originally from the *Albany Centinel*, was reprinted in the *Daily Advertiser*, June 29, 1803, but is more conveniently available in Shane White, "Pinkster in Albany, 1803: A Contemporary Description," *New York History* 70 (1989): 191–99.

65. Eights claims that none of the "colored nobility," including the King, put in an appearance on the Monday. See Eights, "Pinkster Festivities in Albany Sixty Years Ago," 324.

66. A. J. Williams-Myers, "Pinkster Carnival: Africanisms in the Hudson River Valley," *Afro-Americans in New York Life and History* 9 (1985): 7–17, especially 16.

67. Sterling Stuckey, *Slave Culture: Nationalist Theory and the Foundations*

of Black America (New York, 1987), 80–83 and passim. Pinkster is reasonably important in Stuckey's argument, surfacing on 80, 142, 144, 160, 227, and 296.

68. Peter Kolchin, "Reevaluating the Antebellum Slave Community: A Comparative Perspective," *Journal of American History* 70 (1983): 579–601, provides a useful corrective.

69. See the pertinent comments of Elizabeth Fox-Genovese and Eugene D. Genovese in "The Political Crisis of Social History: Class Struggle as Subject and Object," in Fox-Genovese and Genovese, *Fruits of Merchant Capital: Slavery and Bourgeois Property in the Rise and Expansion of Capitalism* (New York, 1983), 179–212, especially 197–98.

70. Alice Morse Earle, *Colonial Days in Old New York* (New York, 1896), 200–201.

71. See in particular Natalie Zemon Davis, "The Reasons of Misrule," in Davis, *Society and Culture in Early Modern France* (Stanford, Calif., 1975), 97–123. See also Peter Burke, *Popular Culture in Early Modern Europe* (London, 1978) and Emmanuel Le Roy Ladurie, *Carnival in Romans: A People's Uprising at Romans, 1579–1580*, trans. Mary Feeney (London, 1981). Historians have begun to consider the continuities between the old and new worlds in various rituals and, more important, the way various groups in America imbued old rituals with new meaning. See, for example, Alfred F. Young, "English Plebeian Culture and Eighteenth-Century American Radicalism," in Margaret Jacob and James Jacob, eds., *The Origins of Anglo-American Radicalism* (London, 1984), 185–212; Sean Wilentz, "Artisan Republican Festivals and the Rise of Class Conflict in New York City, 1788–1837," in Michael Frisch and Daniel J. Walkowitz, eds., *Working Class America: Essays on Labor, Community, and American Society* (Urbana, Ill., 1983), 37–77; Susan G. Davis, "'Making Night Hideous': Christmas Revelry and Public Order in Nineteenth-Century Philadelphia," *American Quarterly* 34 (1982): 185–99; Susan G. Davis, "The Career of Colonel Pluck: Folk Drama and Popular Protest in Early Nineteenth-Century Philadelphia," *Pennsylvania Magazine of History and Biography* 109 (1985): 179–202; Susan G. Davis, *Parades and Power: Street Theater in Nineteenth-Century Philadelphia* (Philadelphia, 1986). Pinkster provides an interesting twist on this type of material.

72. Victor Turner, *The Ritual Process: Structure and Anti-Structure* (Ithaca, N.Y., 1977), 94–203, especially 176–77.

73. Eights, "Pinkster Festivities in Albany Sixty Years Ago," 327.

74. Earle, *Colonial Days in Old New York*, 199.

75. *Albany Register*, January 27, February 3, 1794.

76. Davis, "Reasons of Misrule," 122.

77. Negro Election Day appears to have performed a similar func-

tion in New England. See Joseph P. Reidy, " 'Negro Election Day' and Black Community Life in New England, 1750–1860," *Marxist Perspectives* 1 (1978): 102–17; William D. Piersen, *Black Yankees: The Development of an Afro-American Subculture in Eighteenth-Century New England* (Amherst, Mass., 1988), 117–40.

78. Eights, "Pinkster Festivities in Albany Sixty Years Ago," 325.

79. Ibid., 324, 327.

80. Quoted in Williams-Myers, "Pinkster Carnival," 15.

81. Williams-Myers points out, just a trifle tenuously, that 1811, the year this ordinance was passed, was the year before the War of 1812, the year of the revolt in Louisiana, and only a decade after Gabriel Prosser's conspiracy in Virginia in 1800, which in turn "came on the heels of the Haitian Revolution." Williams-Myers, "Pinkster Carnival," 15–16.

82. See, for example, Eileen Southern, *The Music of Black Americans: A History* (New York, 1971), 53. Epstein more cautiously uses the words "purported to describe events of 1757" (Epstein, *Sinful Tunes and Spirituals,* 67). Not only does Williams-Myers use the novel as evidence of Pinkster's presence in the city, but he also apparently believes that Cooper's explicitness "about the lack of drunkenness" is of some significance. Williams-Myers, "Pinkster Carnival," 15 and passim.

83. Cited in Earle, *Colonial Days in Old New York,* 195.

84. The editors of *American Notes and Queries* quoted in Epstein, *Sinful Tunes and Spirituals,* 67.

85. This is based on my reading of what I would consider to be an extensive amount of primary and secondary material. If Pinkster was important early in the eighteenth century, then its complete omission from Horsmanden's *The New York Conspiracy*, an extensive and lengthy compendium of slave life in New York City in 1740 and 1741, is particularly surprising. See Thomas J. Davis, ed., *The New York Conspiracy by Daniel Horsmanden* (Boston, 1971).

86. The account of Pinkster around New York is my speculation based on Earle's account of the minor celebrations of Long Islanders late in the nineteenth century. See Earle, *Colonial Days in Old New York,* 200.

87. Cited in Epstein, *Sinful Tunes and Spirituals,* 67.

88. "Memoirs of an Emigrant," 215.

89. *Diary of William Dunlap,* 1:65.

90. Statement of Thomas Jackson, *People v. Thomas Jackson,* filed June 5, 1801, box 8, District Attorney's Indictment Papers. For a brief account of the Dutch influence on black culture, see David Steven Cohen, "In Search of Carolus Africanus Rex: Afro-Dutch Folklore in New York and New Jersey," *Journal of the Afro-American Historical and Genealogical Society* 5 (1984): 148–68.

91. The poem is reprinted in Geraldine R. Pleat and Agnes N. Underwood, "Pinkster Ode, Albany, 1803," *New York Folklore Quarterly* 8 (1952): 31–45.

92. See the advertisement in the *New York Evening Post*, May 21, 1804.

93. Ibid., May 16, 1804.

94. Gabriel Furman, *Antiquities of Long Island* (New York, 1874), 266–67.

95. See, for example, the essays in Eric Hobsbawm and Terence Ranger, eds., *The Invention of Tradition* (Cambridge, 1983).

96. Furman, *Antiquities of Long Island*, 266.

97. De Voe, *Market Book*, 344–45.

98. On the task system, see Philip D. Morgan, "Work and Culture: The Task System and the World of Lowcountry Blacks, 1700 to 1880," *William and Mary Quarterly*, 3d ser., 39 (1982): 563–99; Philip D. Morgan, "The Ownership of Property by Slaves in the Mid-Nineteenth–Century Low Country," *Journal of Southern History* 49 (1983): 399–420; Philip D. Morgan, "Task and Gang Systems: The Organization of Labor' on New World Plantations," in Stephen Innes, ed., *Work and Labor in Early America* (Chapel Hill, N.C., 1988), 189–220.

99. *Royal Gazette*, June 27, 1781.

100. Ibid., May 10, 1780.

101. *New York Gazette and Weekly Mercury*, June 1, 1772, March 24, November 10, 1777.

102. Ibid., November 1, 1773.

103. *Minerva*, March 18, 1797.

104. *New York Evening Post*, September 16, 1802.

105. "Memoirs of an Emigrant," 118, 209.

106. *Daily Advertiser*, August 1, 1788.

107. *Greenleaf's New York Journal*, September 16, 1797.

108. *Daily Advertiser*, August 4, 1786.

109. Diary of Dr. Samuel Thompson, August 15, 1800.

110. Moss, "Slavery on Long Island," 332–33.

111. The details of this case have been drawn from Peter Gansevoort to William Walker, October 18, 1807; Gustus to Walker, October 25, 1807; Walker to Gansevoort, November 10, 1807; Gansevoort to Walker, December 4, 1807; Walker to Gansevoort, January 6, 1808, New-York Historical Society.

112. Caesar Brown to Sophia Brown, May 30, 1800, Miscellaneous Collection, New-York Historical Society. The letter is more conveniently available in Robert S. Starobin, ed., *Blacks in Bondage: Letters of American Slaves* (New York, 1974), 102–3.

113. "Memoirs of an Emigrant," 134.

114. Moss, "Slavery on Long Island," 332–33.

115. Statement of Caty, *People v. Caty (a Black)*, filed August 6, 1805, box 24, District Attorney's Indictment Papers.

116. The contract is reprinted in Percy M. Van Epps, "Slavery in Early Glenville, NY," in *Contributions to the History of Glenville* (Glenville, N.Y., 1932), 101–2.

117. The letter, dated January 8, 1913, is quoted in Van Epps, "Slavery in Early Glenville," 103.

118. This is not to suggest that separated families and white interference did not occur in the South, but merely to point out that living on a quarter with perhaps twenty other slaves fostered the creation of a slave community that could help insulate them from their master. A solitary slave living directly underneath his or her master in the cellar kitchen of the house was in a rather different situation.

Chapter Five

1. *New York Journal*, July 26, 1787; *Hudson Weekly Gazette*, August 2, 1787; *Daily Advertiser*, July 28, 1787.

2. For comments on the methodology of such a reconstruction, focusing on "action statements," and for an exemplary reading of the running away of Simon the ox carter from Landon Carter's plantation, see Rhys Isaac, *The Transformation of Virginia, 1740–1790* (Chapel Hill, N.C., 1982), 323–57.

3. Quoted in Philip D. Morgan, "Colonial South Carolina Runaways: Their Significance for Slave Culture," *Slavery and Abolition* 6 (1985): 57–78, especially 57.

4. Carter Woodson included runaway advertisements in his program for collecting documents illustrating the history of American blacks. See "Eighteenth-Century Slaves as Advertised by Their Masters," *Journal of Negro History* 1 (1916): 163–216. For an account of the work of Carter Woodson, see August Meier and Elliot Rudwick, *Black History and the Historical Profession, 1915–1980* (Urbana, Ill., 1986), 1–71. Early essays using runaway advertisements include Lorenzo J. Greene, "The New England Negro as Seen in Advertisements for Runaway Slaves," *Journal of Negro History* 29 (1944): 125–46; Edwin Olson, "Social Aspects of Slave Life in New York," *Journal of Negro History* 26 (1941): 66–77. For more recent studies, see Gerald W. Mullin, *Flight and Rebellion: Slave Resistance in Eighteenth-Century Virginia* (New York, 1972); Peter H. Wood, *Black Majority: Negroes in Colonial South Carolina from 1670 Through the Stono Rebellion* (New York, 1974), 239–68; Daniel E. Meaders, "South Carolina Fugitives as Viewed Through Local Colonial Newspapers with Emphasis on

Runaway Notices, 1732–1801," *Journal of Negro History* 40 (1975): 288–319; Shane White, "Black Fugitives in Colonial South Carolina," *Australasian Journal of American Studies* 1 (1980): 25–40; Michael P. Johnson, "Runaway Slaves and the Slave Communities in South Carolina, 1799 to 1830," *William and Mary Quarterly*, 3d ser., 38 (1981):418–41; Daniel C. Littlefield, *Rice and Slaves: Ethnicity and the Slave Trade to Colonial South Carolina* (Baton Rouge, La., 1981), 115–73; the December 1985 issue of *Slavery and Abolition* was a special issue devoted to studies of runaways in various slave societies. Since the earlier work of Greene and Olson there has been little use of runaway material by historians examining the North. McManus, in his two books, has rather similar chapters in which he eschews quantification and gives little more than a descriptive account of some runaway advertisements. See Edgar J. McManus, *A History of Negro Slavery in New York* (Syracuse, N.Y., 1966), 101–19; Edgar J. McManus, *Black Bondage in the North* (Syracuse, N.Y., 1973), 108–24. But see Billy G. Smith, "Fugitives from Slavery in the Mid-Atlantic Region During the Eighteenth Century" (Paper presented at the Philadelphia Center for Early American Studies, March 31, 1989). I would like to thank Professor Smith for sending me a copy.

5. Occasionally runaway advertisements were printed on handbills. Scholars interested in analyzing the slave narratives have paid more attention to these sorts of points about language. See in particular the excellent William L. Andrews, *To Tell a Free Story: The First Century of Afro-American Autobiography, 1760–1865* (Urbana, Ill., 1986). See also Houston A. Baker, Jr., *Blues, Ideology, and Afro-American Literature: A Vernacular Theory* (Chicago, 1984); Henry Louis Gates, Jr., ed., *Black Literature and Literary Theory* (New York, 1984); Charles T. Davis and Henry Louis Gates, Jr., *The Slave's Narrative* (New York, 1985).

6. For a similar observation, see Allan Kulikoff, *Tobacco and Slaves: The Development of Southern Cultures in the Chesapeake, 1680–1800* (Chapel Hill, N.C., 1986), 396–97.

7. *Daily Advertiser*, May 10, 1793; *American Minerva*, November 15, 1796. More generally, see Charles C. Andrews, *History of the New-York African Free-Schools* (New York, 1830).

8. As Christine Stansell has pointed out, similar limitations were imposed on women. When "Justitia" wrote to the *Diary* in 1793 about the acquittal of Harry Bedlow in a notorious rape case and the linked issue of bawdy houses, the ground of public debate quickly shifted from the substance of Justitia's claims to that of her own virtue. Christine Stansell, *City of Women: Sex and Class in New York, 1789–1860* (New York, 1986), 25–26.

9. *Daily Advertiser*, February 28, March 1, 1788. For an excellent account of the controversy over grave robbing, see Steven Robert Wilf, "Anatomy

and Punishment in Late Eighteenth-Century New York," *Journal of Social History* 22 (1989): 507–30.

10. *New Jersey Gazette*, January 26, February 2, 1780, February 23, 1783, March 1, 8, 1780, June 25, December 23, 1783.

11. This episode, buried among the advertisements, was a precursor of the better-known material published in the *New Jersey Gazette*. Later on that year the *Gazette* printed a series of letters about abolition that, according to Arthur Zilversmit, constituted "perhaps the most extensive newspaper debate of the subject before the 1830s." See, for example, *New Jersey Gazette*, September 20, October 4, November 8, 1780. Two letters from this debate are more conveniently available in Clement Alexander Price, comp. and ed., *Freedom Not Far Distant: A Documentary History of Afro-Americans in New Jersey* (Newark, N.J., 1980), 59–63. See also Arthur Zilversmit, *The First Emancipation: The Abolition of Slavery in the North* (Chicago, 1970), 141–46.

12. There were a few other occasions on which the genre of the newspaper notice or runaway advertisement was subverted, highlighting in much the same fashion the classifying powers of whites. In 1861, for instance, an advertisement was placed in the newspaper edited by Frederick Douglass, in which Sambo Rhett offered a reward for his runaway master Julian Rhett. An advertisement in the *South Carolina Gazette* in 1734 for a runaway baboon had a similar effect, even if the motive of the advertiser was rather different. Here the intention was not to attack the institution of slavery, but to make a racist joke. The Sambo Rhett advertisement is quoted in full in Leon F. Litwack, *Been in the Storm So Long: The Aftermath of Slavery* (New York, 1979), 112–13. The baboon advertisement is quoted in full in Winthrop D. Jordan, *White over Black: American Attitudes Toward the Negro, 1550–1812* (Chapel Hill, N.C., 1968), 238.

13. Mullin, *Flight and Rebellion*, x–xi, 39.

14. *New York Journal*, February 4, 1792.

15. *New Jersey Gazette*, October 23, 1784; *Daily Advertiser*, May 19, 1789. The best account of the debate over the origin of Negroes is Jordan, *White over Black*, 482–541.

16. *Daily Advertiser*, August 1, 1788, February 27, 1795.

17. A useful analogy is the personal notices in the back pages of the *New York Review of Books*. To the cognoscenti, WWF or SJM have an immediate and obvious meaning, but the rest of us have to grope around trying to work it out. Further, such words as "divorced" or "non-smoking" appear to have connotations about life-styles that extend well beyond the literal meaning of the words. Extracting all the information contained in both the personal notices and the runaway advertisements requires a careful analysis of the language used.

18. The following newspapers were used: *American Minerva* (1793–1796); *Argus* (1795–1797); *Daily Advertiser* (1785–1805); *New York Evening Post* (1801–1805); *New York Gazette and Weekly Mercury* (1771–1783); *New York Journal* (1786–1794); *Greenleaf's New York Journal* (1794–1800); *Minerva* (1796–1797); *Rivington's New York Gazette* (varying titles, 1773–1783); *Long Island Courier* (1799–1803); *New Jersey Gazette* (1777–1786); *New Jersey Journal* (1789–1793); *Centinel of Freedom* (1796–1805); *Federalist*; *New Jersey Gazette* (1798–1800). An enormous number of newspapers were published in New York and New Jersey, and this represents only a fraction of the total. Further, the holdings in the various institutions in which I read some of these newspapers were incomplete. Even the microfilm and microcard copies I used were not always complete. Nevertheless I would estimate that I have read a minimum of twelve thousand issues of these newspapers.

19. This figure of 1,232 represents the total number of runaways who left of their own volition and excludes 47 children who ran away with a parent. Thus eight-year-olds absconding by themselves have been counted, but when they fled with a parent they have been left out. Only a fool would claim that this figure represents all the runaways in the newspapers read. Microfilm is bad enough, but many of these newspapers were read on microcard, a medium seemingly designed to send readers both blind and to sleep. Undoubtedly I have missed some runaway advertisements.

20. William Strickland, *Journal of a Tour in the United States of America, 1794–1795*, ed. J. E. Strickland (New York, 1971), 63.

21. Color was mentioned in 47.6 percent (586 of 1,232) of runaway descriptions. Of these 586, 28.6 percent (168) were mulatto, 32.6 percent (191) were "yellowish," 11.3 percent (66) were "not very black," and 27.5 percent were "black." The use of color is one of the codes of the owners that remains impenetrable. What is certain though is that over the period under consideration owners increasingly included such information. In the decade 1776–1785 only 39.3 percent commented on it, but in the next decade, 1786–1795, this figure rose to 50.3 percent, and by the following decade, 1796–1805, it had reached 54.2 percent. The increased interest in this aspect of the slaves' appearance seems to be connected both to the debate over the origins of Negroes and to the influx of Saint Dominguans. The fine gradations of color common in the West Indies can occasionally be discerned in New York in the 1790s and early nineteenth century. The description of Grotis as of a "sambo color," for example, is a technical term used to describe the offspring of a black and a mulatto. This and other matters concerning color are raised in the testimony of several New York physicians in a fascinating lawsuit in which the court was attempting to determine whether the child of a "yellowish" woman was fathered by

a white or by Alexander Whistelo, a black. *The Commissioners of the Alms House, vs Alexander Whistelo, A Black Man, Being a Remarkable Case of Bastardy, Tried and Adjudged by the Mayor, Recorder and Several Aldermen of the City of New York Under the Act Passed 6th. March 1801, For the Relief of Cities and Towns from the Maintenance of Bastard Children* (New York, 1808), 9, 17, and passim; *Daily Advertiser*, June 25, 1802, November 15, 1791; *Greenleaf's New York Journal*, January 17, 1798.

22. *Daily Advertiser*, May 16, 1792, August 30, 1794.

23. On the slave trade to New York and the importation of cargoes direct from Africa in the latter part of the colonial period, see James G. Lydon, "New York and the Slave Trade, 1700 to 1774," *William and Mary Quarterly*, 3d ser., 35 (1978): 375–94.

24. According to Philip Morgan, 60 percent of the 1,525 South Carolina runaways who had their ages noted were in their late teens or early twenties. Morgan, "Colonial South Carolina Runaways," 72–73. It would also appear that a similar pattern prevailed in Virginia and Maryland. See the graph of the age of runaway men in Kulikoff, *Tobacco and Slaves*, 376.

25. *Royal Gazette*, March 17, 1781, May 22, 1782.

26. *Argus*, January 7, March 8, 1797; *Daily Advertiser*, July 15, 1797.

27. *Argus*, October 19, 1795, June 24, 1796. McManus claims that during the whole of the eighteenth century there was only one slave under the age of ten recorded as a runaway. McManus, *History of Negro Slavery in New York*, 107.

28. The New York figures are markedly higher than those from the South. For the period 1736–1801 Gerald Mullin found 141 females out of 1,279 runaways, or 11 percent. In North Carolina for the years 1748–1772 Marvin L. Michael Kay and Lorin Lee Cary found 15 females out of 134 runaways, or 11.2 percent. The situation in South Carolina appears, in this respect at least, to have been the closest to that around New York City. According to Philip Morgan, in the period 1732–1806 there were 1,451 women out of 7,650 adult runaways, or 18.9 percent. For the period 1770–1806 the proportion was higher—833 women out of 4,235 runaways, or 19.7 percent. The percentage figure in and around New York City was 21.7. Mullin, *Flight and Rebellion*, 89, 103; Marvin L. Michael Kay and Lorin Lee Cary, " 'They are Indeed the Constant Plague of Their Tyrants': Slave Defence of a Moral Economy in Colonial North Carolina, 1748–1772," *Slavery and Abolition* 6 (1985): 37–56, especially 43; Philip D. Morgan, "Black Society in the Lowcountry, 1760–1810," in Ira Berlin and Ronald Hoffman, eds., *Slavery and Freedom in the Era of the American Revolution* (Charlottesville, Va., 1982), 83–141, especially 100.

29. I have used the same broad definition of skill that Philip Morgan used in his account of runaways in South Carolina. This article is by far

the best account of the phenomenon of running away; consequently, in order to aid comparisons I have tended to follow or slightly adapt Morgan's categories throughout this chapter. Morgan finds 772 skilled out of 5,599 runaways, or 13.8 percent, in the period 1732–1782. The figure in the New York region is 16.9 percent. Morgan, "Colonial South Carolina Runaways," 64.

30. The figures from the 1786 census, by county, are given in the appendix of McManus, *History of Negro Slavery in New York,* 200.

31. An approximate upper limit can be placed on the number of mulattoes in the population at this time. The 1800 census taker for New York City marked in brackets after the names of Negro heads of households either "black" or "mulatto." Of the 676 free Negro heads of households 170, or 25.1 percent, were mulatto. Further, if it is assumed that the number of blacks in mulatto-headed households was equal to the number of mulattoes living in black-headed households, then the percentage of mulattoes in the free Negro population living in Negro-headed households (i.e., free Negroes living in white households are excluded) was 26.4 (559 out of 2,115). As mulattoes were probably overrepresented in both the free population and the New York City population, I think it can be safely assumed that 25 percent is the upper limit for mulattoes in the whole of the New York region under consideration here.

32. Morgan appears to argue that the South Carolina runaway sample was representative of the slave population as a whole. Although he does demonstrate correlations in the area of skill and the number of Africans in the population, there certainly was none in the sex ratio and there was probably none in terms of age structure. See Morgan, "Colonial South Carolina Runaways," 57–66.

33. *Royal Gazette,* April 24, 1782.

34. *Daily Advertiser,* November 7, 1789.

35. *Greenleaf's New York Journal,* August 23, 1794.

36. *Argus,* April 2, 1796.

37. *Daily Advertiser,* March 25, 1788.

38. *New Jersey Gazette,* May 3, 1781.

39. *Royal Gazette,* September 21, 1782.

40. *Daily Advertiser,* January 27, 1795.

41. Ibid., June 19, 1800.

42. Ibid., February 27, 1795.

43. See, for example, ibid., May 16, 1798.

44. *Centinel of Freedom,* May 18, 1802.

45. *Daily Advertiser,* May 10, 1798.

46. On the reaction of southerners to the behavior of slaves during the Civil War and at the moment of freedom, see, for example, Litwack, *Been in the Storm So Long,* 152–56; Eric Foner, *Nothing but Freedom: Emancipa-*

tion and Its Legacy (Baton Rouge, La., 1983), 80–81; Eugene D. Genovese, *Roll, Jordan, Roll: The World the Slaves Made* (New York, 1974), 97–112. See also Rebecca Scott, "Comparing Emancipations: A Review Essay," *Journal of Social History* 20 (1987), 565–83.

47. The categories used in table 15 and later in tables 16, 17, and 18 to analyze the motivation and destination of runaways have been adapted from Philip Morgan's work. Some changes have been made to accommodate the New York and New Jersey patterns. For example, I have not included a category "to avoid sale" because as far as I can tell no slaves ran away for that reason. I have included a category "Army" in the destinations for the many slaves who were heading not for the city or the countryside but for one or other of the armies. Nonetheless, the material is still very similar to Morgan's organization of the South Carolina data. Morgan's schema has the great advantage of using categories that eighteenth-century Americans observed in their advertisements, and it also allows an assessment of the impact of a number of variables on slave behavior. See Morgan, "Colonial South Carolina Runaways."

48. For the southern states historians have been able to institute a rough check in a few instances when they have been able to match runaway advertisements with the newspaper notices listing where slaves were captured (Mullin, *Flight and Rebellion*, 188–89; Morgan, "Colonial South Carolina Runaways," 66). Both historians agree that the owners' estimates were relatively reliable. It was impossible to make any such check in the case of New York because notices listing where slaves were taken up were very rare and those few I came across did not match any of the runaway advertisements.

49. *Daily Advertiser*, October 11, 1800.

50. *New York Gazette and Weekly Mercury*, September 6, 1779.

51. *Daily Advertiser*, January 6, 1799.

52. Ibid., February 10, 1801.

53. *Greenleaf's New York Journal*, April 26, 1794.

54. *Daily Advertiser*, April 14, 1795. For an excellent account of the role blacks played in a southern city, see Philip D. Morgan, "Black Life in Eighteenth-Century Charleston," *Perspectives in American History*, n.s., 1 (1984): 187–232.

55. *Daily Advertiser*, November 26, 1804.

56. Ibid., May 26, 1802.

57. *New York Gazette and Weekly Mercury*, March 9, 1778.

58. See, for example, *Greenleaf's New York Journal*, December 20, 1794; *Daily Advertiser*, January 26, 1802.

59. *Daily Advertiser*, December 16, 1794. For similar comments on the "French Negroes" from South Carolinians, see Morgan, "Black Life in Eighteenth-Century Charleston," 215.

60. *Daily Advertiser*, June 16, 1801.

61. Ibid., March 26, 1792; Mullin, *Flight and Rebellion,* 108, 120.

62. Statement of Phillis White, *People v. Phillis White,* filed December 6, 1804, box 20, District Attorney's Indictment Papers, Municipal Archives, New York City.

63. *New York Gazette and Weekly Mercury,* May 10, 1773; *Daily Advertiser,* August 15, 1786.

64. *New Jersey Gazette,* October 24, 1785.

65. The term is taken from Thomas M. Doerflinger, *A Vigorous Spirit of Enterprise: Merchants and Economic Development in Revolutionary Philadelphia* (Chapel Hill, N.C., 1986), 283–334.

66. *Philadelphia Magazine and Monthly Review,* January 1799, 28–29.

67. *Greenleaf's New York Journal,* September 23, 1797.

68. *Daily Advertiser,* September 19, 1798.

69. *Centinel of Freedom,* February 9, 1802; *Daily Advertiser,* August 14, 1789.

70. *New York Gazette and Weekly Mercury,* June 9, 1777. On the use of blacks as auxiliaries, see Benjamin Quarles, *The Negro in the American Revolution* (Chapel Hill, N.C., 1961), 134–35.

71. *Royal Gazette,* March 24, 1779.

72. *New Jersey Gazette,* October 28, 1778.

73. *Daily Advertiser,* June 23, 1801.

74. *New York Journal,* August 6, 1790.

75. *Daily Advertiser,* October 7, 1801.

76. Ibid., April 29, 1788.

77. Ibid., May 13, 1800.

78. *Greenleaf's New York Journal,* May 3, 1794.

79. Statement of Toby, *People v. Toby (a Slave of Coventry),* filed October 4, 1804, box 19, District Attorney's Indictment Papers.

80. *Royal Gazette,* December 15, 1779; *New Jersey Gazette,* April 27, 1780; and *New Jersey Gazette,* July 12, 1780, for his subsequent escape from the jail).

81. *Daily Advertiser,* October 17, 1792.

82. Ibid., November 17, 1800.

83. *New York Gazette and Weekly Mercury,* June 30, 1777; *Greenleaf's New York Journal,* April 5, 1797.

84. *New York Journal,* August 6, 1789.

85. *Daily Advertiser,* June 13, 1797.

86. On the role of mulattoes, see Morgan, "Colonial South Carolina Runaways," 69; and also see Mullin's comments on the high number of mulattoes in Virginia who stuttered. Mullin, *Flight and Rebellion,* 101.

87. Morgan found in South Carolina 710 groups totaling 1,999 slaves, or 36 percent of all advertised runaways (Morgan, "Colonial South Caro-

lina Runaways," 72). The groups in the text here include only two or more adults running away—a parent and a child running away have not been counted as a group.

88. *Royal Gazette*, May 12, 1781.

89. On groups in the South, see Morgan, "Colonial South Carolina Runaways," 72, and Johnson, "Runaway Slaves and the Slave Communities in South Carolina, 1799 to 1830."

90. Mullin, *Flight and Rebellion*; Kay and Cary, "Slave Defence of a Moral Economy"; Morgan, "Colonial South Carolina Runaways."

91. The runaway advertisements used in this study were certainly collected from more newspapers. According to Morgan there are approximately 1,750 issues surviving for Virginia and 3,500 for South Carolina in the colonial period. Here I have not used all the surviving newspapers, but have still read in excess of 12,000 issues. Morgan, "Colonial South Carolina Runaways," 75.

92. The population figures are roughly for the midpoints of the periods examined. Mullin, *Flight and Rebellion*, 16; Morgan, "Black Society in the Lowcountry, 1760–1810," 89.

93. *New York Gazette and Weekly Mercury*, August 26, 1776.

94. See Quarles, *Negro in the American Revolution*; Sylvia R. Frey, "Between Slavery and Freedom: Virginia Blacks in the American Revolution," *Journal of Southern History* 49 (1983): 375–98, especially 376.

95. For an account of blacks in New York during the Revolution, see Graham Hodges, "Black Revolt in New York City and the Neutral Zone, 1775–1783" (Paper delivered at the New-York Historical Society conference on New York in the Age of the Constitution, May 15, 1987). I am indebted to Professor Hodges for sending me a copy of his paper.

96. The best and most detailed account of slave resistance in the West Indies is Michael Craton, *Testing the Chains: Resistance to Slavery in the British West Indies* (Ithaca, N.Y., 1982). See also David Geggus, "The Enigma of Jamaica in the 1790s: New Light on the Causes of Slave Rebellions," *William and Mary Quarterly*, 3d ser., 44 (1987): 274–99.

97. Statement of Elizabeth Davison, *People v. Sally Gale*, filed June 7, 1798, box 3, District Attorney's Indictment Papers.

98. Statement of Christopher Prill, *People v. John, Bob, and Harry (black)*, filed June 5, 1801, box 8, District Attorney's Indictment Papers.

99. Statement of J. M. Gervais, *People v. Marcelle, Sam, Benjamin Bandey and 20 Others*, filed October 9, 1801, box 9, District Attorney's Indictment Papers. Timothy Gilfoyle has emphasized the fact that the mob—"a large assemblage of Haitians"—attacked a brothel. My reading of the case is different—the large crowd was principally black and Volunbrun's running a "house of reputed sin" was incidental if not irrelevant. The main purpose

of the blacks was to prevent the twenty slaves being sold to the South. See Timothy J. Gilfoyle, "Strumpets and Misogynists: Brothel 'Riots' and the Transformation of Prostitution in Antebellum New York," *New York History* 68 (1987): 45–65, especially 48–49.

100. On 1741, see Thomas J. Davis, *Rumor of Revolt: The "Great Negro Plot" in Colonial New York* (New York, 1985).

101. William Bradford, *An Enquiry How Far the Punishment of Death . . .* (Philadelphia, 1793), 31–32.

102. The main document for the Albany fire is "Examination of Bet, Slave of Philip S. Van Rensselaer," November 18, 1793, New York State Library, Albany. The fire and consequent executions also received extensive newspaper coverage in both Albany and New York. See, for example, *Albany Register*, November 18, 1793, January 27, February 3, 10, 1794; *American Minerva*, January 6, 17, 20, 1794. See also Don R. Gerlach, "Black Arson in Albany, November 1793," *Journal of Black Studies* 7 (1977): 301–12.

103. Virtually every issue of New York newspapers in these months carried some news of these fires. See, for example, *New York Journal*, November 22, December 16, 27, 30, 1796; *Centinel of Freedom*, December 21, 1796; *American Minerva*, December 15, 1796. Just from reading the New York newspapers it appears that there was a remarkable burst of fires along the eastern seaboard in the middle years of the 1790s. For a story on a fire in Philadelphia, see, for example, *Centinel of Freedom*, July 3, 1798.

104. Lewis Morris to his son, December 29, 1796, New York State Library, Albany.

105. In addition to the blacks being shot down, Morris also claimed that sixty houses in the block from Stuart's store to the Fly Market were burned down. I found no mention of either of these events in the newspapers, although there were several reports of blacks being turned into the authorities.

106. In 1785 an attempt to get a bill through failed on the issue of whether or not free blacks could vote and hold office. In the 1790s, compensation for slaveowners, at least a slightly more plausible issue, led to several defeats of the bill. Zilversmit, *First Emancipation*, 146–50, 175–84.

107. *American Minerva*, June 11, 1796.

108. *Minerva*, April 27, 1797.

109. Constitution and Minutes of the Slave Apprehending Society of Shawangunk, Ulster County, May 21, 1796, New York State Library. On the proliferation of societies of all types in the 1790s, of which this was only one example, see Alfred F. Young, *The Democratic Republicans of New York: The Origins, 1763–1797* (Chapel Hill, N.C., 1967), 392–412.

110. On a smaller and less organized scale this pressure appears to be a precursor of what Michael Craton has argued occurred in the British West Indies in the period 1816–1832. See Michael Craton, "Slave Culture, Re-

sistance and the Achievement of Emancipation in the British West Indies, 1783–1838," in James Walvin, ed., *Slavery and British Society, 1776–1846* (London, 1982), 100–22; Craton, *Testing the Chains,* 241–321.

111. James Oakes has recently run into similar difficulties trying to demonstrate the connection between slave resistance and the Civil War. See James Oakes, "The Political Significance of Slave Resistance," *History Workshop Journal* 22 (1986): 89–107.

Chapter Six

1. *New York Evening Post,* August 20, 1814.

2. Leon F. Litwack, *North of Slavery: The Negro in the Free States, 1790–1860* (Chicago, 1961); see also George M. Fredrickson, *The Black Image in the White Mind: The Debate on Afro-American Character and Destiny, 1817–1914* (New York, 1972), 1–42, 97–129.

3. Harry B. Yoshpe, "Record of Slave Manumissions in New York During the Colonial and Early National Periods," *Journal of Negro History* 26 (1941): 78–107, especially 81, 84, 85.

4. Yoshpe, "Record of Slave Manumissions in New York," 96, 94.

5. Black population growth was so dramatic that it seems unlikely natural growth played much of a role. In support of this, J. P. Brissot de Warville, the French traveler, commented on the high death rate among black children. Unfortunately, as far as I know, death records for New York are fragmentary. In the early 1800s the *Daily Advertiser* published a weekly table of burials in the city, and from 1804 they included some details of age. The *Daily Advertiser* for April 26, 1803, gave a list of interments in New York City burial grounds from November 1, 1801, to December 31, 1802 — 61 percent of the 203 black burials were classified as children. The death rate was also high among white children. The white death rate cannot be worked out exactly because of the high number of whites who were not classified as adults or children, but it was lower than the rate among blacks. J. P. Brissot de Warville, *New Travels in the United States,* ed. Durand Echeverria (Cambridge, Mass., 1964), 232.

6. *New York Gazette and General Advertiser,* January 3, 1803.

7. In order to focus on the rural hinterland of New York City I have excluded Brooklyn from the Kings County figures. In 1790, 456 out of 888 white households owned slaves (see table 12).

8. Not all free blacks went to the city. For an account relying on historical archaeology of a rural black community that formed in New Jersey in the aftermath of the Gradual Manumission Act of 1804, see Joan H. Geismar, *The Archaeology of Social Disintegration in Skunk Hollow: A Nineteenth-Century Rural Black Community* (New York, 1982).

9. On their importance in the South, see for example, Ira Berlin, "The

Structure of the Free Negro Caste in the Antebellum United States," *Journal of Social History* 9 (1976): 297–318.

10. John Baur, "International Repercussions of the Haitian Revolution," *Americas* 26 (1970), 394–418.

11. Quantifying the number of free blacks with French names in the census would be of little value — the census takers and the blacks anglicized their surnames very quickly. This process can occasionally be observed when the directories listed the French names. The surnames Arnauld and Pierre, for example, became Arnold and Peer.

12. Over the period 1791–1805 a minimum of 47 out of the 621 runaways were French speaking. Many others in the sample undoubtedly spoke French, but the slaveowners did not give full details. At certain periods awareness of the French appears to have been higher and slaveowners were more forthcoming. In the six-month period from July 1, 1794, to December 31, 1794, for example, the *Daily Advertiser* contained advertisements describing 39 runaways, of whom at least 11 were French speaking.

13. *Daily Advertiser*, July 3, 1792.

14. [Thomas Eddy], *An Account of the State Prison or Penitentiary House in the City of New York* (New York, 1801), 84–87.

15. Some of the West Indian arrivals who caused trouble appear to have been deported. A newspaper report in the *Daily Advertiser*, April 26, 1803, related that the captain of an American schooner had been taken before a magistrate in Kingston, Jamaica, for bringing in a "foreign negro of a description dangerous to the welfare of the community." The black had been placed "on board at New York by the Police of that city." The captain had apparently been instructed to take the black to Saint Thomas, but the authorities there refused to allow him ashore.

16. There was another alarm about French blacks in 1802. Rumors were published all over the state. A Catskill newspaper, for example, included a report of French blacks swimming ashore from the French frigates moored near Staten Island. The numerous blacks were illuminated by flashes of lightning and looked like "flocks of ducks making for the land." *New York Evening Post*, September 10, 13, 1802; *Western Constellation*, September 13, 1802.

17. See Litwack, *North of Slavery*, 153–86; Leonard P. Curry, *The Free Black in Urban America, 1800–1850: The Shadow of the Dream* (Chicago, 1981), 15–36.

18. See A Note to the Reader for a more detailed account of the method used.

19. William Strickland, *Journal of a Tour in the United States of America, 1794–1795*, ed. J. E. Strickland (New York, 1971), 63–64.

20. See Ira Dye, "Early American Merchant Seafarers," *Proceedings of*

the American Philosophical Society 120 (1976): 349; Gary B. Nash, "Forging Freedom: The Emancipation Experience in the Northern Seaports, 1775–1820," in Ira Berlin and Ronald Hoffman, eds., *Slavery and Freedom in the Era of the American Revolution* (Charlottesville, Va., 1982), 8–10.

21. Statements of Gabriel Therior and John, *People v. John (a Black)*, filed October 8, 1801, box 9, District Attorney's Indictment Papers, Municipal Archives, New York City.

22. Coroner's Report for John Richards, a Black Man, January 20, 1804, Historical Documents Collection, Queens College, City University of New York.

23. I have based my definition of "artisan" on Howard B. Rock, *Artisans of the New Republic: The Tradesmen of New York City in the Age of Jefferson* (New York, 1979), 9–14. I agree with Sean Wilentz's criticisms of Rock, but there were no blacks in the occupations in dispute. See Sean Wilentz, *Chants Democratic: New York City and the Rise of the American Working Class, 1788–1850* (New York, 1984), 27.

24. Statement of Timothy Weeks, *People v. Sally Gale*, filed June 7, 1798, box 3, District Attorney's Indictment Papers.

25. Free blacks even appeared in the debtor's prison; according to the 1810 census there were fourteen free black inmates. For an account of a black barber in the debtor's prison who carried on his trade, see Statement of John Albert, *People v. John Albert*, filed February 9, 1804, box 16, District Attorney's Indictment Papers.

26. See Diary of Alexander Anderson, 1793–1799, June 25, 1793, April 22, 1794, July 3, August 15, 1795, New-York Historical Society.

27. John W. Francis, *Old New York: or, Reminiscences of the Past Sixty Years* (New York, 1858), 150.

28. Nash, "Forging Freedom," 15–19.

29. Nash is not explicit about his definition of artisan, but as far as I can tell the sawyers are the only group in dispute. In New York there were eleven free black sawyers in the 1800 figures and thirteen in 1810. If these are taken out of the New York figures the artisan percentage drops from 37.8 to 27.9 in 1800, and from 28.6 to 23.7 in 1810. The new percentages are still substantially larger than Nash's figures for Philadelphia — 12.0 percent in 1795 and 12.6 percent in 1816.

30. This labeling presents problems that parallel those historians have had to grapple with when using later material, such as the 1850 census. The census taker probably categorized the blacks by skin color, but in this case, as only one census taker was involved, the problems of inconsistent application are minimized. For an account of these problems, see Theodore Hershberg and Henry Williams, "Mulattoes and Blacks: Intragroup Color Differences and Social Stratification in Nineteenth-

Century Philadelphia," in Theodore Hershberg, ed., *Philadelphia: Work,
Space, Family, and Group Experience in the Nineteenth Century: Essays Toward
an Interdisciplinary History of the City* (New York, 1981), 392–94. Unfortunately it is impossible to test the reliability of this data in the same way,
as there is no other list separating blacks from mulattoes. Also see Joel
Williamson, *New People: Miscegenation and Mulattoes in the United States*
(New York, 1980).

31. The Jersey blacks, for example, frequented the Buttermilk Market
on the Hudson. See Thomas F. De Voe, *The Market Book: A History of the
Public Markets of the City of New York* (New York, 1970 [orig. pub. 1862]),
322.

32. John M. Kochiss, *Oystering from New York to Boston* (Middletown,
Conn., 1974), 24–40.

33. One of the first and best known of the black tavern owners was
Samuel Fraunces, about whose color, however, there is some controversy.
See Kym S. Rice, *Early American Taverns: For the Entertainment of Friends
and Strangers* (Chicago, 1983), 125–33. In a note Rice discusses the evidence
and concludes, not very convincingly, that Fraunces was not black.

34. A very few blacks can be matched with the directories in both years
and traced from census to census—William Hamilton was a carpenter in
both 1800 and 1810, as was Edward West; Francis Paulin was a "segar"
maker in 1800 and a tobacconist in 1810; and John Boyd was a hairdresser
in both years. However, because the majority of heads of households cannot be matched with the directories and because many blacks used very
common surnames (as we saw in the last chapter almost 11 percent of the
free black heads of households in New York City in 1810 were called Williams, Smith, or Johnson), it was impossible to trace more than a few blacks
through with any degree of certainty. Of the blacks heading households
and listed with a surname in the 1800 and 1810 censuses, an absolute maxi-
mum of 147 were present in both lists. This is 23.1 percent of the blacks
listed with a surname in the 1800 census and 13.1 percent of those in the
1810 census. The actual figures were probably much smaller.

35. *The Commissioners of the Alms House, vs Alexander Whistelo, A Black
Man, Being a Remarkable Case of Bastardy, Tried and Adjudged by the Mayor,
Recorder and Several Aldermen of the City of New York Under the Act Passed
6th. March 1801, For the Relief of Cities and Towns from the Maintenance of
Bastard Children* (New York, 1808), 4, 9–13, and passim.

36. Statement of Diana Lawrence, *People v. Diana Lawrence*, filed December 7, 1803, box 14, District Attorney's Indictment Papers.

37. Statement of William Thomas, *People v. William Thomas*, filed February 4, 1802, box 11, District Attorney's Indictment Papers.

38. Statement of Sally Gale, *People v. Sally Gale*, filed June 7, 1798, District Attorney's Indictment Papers.

39. De Voe, *Market Book*, 219–20. For an account of black women and their cries as they sold hot corn and baked pears, see Charles H. Haswell, *Reminiscences of an Octogenarian of the City of New York (1816–1860)* (New York, 1897), 35.

40. Statement of Nancy, *People v. Nancy (a Black)*, filed June 5, 1804, box 17, District Attorney's Indictment Papers.

41. Statement of Betsey Miller, *People v. Betsey Miller*, filed April 5, 1802, box 11, District Attorney's Indictment Papers.

42. Kenneth Roberts and Anna M. Roberts, trans. and eds., *Moreau de St. Méry's American Journey, 1793–1798* (Garden City, N.Y., 1947), 156.

43. Diary of Alexander Anderson, October 21, 1793.

44. Statement of Anthony Delacroix, *People v. Anthony Delacroix*, filed December 1803, box 14, District Attorney's Indictment Papers.

45. Statement of Amos Curtis, *People v. Nancy Cobus*, filed August 6, 1802, box 13, District Attorney's Indictment Papers.

46. Statements of Gabriel Therior and John, *People v. John (a Black)*, filed October 8, 1801, box 9, District Attorney's Indictment Papers.

47. James E. Cronin, ed., *The Diary of Elihu Hubbard Smith (1771–1798)* (Philadelphia, 1973), 89, 105 (quotation), 124, 131.

48. Nash, "Forging Freedom," 35.

49. *New York Evening Post*, September 26, 1803.

50. A substantial challenge to such stereotypes about sexual relations in the South is presented by Gary B. Mills, "Miscegenation and the Free Negro in Antebellum 'Anglo' Alabama: A Re-examination of Southern Race Relations," *Journal of American History* 88 (1981): 16–34.

51. Wilentz, *Chants Democratic*, 264. Two households headed by black females contained whites. For example, one of them, Amanda Wright, a mulatto, headed a household that contained three blacks apart from herself, one white male under ten, and one white female between the ages of seventeen and twenty-six.

52. Statements of David Smith and Sarah Thomas, *People v. David Smith*, filed December 16, 1802, box 13, District Attorney's Indictment Papers.

53. *Centinel of Freedom*, May 28, October 8, 1805.

54. Statement of John Vallier, *People v. John Vallier*, filed June 5, 1805, box 23, District Attorney's Indictment Papers.

55. Statement of William Thomas, *People v. William Thomas*, filed February 4, 1802, box 11, District Attorney's Indictment Papers.

56. Statement of George Pollock, *People v. Peter*, filed December 8, 1801, box 10, District Attorney's Indictment Papers.

57. *New York Evening Post*, September 9, 1803.

58. Ibid., November 29, 1805.

59. Statements of Sarner(?) Miller and Savinah King, *People v. Jupiter Abels*, filed November 4, 1801, box 10, District Attorney's Indictment Papers.

60. See Litwack, *North of Slavery*, 168–70. One historian has stated that Bancker Street "lay at the heart of a large black ghetto spreading between City Hall and the East River," but this statement is probably incorrect. See Raymond A. Mohl, *Poverty in New York, 1783–1825* (New York, 1971), 21. The most detailed discussion of black residential patterns in northern cities is in Curry, *Free Black in Urban America*, 49–95, but his analysis centers on the 1850 census and the directories from that period.

61. The index of dissimilarity measures the number of black households (as a percentage of all black households) that would have to move into another ward for black households to constitute the same percentage of the total number of households in each ward. See Ira Berlin, *Slaves Without Masters: The Free Negro in the Antebellum South* (New York, 1974), 254–55; Curry, *Free Black in Urban America*, 54–55. The figures were 22.17 in 1790, 11.26 in 1800, and 22.29 in 1810.

62. The clustering is similar to the pattern found in Cincinnati. See Henry Taylor, "The Use of Maps in the Study of the Black Ghetto-Formation Process: Cincinnati, 1802–1910," *Historical Methods* 17 (1984): 44–58; Henry L. Taylor, "On Slavery's Fringe: City-Building and Black Community Development in Cincinnati, 1800–1850," *Ohio History* 95 (1986): 5–33; and Henry L. Taylor, "Spatial Organization and the Residential Experience: Black Cincinnati in 1850," *Social Science History* 10 (1986): 45–69.

63. On the mixed neighborhoods of the colonial city, see Carl Abbott, "The Neighborhoods of New York City, 1760–1775," *New York History* 55 (1976): 35–53. On the spatial transformation of the city, see Betsy Blackmar, "Re-walking the 'Walking City': Housing and Property Relations in New York City, 1780–1840," *Radical History Review* 21 (1979): 131–48; Elizabeth Strother Blackmar, "Housing and Property Relations in New York City, 1780–1850" (Ph.D. diss., Harvard University, 1980); Allan R. Pred, *The Spatial Dynamics of U.S. Urban-Industrial Growth, 1800–1914: Interpretive and Theoretical Essays* (Cambridge, Mass., 1966). For a brilliant and provocative account of the larger process of which this was a part, see Wilentz, *Chants Democratic*.

64. *Daily Advertiser*, May 11, 1798.

65. See Jonathan Greenleaf, *A History of the Churches of All Denominations, in the City of New York, From the First Settlement to the Year 1846* (New York, 1846), 321–22; *American Citizen*, March 21, July 29, 1800.

66. On the importance of the black church in northern cities, see Gary B. Nash, " 'To Arise Out of the Dust': Absalom Jones and the African Church of Philadelphia, 1785–95," in Gary B. Nash, *Race, Class, and Politics: Essays on American Colonial and Revolutionary Society* (Urbana, Ill., 1986), 323–55; Nash, "Forging Freedom," 43–48; Doris Elisabett Andrews, "Popular Religion and the Revolution in the Middle Atlantic Ports: The Rise of the Methodists, 1770–1800" (Ph.D. diss., University of Pennsylvania, 1986); Carol V. R. George, *Segregated Sabbaths: Richard Allen and the Emergence of Independent Black Churches, 1760–1840* (New York, 1973). On community, see for example the case of an eighty-year-old black woman who had been burnt out in a fire. On being asked if she was all right, she replied, "O a sister in the church has promised to take me in." Ezra Stiles Ely, *Visits of Mercy: Being the Journal of the Stated Preacher to the Hospital and Alms House in the City of New York for the Year of Our Lord, 1811* (New York, 1812), 101–2.

67. Statement of Robert Havens, *People v. Robert Havens*, filed June 4, 1800, box 4, District Attorney's Indictment Papers.

68. Statement of Silvey [sic], *People v. Silvia (a Slave)*, filed August 11, 1800, box 5, District Attorney's Indictment Papers.

69. Statement of Jacob Spellman, *People v. Jacob Spellman*, filed November 12, 1801, box 10, District Attorney's Indictment Papers.

70. Statements of Mathew, Caesar, Jersey, and Claire, *People v. Newall*, filed December 1799, box 4, District Attorney's Indictment Papers.

71. *Commissioners of the Alms House*, 15.

72. *Abstracts of Wills on File in the Surrogate's Office, New York City, 1665–1800*, 17 vols. (New York, 1892–1909), 15:330.

73. Statement of Ruth Dusenbury, *Coroner's Report on Aury Slater*, February 17, 1802, box 11, District Attorney's Indictment Papers.

74. Blackmar, "Housing and Property Relations in New York City, 1780–1850," 148–52.

75. Statements of Ruth Smith and John Young, *People v. Thomas Cooney and Others*, filed April 7, 1804, box 16, District Attorney's Indictment Papers.

76. *New York Evening Post*, March 13, 1802.

77. Ralph Ellison, *Invisible Man* (New York, 1952), especially 9; James Ford, *Slums and Housing with Special Reference to New York City* (Cambridge, Mass., 1936), 86. For another example of vertical segregation, see Peter A. Coclanis, "The Sociology of Architecture in Colonial Charleston: Pattern and Process in an Eighteenth-Century Southern City," *Journal of Social History* 18 (1985): 607–23, especially 610.

78. *New York Evening Post*, August 23, 1805. Extracts from many of the medical reports are reprinted in Ford, *Slums and Housing*, 60–71.

79. Statement of Susan Brasher, *People v. John Stoddart*, filed February 8, 1800, box 4, District Attorney's Indictment Papers.

80. Statements of George Duryee and John White, *People v. York Loyal*, filed October 8, 1804, box 19, District Attorney's Indictment Papers.

81. *Daily Advertiser*, February 15, May 7, 1799.

82. Statement of Daniel Course, *People v. Henry Thompson*, filed April 9, 1802, box 11, District Attorney's Indictment Papers.

83. Statement of Caty Thomas, *People v. Harry (a Black)*, filed April 4, 1805, box 22, District Attorney's Indictment Papers.

84. Statement of Samuel Tonkin, *People v. Samuel Tonkin*, filed December 4, 1802, box 13, District Attorney's Indictment Papers.

85. Statement of Sannon, *People v. Sannon (a Slave)*, filed April 5, 1802, box 11, District Attorney's Indictment Papers.

86. Statements of James Curran and James Clark, *People v. James Clark*, filed August 8, 1804, box 18, District Attorney's Indictment Papers.

87. Statement of Andrew Kevan, *People v. John Obree*, filed December 6, 1798, box 3, District Attorney's Indictment Papers; Statement of Hezekiah Rogers, *People v. Hannah (a black)*, filed October 10, 1800, box 5, District Attorney's Indictment Papers.

88. Statements of Mathew, Caesar, Jersey, and Claire, *People v. Newall*, filed December 1799, box 4, District Attorney's Indictment Papers.

89. *Daily Advertiser*, January 15, 1799.

90. Statement of Luther Baldwin, *People v. John Hunter*, filed January 4, 1798, box 2, District Attorney's Indictment Papers.

91. *Daily Advertiser*, February 25, 1786.

92. *People v. Edward Jones*, filed June 4, 1800, box 4, District Attorney's Indictment Papers.

93. Statement of Moses Helmes, *People v. John Moore*, filed July 12, 1802, box 12, District Attorney's Indictment Papers.

94. *New York Journal*, April 26, 1790.

95. *Centinel of Freedom*, August 5, 1800; *New York Journal*, September 3, 1790.

96. Statement of Tobias, *People v. Tobias (a black man)*, filed December 6, 1798, box 3, District Attorney's Indictment Papers.

97. Statement of William Hayslop, *People v. William Hayslop*, filed August 8, 1804, box 18, District Attorney's Indictment Papers.

98. Statement of William Rollins, *People v. William Rollins*, filed February 2, 1802, box 11, District Attorney's Indictment Papers.

99. Statement of John Primrose, *People v. John Primrose*, filed April 3, 1805, box 22, District Attorney's Indictment Papers.

100. Statement of Abraham Joseph, *People v. Solomon Lane or Solomon Lang*, filed December 5, 1804, box 19, District Attorney's Indictment Papers.

101. Statement of Tom Peters, *People v. Tom Peters*, filed June 6, 1801, box 8, District Attorney's Indictment Papers.

102. Statement of Dick Smock, *People v. Richard Smock*, filed October 2, 1804, box 18, District Attorney's Indictment Papers.

103. For an account of a similar phenomenon in nineteenth-century Philadelphia, see Allen Steinberg, "'The Spirit of Litigation': Private Prosecution and Criminal Justice in Nineteenth Century Philadelphia," *Journal of Social History* 20 (1986): 231–49.

104. Statement of Cesar Jackson, January 12, 1805, Papers of the Common Council, Municipal Archives, New York City.

105. Statement of Exodus Thompson, *People v. Exodus Thompson*, filed November 14, 1801, box 10, District Attorney's Indictment Papers.

106. Statements of Diana Lawrence and Elizabeth Hazelton, *People v. Diana Lawrence*, filed December 7, 1803, box 14, District Attorney's Indictment Papers.

107. Rhys Isaac observed that on Landon Carter's plantation "liquor and the theft needed to acquire it were integral to the life of the plantation community." See Rhys Isaac, "Communication and Control: Authority Metaphors and Power Contests on Colonel Landon Carter's Virginia Plantation, 1752–1778," in Sean Wilentz, ed., *Rites of Power: Symbolism, Ritual, and Politics Since the Middle Ages* (Philadelphia, 1985), 275–302, especially 288. On the role of crime and theft in the black community in Philadelphia at this time, see G. S. Rowe, "Black Offenders, Criminal Courts, and Philadelphia Society in the Late Eighteenth-Century," *Journal of Social History* 22 (1989): 685–721; for a treatment of theft on the plantation, see Alex Lichenstein, "'That Disposition to Theft, With Which They Have Been Branded': Moral Economy, Slave Management, and the Law," *Journal of Social History* 21 (1988): 413–40.

Chapter Seven

1. James E. Cronin, ed., *The Diary of Elihu Hubbard Smith (1771–1798)* (Philadelphia, 1973), 73.

2. Ira Berlin provides a very good discussion of much of the innovative work on eighteenth-century black culture published in the 1970s. See Ira Berlin, "Time, Space, and the Evolution of Afro-American Society on British Mainland North America," *American Historical Review* 85 (1980): 44–78. Recently, however, a few of the southern urban centers have received some attention. See Suzanne Lebsock, *The Free Women of Petersburg: Status and Culture in a Southern Town, 1784–1860* (New York, 1984); Philip D. Morgan, "Black Life in Eighteenth-Century Charleston," *Perspectives in American History*, n.s., 1 (1984): 187–232. Most of the well-known studies of black culture in the antebellum South also concentrate on

the rural areas. See, for example, Eugene D. Genovese, *Roll, Jordan, Roll: The World the Slaves Made* (New York, 1974); Lawrence W. Levine, *Black Culture and Black Consciousness: Afro-American Folk Thought from Slavery to Freedom* (New York, 1977).

3. See Stuart Hall and Tony Jefferson, eds., *Resistance Through Ritual: Youth Subcultures in Post-War Britain* (London, 1976); Dick Hebdige, *Subculture: The Meaning of Style* (London, 1979); Dick Hebdige, *Hiding in the Light: On Images and Things* (London, 1988).

4. As the text is meant to suggest, I am skeptical about the existence of any precise correlation between running away and the cultural traits described in this chapter. Arguments that the "resistance" demonstrated by running away would flow into such areas as clothing or hairstyles are based on misapprehensions about what running away meant. As Philip Morgan has pointed out, one should avoid wrenching running away out of its context and simplistically equating it with resistance. Nevertheless, in an attempt to forestall such criticism, I have placed my findings within this more tentative framework. See Philip D. Morgan, "Colonial South Carolina Runaways: Their Significance for Slave Culture," *Slavery and Abolition* 6 (1985): 57–78, especially 57.

5. Gerald W. Mullin, *Flight and Rebellion: Slave Resistance in Eighteenth-Century Virginia* (New York, 1972); Peter H. Wood, *Black Majority: Negroes in Colonial South Carolina from 1670 Through the Stono Rebellion* (New York, 1974), 191 and passim.

6. Charles W. Joyner, "The Creolization of Slave Folklife: All Saints Parish, South Carolina as a Test Case," *Historical Reflections* 6 (1979): 435–53. See also Charles W. Joyner, *Down by the Riverside: A South Carolina Slave Community* (Urbana, Ill., 1984); Charles W. Joyner, "History as Ritual: Rites of Power and Resistance on the Slave Plantation," *Australasian Journal of American Studies* 5 (1986): 1–9; Patricia Jones-Jackson, *When Roots Die: Endangered Traditions on the Sea Islands* (Athens, Ga., 1987).

7. Much of the following discussion is indebted to these linguists. See William A. Stewart, "Sociolinguistic Factors in the History of American Negro Dialects," in J. Dillard, ed., *Perspectives on Black English* (The Hague, 1975), 222–32; William A. Stewart, "Continuity and Change in American Negro Dialects," in Dillard, *Perspectives on Black English*, 233–47; J. L. Dillard, *Black English: Its History and Usage in the United States* (New York, 1972).

8. Dillard, *Black English*, 55–56, 73–138, especially 108.

9. See chapter 3 above and, for later in the nineteenth century, William J. Mahar, "Black English in Early Blackface Minstrelsy: A New Interpretation of the Sources of Minstrel Show Dialect," *American Quarterly* 37 (1985): 260–85.

10. *Centinel of Freedom*, November 27, 1804; *Daily Advertiser*, September 2, 1788.

11. *Daily Advertiser*, June 25, 1802.

12. Ibid., April 14, 1795.

13. This figure considerably underestimates the influence of the Dutch language. Dutch-speaking slaveowners probably did not advertise in the press for their runaways. Most of the owners of Dutch-speaking slaves in fact had non-Dutch names and had presumably purchased these slaves from owners of Dutch origin. Sambo, for example, spoke good English but his owner, Caleb Morgan, advertised in the *New York Gazette and Weekly Mercury* of November 2, 1772, that he believed Sambo spoke Dutch, as he "was brought up among the Dutch on the west side of the [Hudson] river." As we saw in the last chapter there was a flurry of slave runaway activity in the Dutch stronghold of Ulster County in 1796 as a result of the legislative debates over the abolition of slavery. Locals, the vast majority with Dutch names, formed the Slave Apprehending Society of Shawangunk, but there is no indication at all in newspaper advertisements of the existence of this flurry of slave runaways. English-speaking newspapers are not a very good guide to the activities of Dutch-speaking New Yorkers.

14. Carl Bridenbaugh, ed., *Gentleman's Progress: The Itinerarium of Dr. Alexander Hamilton, 1744* (Chapel Hill, N.C., 1948), 40–41. See also Geoffrey D. Needler, "Linguistic Evidence from Alexander Hamilton's Itinerarium," *American Speech* 42 (1967): 211–18.

15. Dillard, *Black English*, 223–24.

16. *Daily Advertiser*, July 21, 1792.

17. *New Jersey Journal*, December 16, 1789; *Centinel of Freedom*, February 9, 1802.

18. *New York Evening Post*, July 20, 1802; Stewart, "Sociolinguistic Factors in the History of American Negro Dialects," 226–29.

19. *Daily Advertiser*, September 4, November 27, 1800.

20. See, for example, Statement of Jack St. Domingo, *People v. Jack St. Domingo*, filed October 7, 1801, box 9, District Attorney's Indictment Papers, Municipal Archives, New York City.

21. *Daily Advertiser*, August 30, 1794.

22. *New York Evening Post*, July 1, 1805.

23. *Daily Advertiser*, May 19, 1789.

24. See *Royal Gazette*, March 3, 1781. On the importance of names, see Herbert G. Gutman, *The Black Family in Slavery and Freedom, 1750–1925* (New York, 1976), 230–56; John C. Inscoe, "Carolina Slave Names: An Index to Acculturation," *Journal of Southern History* 49 (1983): 527–54. Nash has analyzed northern black names, and his work has strongly influenced my interpretation. See Gary B. Nash, "Forging Freedom: The

Emancipation Experience in the Northern Seaports, 1775–1820," in Ira Berlin and Ronald Hoffman, eds., *Slavery and Freedom in the Era of the American Revolution* (Charlottesville, Va., 1982), 20–27.

25. *Daily Advertiser*, August 4, 1786.

26. *The Federalist; New Jersey Gazette*, July 8, 1799; *Daily Advertiser*, June 15, 1790.

27. The runaway advertisements are heavily biased against women, but a few indicate that the same pattern may have occurred with females as well. An advertisement in the *Daily Advertiser*, January 12, 1792, identified a sixteen-year-old runaway by the name Jane but noted that "sometimes she calls herself Sarah."

28. Whites associated these names with slavery as well, as the following piece of political abuse from the *Centinel of Freedom*, April 10, 1804, demonstrates. The editor of the *Centinel* attacked the editor of another newspaper whose name was Toby: "Let's see—Toby—Surely that's an African name. Tis how the editor's name corresponds with the color of his sheet, which is blacker than the blackest Ethiopian."

29. *Daily Advertiser*, May 26, 1801.

30. Ibid., September 20, 1793.

31. Although the census is the most satisfactory means of examining black names, it is not without problems. Blacks dealing with whites, and the census takers were of course white, assumed new names with great ease. Perhaps one can detect a slight note of frustration in one slaveowner's description of his nineteen-year-old slave in the *Daily Advertiser*, September 14, 1799. The runaway was "named Peter, Victor, Le Sauce or any of these names." Even a cursory look at the court records demonstrates that many blacks used more than one surname when dealing with whites. However, as *People v. John Smith alias David Brown and John Scott alias Stephen Williams* illustrates, they were still very common names. On the ease of changing names, see Melville J. Herskovits, *The Myth of the Negro Past* (Boston, 1958), 193–94.

32. There were 157 free black households in New York City in the 1790 census, 676 in 1800, and 1,228 in 1810.

33. See Nash, "Forging Freedom," 20–27.

34. Unfortunately the material from New York is nowhere near detailed enough to allow a generational study of black names through time and within families. If suitable data can ever be found for New York an analysis of this sort may well detect distinctively black patterns in naming. For examples of this sort of analysis, see Cheryll Ann Cody, "Naming, Kinship, and Estate Dispersal: Notes on Slave Family Life on a South Carolina Plantation, 1786 to 1833," *William and Mary Quarterly*, 3d ser., 39 (1982): 192–211; Cheryll Ann Cody, "There Was No 'Absalom' on the Ball

Plantations: Slave-Naming Practices in the South Carolina Low Country, 1720–1865," *American Historical Review* 92 (1987): 563–96.

35. Quoted in Vivienne L. Kruger, "Born to Run: The Slave Family in Early New York, 1626–1827" (Ph.D. diss., Columbia University, 1985), 87–88.

36. William Strickland, *Journal of a Tour in the United States of America, 1794–1795*, ed. J. E. Strickland (New York, 1971), 63.

37. See, for example, Genovese, *Roll, Jordan, Roll*, 550–61; Robert William Fogel and Stanley L. Engerman, *Time on the Cross: The Economics of American Negro Slavery* (Boston, 1974), 116–18.

38. The approach used here has been influenced by the essays in Hall and Jefferson, *Resistance Through Ritual;* Hebdige, *Subculture;* Alison Lurie, *The Language of Clothes* (New York, 1981); Stuart Cosgrove, "The Zoot Suit and Style Warfare," *History Workshop Journal* 18 (1984): 77–91; Steve Chibnall, "Whistle and Zoot: The Changing Meaning of a Suit of Clothes," *History Workshop Journal* 20 (1985): 56–81. But see also Grant McCracken, *Culture and Consumption: New Approaches to the Symbolic Character of Consumer Goods and Activities* (Bloomington, Ind., 1988), especially 57–70.

39. This is based on my reading of the runaway advertisements. For a more detailed description of the clothing worn, see Edwin Olson, "Social Aspects of Slave Life in New York," *Journal of Negro History* 26 (1941): 66–77.

40. *Daily Advertiser*, October 8, 1793, September 14, 1795.

41. Ibid., May 19, 1789.

42. Statement of Isabella Thomas, *People v. Isabella Thomas*, filed June 4, 1802, box 12, District Attorney's Indictment Papers.

43. Statement of Frank Pero, *People v. John Jackson & Frank Pero*, filed December 11, 1802, box 13, District Attorney's Indictment Papers.

44. Statement of Samuel Robertson, *People v. Samuel Robertson*, filed January 4, 1798, box 2, District Attorney's Indictment Papers.

45. Statement of John Young, *People v. Thomas Cooney and others*, filed April 7, 1804, box 16, District Attorney's Indictment Papers.

46. Statement of John Sickles, *People v. John Thomas*, filed April 4, 1804, box 16, District Attorney's Indictment Papers.

47. Statement of Sally Smith, *People v. Sally Smith*, filed November 4, 1805, box 24, District Attorney's Indictment Papers.

48. Statement of Nancy, *People v. Nancy (a Black)*, filed June 5, 1804, box 17, District Attorney's Indictment Papers.

49. *Argus*, April 27, 1796.

50. *Daily Advertiser*, December 22, 1794.

51. Joyner, *Down by the Riverside*, 113; see also Genovese, *Roll, Jordan, Roll*, 558–59.

52. *Daily Advertiser,* June 23, 1801; *New York Evening Post,* December 20, 1804.

53. *Daily Advertiser,* May 19, 1789.

54. *Centinel of Freedom,* August 10, 1802. Little appears to be known about the wearing of jewelery in the West Indies. See Jerome S. Handler and Frederick W. Lange, *Plantation Slavery in Barbados: An Archaeological and Historical Investigation* (Cambridge, Mass., 1978), 153–54.

55. Orlando Patterson, *Slavery and Social Death: A Comparative Study* (Cambridge, Mass., 1982), 61.

56. *Daily Advertiser,* June 24, 1801.

57. Ibid., November 23, 1798.

58. Ibid., May 24, 1793.

59. Ibid., September 6, 1792; *New York Evening Post,* May 11, 1804.

60. *Minerva,* March 15, 1797.

61. *Centinel of Freedom,* July 14, 1807.

62. Thomas F. De Voe, *The Market Book: A History of the Public Markets of the City of New York* (New York, 1970 [orig. pub. 1862]), 345.

63. *Daily Advertiser,* July 26, 1799, March 3, 1800; Herskovits, *Myth of the Negro Past,* 148–49.

64. Herskovits, *Myth of the Negro Past,* 148–49.

65. *Greenleaf's New York Journal,* December 19, 1795.

66. De Voe, *Market Book,* 345.

67. *Daily Advertiser,* July 30, 1794 (emphasis mine).

68. For Lévi-Strauss's use of the term, see Claude Lévi-Strauss, *The Savage Mind* (London, 1966), and also Terence Hawkes, *Structuralism and Semiotics* (London, 1977), 49ff. However, I have used the term in a similar fashion to some of the scholars at the Centre for Contemporary Cultural Studies in Birmingham. See the essays in Hall and Jefferson, *Resistance Through Ritual,* especially John Clarke, "Style," 175–91; Hebdige, *Subculture,* 102–6. Also see T. J. Jackson Lears, "The Concept of Cultural Hegemony: Problems and Possibilities," *American Historical Review* 90 (1985): 567–93, especially 590–91.

69. Stan Cohen quoted in Dick Hebdige, "The Meaning of Mod," in Hall and Jefferson, *Resistance Through Ritual,* 88. See also Hebdige, *Subculture,* 52–54.

70. John Bernard, *Retrospections of America, 1797–1811* (New York, 1887), 195–96. Another traveler recorded a similar comment. See John Davis, *Travels of Four Years and Half in the United States of America During 1798, 1799, 1800, 1801, and 1802* (New York, 1909), 47.

71. *Greenleaf's New York Journal,* September 23, 1797.

72. *American Minerva,* September 3, 1796.

73. *New Jersey Journal*, August 14, 1793.
74. Herskovits, *Myth of the Negro Past*, 145–46.
75. *New Jersey Gazette*, August 29, 1785.
76. *Centinel of Freedom*, February 9, 1802.
77. *Daily Advertiser*, December 13, 1789; *New York Journal*, October 10, 1792; *New Jersey Gazette*, October 31, 1785.
78. *American Minerva*, August 29, 1796; *Argus*, October 24, 1795; Kenneth R. Johnson, "Black Kinesics—Some Non-Verbal Communication Patterns in Black Culture," in Dillard, *Perspectives on Black English*, 296–306, especially 301.
79. *Daily Advertiser*, June 25, 1801, September 20, 1793.
80. Ibid., September 3, 1787. This section has been influenced by Mullin's innovative work, *Flight and Rebellion*.
81. *Daily Advertiser*, February 1, 1787.
82. Ibid., September 20, 1793. In many cases this aggressive behavior was associated with alcohol: see, for example, *Centinel of Freedom*, August 5, 1800; *New York Journal*, September 3, 1790.
83. Johnson, "Black Kinesics," 298–99.
84. *New York Evening Post*, August 10, 1804.
85. Johnson, "Black Kinesics," 299.
86. *New Jersey Journal*, December 16, 1789; *New York Evening Post*, July 6, 1803.
87. *Daily Advertiser*, November 8, 1793, June 2, 1801.
88. Roger A. Ekirch, *Bound for America: The Transportation of British Convicts to the Colonies, 1718–1775* (Oxford, 1987), 197. I am very grateful to Professor Ekirch for sending me an advance copy of his chapter on convict runaways.
89. *Centinel of Freedom*, February 13, 1810.
90. Herskovits, *Myth of the Negro Past*, 150–52. See also Bertram Wyatt-Brown, "The Mask of Obedience: Male Slave Psychology in the Old South," *American Historical Review* 93 (1988): 1228–52.
91. *New York Evening Post*, December 16, 1802.
92. Gerald Mullin developed an elaborate theory about the "stuttering" of the runaways in Virginia demonstrating the "assimilated's divided self and cultural marginality." Herskovits, however, makes the intriguing observation in *The Myth of the Negro Past* that in Dutch Guiana a young man speaking to his elders used "a low voice, and introduced a conventionalized stammer into his speech." It remains little more than speculation, but possibly the stammer of some blacks has been misinterpreted by both slaveowners and historians. Mullin, *Flight and Rebellion*, 98–103; Herskovits, *Myth of the Negro Past*, 152.

93. Bound Volume, Forman Papers, New-York Historical Society.

94. On the meanings of the name Sambo, see Dillard, *Black English*, 130–32.

95. On the importance of a shaved head in various slave systems, see Patterson, *Slavery and Social Death*, 60–62. See also Raymond Firth, *Symbols Public and Private* (London, 1973), 287–91. See also the example cited in Wyatt-Brown, "Mask of Obedience," 1228–29.

96. See, for example, John W. Blassingame, *The Slave Community: Plantation Life in the Antebellum South* (New York, 1979). However, see also Peter Kolchin, "Reevaluating the Antebellum Slave Community: A Comparative Perspective," *Journal of American History* 70 (1983): 579–601; Jean Butenhoff Lee, "The Problem of Slave Community in the Eighteenth-Century Chesapeake," *William and Mary Quarterly*, 3d ser., 43 (1986): 333–61.

Epilogue

1. See the comments of Erastus Root cited in Dixon Ryan Fox, "The Negro Vote in Old New York," *Political Science Quarterly* 32 (1917): 252–75, especially 257.

2. Statement of William Waldron, *People v. Henry Stanton*, filed November 14, 1801, box 10, District Attorney's Indictment Papers, Municipal Archives, New York City.

3. Statement of Louis Hart, *People v. Lewis Humphrey*, filed June 9, 1803, box 14, District Attorney's Indictment Papers.

4. The members of the watch in Cooney's case were listed in the indictment papers as "laborers." On the background of the watch in this period, see James F. Richardson, *The New York Police: From Colonial Times to 1901* (New York, 1971), 19–21. For a very suggestive account of similar behavior by poor whites in Philadelphia in the 1830s, see Emma Jones Lapsansky, " 'Since They Got Those Separate Churches': Afro-Americans and Racism in Jacksonian Philadelphia," *American Quarterly* 32 (1980): 54–78.

5. See, for example, Leon F. Litwack, *North of Slavery: The Negro in the Free States, 1790–1860* (Chicago, 1961); Leonard P. Curry, *The Free Black in Urban America, 1800–1850: The Shadow of the Dream* (Chicago, 1981). This suggested connection between "industrialization" and a savage attack on the status and persons of the blacks has strong resonances with later developments in the South and in South Africa. See John W. Cell, *The Highest Stage of White Supremacy: The Origins of Segregation in South Africa and the American South* (Cambridge, 1982), especially 131–35; Armstead L. Robinson, "The Difference Freedom Made: The Emancipation of Afro-Americans," in Darlene Clark Hine, ed., *The State of Afro-American History:*

st, Present, and Future (Baton Rouge, La., 1986), 51–74, especially 51. On
cial violence, see Leonard L. Richards, *Gentlemen of Property and Stand-
ɜ: Anti-Abolition Mobs in Jacksonian America (New York, 1971); Paul O.
einbaum, *Mobs and Demagogues: The New York Response to Collective Vio-
ıce in the Early Nineteenth Century (Ann Arbor, Mich., 1979); the best and
ost detailed account, however, is Paul A. Gilje, *The Road to Mobocracy:
pular Disorder in New York City, 1763–1834 (Chapel Hill, N.C., 1987),
5–70.

Index

Polhemus, Abraham, 11, 197
Poor Richard, 66
Potts, Stacy, 118
Poulson's Town and Country Almanac, 67
Powlis, Andrew, 94
Prill, Christopher, 144
Primrose, John, 182
Prostitution, 165, 170

Queens County, 4, 16, 52–53, 89, 120

Richards, John, 159–60
Richmond County, 4, 16, 51–53,
    89, 120
Rivers, Hudson, 193
Rivington, James, 11
Robertson, Samuel, 195
Robinson, Armstead, xxiv
Rogers, Henry, 197
Rollins, William, 182
Roosevelt, Mingo, 193
Root, Erastus, 20
Roper, George, 49
Rousseau, C., 12
Rudwick, Elliot, xix
Runaways: ages of, 122–24, 148;
    clothing, 194–97; in context of black
    resistance in New York, 141–49;
    female, 124, 134–38; groups, 138–39;
    hairstyles, 197–99; historiography,
    115–16; kinesics, 200–202; language
    ability, 122, 134, 188–94; language of
    advertisements, 116–20; mulatto,
    122, 124, 139; number of
    advertisements in sample, 120;
    numbers of, 140–41; origins, 121–22;
    owners' views of runaway slaves'
    destinations, 132–39; owners' views
    of runaway slaves' motivations, 126–
    32; and Revolution, 122, 130–31,
    142–43; variety of, 121. *See also*
    Slaves
Rural Magazine, 61
Rush, Benjamin, 58, 59, 60, 63, 65–66

Saint Domingue, 31–32, 61, 65, 67–68,

85, 87, 122, 143–45, 146, 155–56,
    161, 191
Salinger, Sharon, 36
Satanstoe (Cooper), 102
Shaw, George, 131
Sickles, John, 196
Sipson, John, 104
Slave Apprehending Society of
    Shawangunk, 147
Slaveowners: in 1790, 5–14; in 1800,
    31–38; in 1810, 40–41; artisan, 8, 10–
    12, 34, 35–37, 45; Dutch, 18–21, 55;
    and end of slavery, 46–50; French
    émigrés, 31–32, 65; merchant, 8, 34,
    40–41, 44; professional, 8, 34; size of
    holdings, 9–10; spatial distribution
    in New York City, 13–14, 41–46;
    turnover in, 30–36, 38, 90, 91;
    women, 8–9, 32, 37–38, 40
Slavery: historiography, xix–xxiv; as
    investment, 13; "mildness" of in
    New York, 79–80, 85, 113, 115; views
    of in magazines, newspapers, and
    almanacs, 57–73
Slavery and Social Death
    (Patterson), 197
Slaves: and alcohol, 181–82; clothing,
    101, 194–200, 203–5; and crime,
    180–81; dancing, 95, 96–97, 105–6,
    112–13, 179; family, 88–92, 113, 134–
    39; females, 12–13, 90, 134–38;
    "French Negroes," 122, 128–29,
    143–45, 155–56, 183, 191; kinesics,
    200–202; names, 192; negotiating
    with masters, 106–13; networks, 92,
    93, 179; number in New York City,
    3–4, 153; occupations, 10, 12, 21–22,
    44, 94; religion, 95, 173; residences,
    92, 175, 179; resistance of, xxi, 64–
    65, 143–49; role in their
    emancipation, 49–50, 108–13,
    148–49, 151–53; sales of, 89–92
— mentioned by name: Aaron, 202;
    Abraham, 130; Abraham (Rogers's),
    197; Adam (allegedly Cowell's), 117–
    19, 148; Alcindor, 128; Beliour, 191;

Ben, 92; Ben (Thompson), 94;
Benoit, 82; Bet, 126; Bet (Albany
slave), 100, 145; Bill, 22, 201; Bill
(Metcalf Eden's), 29; Bret, 129;
Calypso, 128; Caster, 141–42;
Catharine, 124; Cato, 131; Caty, 198;
Charity, 137; Charles, 11, 202;
Charles (King at Pinkster), 96–97,
98–99; Constance, 137; Cook, 129;
Cudjo, 201; Cuff, 21, 94, 195, 201;
Cuff (Allen's), 190; Cuff
(Coventry's), 103; Daniel, 130, 197;
David, 127; Dean, 100, 145; Dianna,
29; Dinah, 13; Dromo, 190; Duke,
127; Esmal, 138; Flora, 13;
Flummary, 108, 192; Fortune, 29;
Franklin, 21, 94; Grace, 134; Grotis,
121, 189; Gustus, 108–9; Hagar, 29;
Hannah, 29; Hannah (Baxter's), 110;
Harry, 29; Isaac, 29; Isabella, 197;
Ishmael, 95; Jack, 28, 94, 95; Jack
(Caldwell's), 125; Jack (Griffin's),
194; Jack (Metcalf Eden's), 29; Jack
(Polhemus's), 197; Jack (from Rocky
Hill Mills), 127; Jack (Mrs.
Upham's), 110; Jack (Van Alstine's),
107; Jack (Woodruff's), 197; Jacob,
181; Jacob (Mulford's), 189; Jacob
(York), 192; Jake, 92; James, 121;
Jane, 29; Jane (Mary Thomas's), 30;
Japhet, 22; Jim, 22, 197, 198; Jim
(Thompson's), 126; Jo, 123; Joseph,
191; Joshua, 10; Jude, 132; Killis, 95,
108; King, 28; Lindor, 120, 191, 195,
197; Lydia, 108; Margaret, 131, 137;
Margaret (Fine's), 152; Maria, 189;
Mary, 137, 198; Mingo, 197; Mink,
138; Molly, 195; Morris, 10, 197;
Nan, 30; Nan (Thompson's), 94;
Nassau, 191; Nat, 200; Nero, 202;
Nero (Baxter's), 108; Nicholas, 12;
Paris, 120; Peggy, 196; Peter, 29,
170; Peter (mulatto runaway), 179;
Phillis, 49; Phillis (Spingler's), 191;
Plato, 22; Polly, 128; Pomp, 145;
Pompey, 100; Pompy, 201–2;

Primus, 132; Prince, 30; Pro, 22, 127,
181; Rob, 30; Robin, 21, 94; Roe,
181; Rose, 138; Ruth, 125; Sal, 29;
Sam, 152; Sambo, 93–94, 203–5;
Samuel, 129; Sannon, 180; Sarah,
131; Saul, 29; Scip, 201; Scipio, 30;
Sharp, 128; Sharp (Condit's), 189;
Sharper, 21, 94; Silvey, 29; Silvia,
175; Suke, 131, 197; Telmaque, 128,
189; Toby, 132; Tom, 11, 200;
Wanno, 197; West, 11; Will, 120,
130, 200; Will (Banks's), 190; Will
(Wykham's), 108; William, 12;
William (Caesar), 192; Yaff, 125; Yat,
111–12; York, 123; York (accused of
arson), 132; Zamor, 155
See also Blacks; *names of other*
individuals
Smith, David, 169
Smith, Elihu, 167, 185, 196
Smith, Ruth, 177
Smith, Sally, 196
Smith, Stanhope, 58
Smith, Thomas, 4–5
Smock, Richard, 183
Sonthonax, L. F., 65
South Carolina, 16
Spellman, Jacob, 175
Spingler, Henry, 191
Stackhouse, Hastings, 6
Stansell, Christine, xxiv
Stedman, John, 61
Stevenson, Cornelius, 12
Stewart, William, 188
St. Méry, Médéric Moreau de, 20,
87, 165
Stoddart, John, 178
Stoothoff, John W., 108
Strickland, William, 3, 4, 10, 18, 19,
24, 26, 27, 121, 159, 194
Stuckey, Sterling, 97
Study of Slavery in New Jersey, A
(Cooley), xxi
Style, 186–206
Stymets, William, 6
Suffolk County, 16

Printed in the United States
6165